Equitable Access to High-Cost Pharmaceuticals

Equitable Access to High-Cost Pharmaceuticals

Edited by

Zaheer-Ud-Din Babar

University of Huddersfield, Queensgate, Huddersfield, United Kingdom
and
University of Auckland, Auckland, New Zealand

ELSEVIER

ACADEMIC PRESS

An imprint of Elsevier

Academic Press is an imprint of Elsevier
125 London Wall, London EC2Y 5AS, United Kingdom
525 B Street, Suite 1800, San Diego, CA 92101-4495, United States
50 Hampshire Street, 5th Floor, Cambridge, MA 02139, United States
The Boulevard, Langford Lane, Kidlington, Oxford OX5 1GB, United Kingdom

Library of Congress Cataloging-in-Publication Data

A catalog record for this book is available from the Library of Congress

British Library Cataloguing-in-Publication Data

A catalogue record for this book is available from the British Library

ISBN: 978-0-12-811945-7

For information on all Academic Press publications visit our website at https://www.elsevier.com/books-and-journals

Publisher: Candice Janco
Acquisition Editor: Graham Nisbet
Editorial Project Manager: Susan Ikeda
Production Project Manager: Poulouse Joseph
Designer: Miles Hitchen

Typeset by Thomson Digital

DEDICATION

I dedicate this book to two great women:

To my grandmother, who has been a source of inspiration to me for all my life!

To Margaret Ewen, a leading public health advocate and a fellow New Zealander from whom I have learned a lot about access to medicines and pharmaceutical prices.

CONTENTS

CONTRIBUTORS

Zaheer-Ud-Din Babar
University of Huddersfield, Queensgate, Huddersfield, United Kingdom;
University of Auckland, Auckland, New Zealand

Darrin Baines
Bournemouth University, Bournemouth, Dorset, United Kingdom

Robert Bracchi
All Wales Therapeutics and Toxicology Centre, Academic Centre, University Hospital Llandough, Wales, United Kingdom

Nadeem Irfan Bukhari
Punjab University College of Pharmacy, University of the Punjab, Lahore, Pakistan

Louise E. Curley
University of Auckland, Auckland, New Zealand

Filipa Alves da Costa
Centro de Estudos Interdisciplinar Egas Moniz (CiiEM), Instituto Universitário Egas Moniz (IUEM), Campus Universitário, Quinta da Granja, Monte da Caparica; Portuguese Pharmaceutical Society, Rua da Sociedade Farmacêutica, Lisboa, Portugal

Syed Shahzad Hasan
University of Huddersfield, Queensgate, Huddersfield, United Kingdom

Dyfrig A. Hughes
Centre for Health Economics and Medicines Evaluation, Bangor University, Bangor, Wales, United Kingdom

Maree Jensen
University of Auckland, Auckland, New Zealand

Claudio Jommi
Università del Piemonte Orientale, Novara; Cergas (Centre for Research on Health and Social Care Management), SDA Bocconi School of Management, Milano, Italy

Brendan Kwesiga
Management Sciences for Health, Kampala, Uganda

Christine Y. Lu
Harvard Medical School and Harvard Pilgrim Health Care Institute, Boston, MA, USA

Ana Paula Martins
Portuguese Pharmaceutical Society, Rua da Sociedade Farmacêutica; Research Institute for Medicines (iMED.ULisboa), Universidade de Lisboa, Lisboa, Portugal

Katrina Perehudoff
University Medical Center Groningen, Department of Health Sciences - Global Health Unit, University of Groningen, Groningen, The Netherlands

Sanya Ram
University of Auckland, Auckland, New Zealand

Khurram Rehman
Lahore Pharmacy College (A Project of Lahore Medical and Dental College), Lahore, Pakistan

Sabrina Rind
All Wales Therapeutics and Toxicology Centre, Academic Centre, University Hospital Llandough, Wales, United Kingdom

Philip A. Routledge
All Wales Therapeutics and Toxicology Centre, Academic Centre, University Hospital Llandough, Wales, United Kingdom

Karen Samuels
All Wales Therapeutics and Toxicology Centre, Academic Centre, University Hospital Llandough, Wales, United Kingdom

Morries Seru
Ministry of Health Pharmacy Department, Kampala, Uganda

Russell Shute
Sansom Institute, University of South Australia, SA, Australia

Ellen 't Hoen
University of Groningen, University Medical Center Groningen, Global Health Unit, Groningen, The Netherlands

Birna Trap
Management Sciences for Health, Kampala, Uganda

Alice Varnava
All Wales Therapeutics and Toxicology Centre, Academic Centre, University Hospital Llandough, Wales, United Kingdom

Agnes Isabelle Vitry
Sansom Institute, University of South Australia, SA, Australia

Sabine Vogler
Gesundheit Österreich GmbH (GÖG/Austrian Public Health Institute), Vienna, Austria

Anita Katharina Wagner
Harvard Medical School and Harvard Pilgrim Health Care Institute, Boston, MA, USA

Jennifer A. Whitty
Norwich Medical School, University of East Anglia, Norwich, United Kingdom

Inthira Yamabhai
International Trade and Health Programme, International Health Policy Program, Ministry of Public Health, Nonthaburi, Thailand

FOREWORD

Never before has access to medicines been so high on health care decision-makers' agenda as it is now. Access to medicines is a pillar in most OECD countries' pharmaceutical policies and has significant consequences for patients and society. In recent years, public policy focus has continued to grow due to the combination of rising medicine costs and budgetary limitations in most healthcare systems. The high prices of new medicines are at the centre of this conundrum: is it fair or acceptable that important new medicines are unaffordable, even for the most advanced economies?

There have been numerous responses to this in different jurisdictions, not entirely uncoordinated, explicitly or implicitly. In Europe, recent examples of relevant developments at institutional level include the 'European Council conclusion on strengthening the balance in pharmaceutical systems in the EU and its Member States' and the legislative proposal by the European Commission to 'Strengthening EU cooperation on Health Technology Assessment amongst Member States beyond 2020'. In the USA, historic increases in prescription medicine prices contribute to the ever increasing and unsustainable healthcare spending while the current administration has publicly criticised the pricing strategies of the pharmaceutical industry.

From an international standpoint, the initiative of the 'UN Secretary-General's High Level Panel on Access to Medicines' calling for a 'new deal to close the health innovation and access gap' comes as a consequence of the distress that several governments face with the introduction of new medicines. Partly to address some of these concerns, the WHO Health Technologies and Pharmaceuticals (HTP) Programme has expanded aiming to provide technical assistance and training to countries linked to access to medicines and universal health coverage (UHC).

In parallel, several regional efforts have taken shape in the past few years aiming to increase the collaboration amongst participating countries, share expertise and carve common pathways to deal with the introduction of new and expensive medicines. The BeNeLuxA initiative is probably the most advanced amongst regional collaborative efforts, but some momentum exists around other efforts such as the Valetta Declaration. One underlying theme is that cross-country collaborations could transition into becoming more effective buyers and use their monopsony power to their advantage.

National decision makers have to strike a balance between strengthening equity in access and the financial and budgetary impact of their decisions. Such a delicate balancing act becomes even more challenging when combined with the need to incentivise innovation. Industry critics increasingly point towards the unethical leverage of patient need by manufacturers, driven by monopolistic power granted by generous Intellectual Property (IP) rights. Others contend that the current pharmaceutical R&D model and regulatory policies need a complete overhaul; this would imply a change of rules rather than a change of tools. If prohibitive drug prices are often the result of strong intellectual property, then, the argument goes, the latter may need to be relaxed. This may sound extreme but is indicative of the prevailing sentiment amongst policy makers. Industry supporters and investors, on the other hand, argue that for new and effective (bio)pharmaceutical products, high prices are an unavoidable necessity if high-risk financing decisions are to deliver positive returns on investment (ROI) in the wake of continuously rising R&D costs and high failure rates.

At the same time, what is urgently needed is better incentives for socially desirable R&D as current funding at aggregate level is not aligned with disease burden and several important disease areas remain underfunded. What is happening instead is that the pursuit of marginal indications or 'Me-Too' drugs may have the unintended consequence of inhibiting innovation and creativity, particularly in key therapy areas such as cancer. A number of HTA bodies estimate that over half of new drugs have little or no added clinical benefit. A related inefficiency is that society seems to be paying twice to some degree for a number of new medicines, first in the form of early basic research, sponsored largely by public funds and then again for the final marketed product at the point of use. Pharmaceutical manufacturers have been criticised that they often mirror the behaviour of financial institutions, magnifying development costs through acquisition strategies for companies with promising compounds rather than real R&D investment.

However, should all these issues be attributed solely to the strategic behaviour of the pharmaceutical industry? Regulators and decision makers also face important dilemmas as access to market and reimbursement decisions are increasingly based on incomplete or inadequate evidence. This may explain – in part – the different approaches to value interpretation and the variability in reimbursement decisions across countries, not terribly satisfactory for patients.

But considering just one side solely responsible for escalating pharmaceutical prices is one-sided and probably naive. Value assessment frameworks are in need of reform as much as the R&D financing model. Current approaches to value assessment, whether based on comparative clinical benefit assessment or clinical and cost effectiveness have been criticised as partial and in need of reform. Additional parameters of value are known to influence decision making, but their role is ad hoc.

When deciding to invest in R&D, manufacturers need to be given clear signals. Value preferences of decision makers and the appropriate stakeholders should be incorporated in a transparent way early in the product lifecycle of new medicines to shape their development, regulation, coverage and use. Imposing stricter regulations that require adequate evidence on comparative benefit as part of marketing authorisation could be used to generate real world evidence on comparative effectiveness, therefore laying out long-term incentives for tackling an 'innovation deficit'. This should take place while aiming to streamline evidence needs between licensing and HTA bodies.

Equitable Access to High-Cost Pharmaceuticals seeks to aid the development and implementation of equitable public health policies by pharmaco-economic professionals and policy makers. Written by a number of well-known experts in the field under the accomplished editorial guidance of Professor Zaheer-Ud-Din Babar, the book provides country-by-country analyses and empirical evidence on different policies, practices, regulations and tools in pharmaceutical policy making, while comparing and contrasting different healthcare systems. Through these, the reader obtains a more holistic perspective of the problems in this area and the way they have been addressed in different settings. Starting with a comprehensive overview of Access to High Cost Medicines and Public Health Policies, it transitions from the fundamentals of Health Technology Assessment to tools such as Managed Entry Agreements, before touching upon more complex issues relating to national Public Health Agendas and Intellectual Property. A number of case-specific experiences on Access to High Cost Medicines provide an interesting expose of how the same problem has been addressed in different regulatory settings. Key features of the book include the evaluation of current regulatory policies on access and pricing, the provision of existing guidelines and recommendation by international organisations and the exploration of novel emerging policies and methods. The book rises to the challenge and the complexity of issues surrounding access to and cost of new medicines and provides an excellent source of information on and analysis of policies, practices and tools used in different settings. It is useful to any reader interested in the topic, ranging from current health economics professionals and policy makers, to health policy leaders and future graduate students.

Aris Angelis, Panos Kanavos
London School of Economics and Political Science, London, United Kingdom

CHAPTER 1

Access to High Cost Medicines: An Overview

Syed Shahzad Hasan*, Christine Y. Lu, Zaheer-Ud-Din Babar*,†**
*University of Huddersfield, Queensgate, Huddersfield, United Kingdom
**Harvard Medical School and Harvard Pilgrim Health Care Institute, Boston, MA, USA
†University of Auckland, Auckland, New Zealand

ABBREVIATIONS

CDF	Cancer Drugs Fund
DMARDs	Disease modifying anti-rheumatic drugs
HCMs	High-cost medicines
HTA	Health technology assessment
NICE	National Institute of Clinical Excellence
MEAs	Managed entry agreements
MOA	Mechanisms of action
QALY	Quality-adjusted life years
SMART-D	State Medicaid Alternative Reimbursement and Purchasing Test for High-Cost Drugs
UK	United Kingdom
US	United States
VBP	Value-based pricing
WHO	World Health Organisation

1.1 DEFINING HCMs

Date back to 1990s, in a time where only little attention was paid to high-cost medicines (HCMs), several groups of researchers have commenced to conceptualise 'high-cost' or 'high-priced' medicines. Although some referred to certain medicines as being 'high-cost' without pre-specified criteria, others provided the price point at which a medicine can be defined as being 'high-cost'. For instance, Powe et al. (1994) considered cyclosporine and erythropoietin as HCMs. The cost of treatment with these medicines in 1994 was US $4000–US $6000 per patient per year in the United States (Powe et al., 1994). In 1995, Poirier et al. defined foscarnet, monoclonal antibodies for septic shock treatment, and granulocyte colony-stimulating factors, as HCMs with no reference being made to the cost of these medicines (Poirier and Gianetti, 1995). In that same year, Crump et al. (1995)

Equitable Access to High-Cost Pharmaceuticals
http://dx.doi.org/10.1016/B978-0-12-811945-7.00001-4

defined 'expensive treatments' as those costing more than £2000 per patient per year.

The more contemporary definitions of 'high-cost' or 'high-priced' medicines almost exclusively provided the cut-off price point beyond which a medicine would be classified as 'high-cost' or 'high-priced'. This is illustrated in a 2015 report by the World Health Organisation (WHO) Regional Office for Europe which defines a medicine as high-priced if the therapy exceeds €10,000 per patient per year to be reimbursed by a public payer (WHO, 2015). This definition is limited to European countries which use Euro as their currency. On the other hand, in British Columbia, Canada, the minister may designate a medicine as a HCM if the minister determines that the maximum daily amount the minister may pay for the medicine when averaged over a 1-year period is equal to or greater than Can $40 (for the typical prescribed dose or the typical number of doses per year), as stipulated in the Drug Price Regulation of Pharmaceutical Services Act of British Columbia (British Columbia, 2017). While in New Zealand, McCormack et al. (2013) acknowledged that there is no precise definition for New Zealand and considered HCMs to be more than NZ $20,000 per patient per year in their report to Minister of Health of New Zealand.

Definitions could also vary within the same country according to who defines it and how they are defined. This is exemplified in both the United States and Australia. In the United States, while the Office of Inspector General of the Department of Health & Human Services considered HCMs as those with an average price of more than US $1000 per month, the researchers at State Medicaid Alternative Reimbursement and Purchasing Test for High-Cost Drugs (SMART-D) project defined HCMs as those that have reimbursement of more than US $600 per prescription amounting to a total Medicaid reimbursement of US $72 million per year (these numbers may be subject to change every year) (Department of Health and Human Services, 2017; State Medicaid Alternative Reimbursement and Purchasing Test for High-Cost Drugs (SMART-D), 2016). In Australia, price is not the only consideration factor in determining HCMs. Medicines with modest acquisition cost but used in high volume are also considered to be HCMs in addition to medicines with high acquisition cost (Rickard, 2002). With the former definition, medicines such as atorvastatin, omeprazole and celecoxib are classified as being 'high-cost' because they are used in high volume in Australia (Rickard, 2002). With the latter definition, HCMs are defined as those which incur an acquisition cost equivalent to, or more than Aus $500 per week per medicine per patient and require particular expertise for management of patient care as stipulated by the government of New South Wales of Australia (New South Wales Department of Health, 2004). Nevertheless, in Victoria, Australia, the Victorian Therapeutic Advisory Group defined HCMs for inpatient use in government-funded tertiary care facilities as those costing more than Aus $1000 per treatment episode and for outpatient visits as costing more than Aus $100 per week per beneficiary (Victorian Therapeutic Advisory Group VicTAG, 2004). While in South Australia, HCMs are defined as medicines for which the predicted annual expenditure is Aus $10,000 and above per patient per treatment course or; Aus $100,000 and above for an individual public hospital; or Aus $300,000 and above across the South Australia public health system as defined by the South Australian Medicines Advisory Committee (South Australian Medicines Advisory Committee, 2013). In Western Australia, Western Australian Therapeutics Advisory Group defines HCMs as those with a cost of more than Aus $250,000 annually within the Western Australia public health system (Government of Western Australia Department of Health, 2014).

In non-monetary terms, HCMs also encompass innovative specialty medications that involve costly medication delivery, such as requirements for special handling, complex treatment administration and complex molecule composition (i.e. biological agents with complex mechanisms of actions; Fendrick et al., 2014; Lu et al., in press). HCMs provide therapeutic advantages for a range of life-threatening diseases, including cancer, hepatitis C, rheumatoid arthritis and multiple sclerosis.

1.2 VALUE OF HCMs

The global medicine spending rises constantly as use of medicines expands. HCMs by their very nature are expected to increase pharmaceutical expenditures for either the individual patient or the healthcare system (Bach, 2009). HCMs, especially those of specialty medicines that offer highly effective treatments for many life-threatening diseases, could cost 10 times more than the cost of traditional medicines (Pharmacy Benefit Management Institute, 2013, 2014). Therefore, questions have been raised if the high cost of these medicines is worth the clinical benefits that these specialty medicines provide. Despite being expensive, HCMs are often reported to have high ‘cost per quality-adjusted life years’ (QALY) gained (McCormack et al., 2009). Chambers et al. (2014) evaluated incremental health improvements and incremental costs associated with high-cost specialty medicines upon their introduction into the market, in comparison with existing medicine or non-medicine treatments (Chambers et al., 2014). Incremental health improvements were reported as the additional QALYs gained by the high-cost specialty medicines relative to existing treatment options, while incremental costs were reported as the additional costs associated with a new treatment relative to existing treatment options. It was reported that the mean incremental QALY gain across the included 58 high-cost specialty medicines was 0.25 QALYs, with 14 of the included specialty medicines and two traditional medicines offered more than half a QALY gained (Chambers et al., 2014). However, specialty medicines were associated with greater additional (median = US $12,238) and incremental (mean = US $72,917) costs. High-cost specialty medicines tended to offer greater health improvements over pre-existing care than did traditional medicines, with 13 of the 15 medicines with the largest health gains were specialty medicines. Nevertheless, these high-cost specialty medicines also tended to be associated with larger incremental costs than traditional medicines; all the 15 medicines with the largest additional costs were specialty medicines (Chambers et al., 2014). There was no significant difference in cost-effectiveness between specialty and traditional medicines, which indicated that although high-cost specialty medicines were associated with greater incremental costs they were also associated with larger QALY gains; thus, the authors concluded that these high-cost specialty medicines may offer reasonable value for money (Chambers et al., 2014).

1.3 ACCESSIBILITY OF HCMs

Given that HCMs are both efficacious and expensive, it is of utmost importance to understand how to cover and pay for these medicines. Yazdany et al. (2015) examined the nationwide coverage of nine high-cost biological disease-modifying anti-rheumatic drugs (DMARDs) for rheumatoid arthritis treatment in the United States' Medicare Part D standalone plans and Medicare Advantage prescription medicine plans. The potential out-of-pocket cost that Medicare beneficiaries might experience for a single high-cost biological DMARD was also evaluated. It was reported that although all Medicare Part D standalone and Medicare Advantage plans covered at least one high-cost biological DMARD, access is highly controlled with 97% of these plans required prior authorisation approval, which limits access to these medicines (Yazdany et al., 2015). Coverage for individual high-cost biological DMARDs ranged from 30% to 100% of plans. Medicare Advantage prescription medicine plans were more likely to cover high-cost biological DMARDs (mean: 79%) compared to Part D standalone plans (mean: 69%). Even with biological DMARDs covered by the plan, Medicare beneficiaries would still experience very high out-of-pocket costs, requiring to pay on average 30% of coinsurance that translates to about US $2712–US $2774 for high-cost biological DMARDs before reaching catastrophic threshold, after which patients share a relatively small portion of drug costs (5%) (Yazdany et al., 2015).

Given the significant high prices of HCMs, it is not surprising that the public demand for subsidy of HCMs persists. It is imperative to engage patient and the general public, who are often the most directly affected populations, in coverage and reimbursement decisions. MacLeod et al. (2016) critically reviewed and compared the funding preferences of patients with cancer and the general public against the criteria used by payers making coverage decisions relating to high-cost cancer medicines. Overall, payers considered the broadest range of issues in the criteria (n = 35), the general public considered a moderate number in the criteria (n = 24) and patients with cancer considered the fewest criteria (n = 12). Nearly half (n = 16/35) of criteria prioritised by payers were not shared by both patients and the public, and more than two-thirds (n = 27/35) of criteria prioritised by payers were not explicitly shared by either patients or the general public. The criteria that payers consider when making decisions on the funding of high-cost cancer medicines include health outcomes, clinical need (whether alternative treatment exists), incremental health gain compared to existing therapies, economic impact and quality of evidence (MacLeod et al., 2016). Patients with cancer prefer funding for high-cost cancer medicines that improve patient health outcomes expressed by efficacy, extended survival and/ or better quality of life (MacLeod et al., 2016). Although the payers have the moral responsibility to implement care, costs of these medicines and in many situations insufficient scientific evidence are challenges for coverage decisions. On the other hand, the general public should appreciate the coverage by payers for HCMs that are efficacious and offer wider societal benefits.

The bureaucratic constraints of public health service provision impede access to medicines including HCMs (Souliotis et al., 2014). At times, the registration approval and subsequent funding of HCMs within the healthcare system is not efficient. For instance, almost all oncologists (97%) surveyed in a Canadian study were concerned about the design of the Canadian drug approval and reimbursement processes, particularly with decision-making time (Chan et al., 2012). The reimbursement of anti-cancer medicines by publicly funded programs varies by country, with Finland, France, Germany, Sweden, and the United States reimbursed the highest percentage of indications (range: 90%–100%) (Cheema et al., 2012). The healthcare focus is shifting from the number of services delivered to the value created for patients, with 'value' defined as the outcomes achieved relative to the costs (Porter et al., 2016). The strategy of 'value for money' promotes policy makers to employ rigorous, comprehensive evaluation of drugs for coverage and reimbursement decisions which could lead to restricted, denied or delayed access to HCMs.

1.4 APPROACHES FOR PROMOTING ACCESS TO HCMs

Evaluating HCMs for coverage and reimbursement may be a lengthy process and the turnaround time for this process depends on how this process is structured within a health system. Health technology assessment (HTA) refers to the systematic evaluation of properties, effects and/or impacts of health technology, which in its broadest context, includes pharmaceuticals, vaccines, medical devices, medical and surgical procedures, and the systems within which health is protected and maintained (WHO, 2017a). Since it would be impossible for health systems to financially support every new health technology that is being introduced onto the market, HTA serves to direct funding, in the form of reimbursement, to health technologies that address clinical needs and are efficacious, safe and cost-effective. Therefore, with well-performed HTA, patient access to HCMs that improve health outcomes would be made possible. HTA could ensure value for money investments in HCMs within the setting of limited healthcare resources.

However, there are often uncertainties about the clinical evidence and/or financial impact of HCMs. Therefore, to limit the impact of high prices and uncertainty, managed entry agreements (MEAs), also known as patient access schemes, have been implemented (Carlson et al., 2009; Lu et al., 2015). MEAs represent contractual agreements between the marketing authorisation holder and healthcare payers that allow market access of HCMs, particularly those for cancer and orphan diseases (Howard et al., 2015; WHO, 2017b). Although the nature of MEAs may vary between and within countries, they have a common framework of sharing the cost of uncertainty between the payer and the marketing authorisation holder to facilitate access to new HCMs.

Payers may also set up special access schemes by allocating funds to HCMs that are not publicly reimbursed. One such example is Cancer

Drugs Fund (CDF), which has been established in England in 2010 to provide patient access to cancer medicines that are not available through the National Health Service (NHS) (Aggarwal et al., 2017). Drugs for rare diseases that National Institute of Health and Care Excellence (NICE) would ordinarily not appraise can also receive funding through this channel (Davies et al., 2012). Despite significant spending channelled through CDF, Aggarwal et al. (2017) found no evidence that CDF delivers meaningful value to patients with cancer. The authors considered HTA processes as the best approach to evaluating available evidence that ensure coverage decisions maximise value for patients (Aggarwal et al., 2017).

Prices of medicines are normally determined by market forces with hardly any scrutiny by regulatory bodies. The older cost-based pricing primarily aims for profit maximisation, often leading to overpricing of medicines. However, significant changes in pharmaceutical pricing model across the world have been observed in the past few years. This is driven primarily by payers to curb the price of new HCMs. This paradigmatic shift has led to the implementation of some of the newer concepts including the value-based pricing (VBP) method. In this method, the price of a medicine is linked to actual observed real-world performance, based on willingness to pay or the perceived additional benefit of new medicines relative to established comparator therapies (Dang et al., 2016). This would permit better allocation of resources and ultimately benefit consumers, who are likely to receive the most benefit through access to new HCMs that address previously unmet needs.

The high cost of biological medicines often limits access to effective treatment for many patients. Biosimilars have been developed as interchangeable, safe, effective and cheaper alternatives to the existing biological medicines. The European Union defines a biosimilar medicine as a medicinal product, which is a copy of a biological product (the reference product) that has already received authorisation (Müller et al., 2014). Since the approval of the first biosimilar, somatotropin for injection, by the European Medicines Agency in 2009, 20 biosimilars have been approved in Europe; these medicines are based on hematopoietic growth factors (such as filgrastim and epoetin), insulin, follitropin and monoclonal antibodies (such as infliximab and etanercept) (European Medicines Agency: Epoetin Alfa Hexal, 2017; First Biosimilar Drug Gets EU Market Authorisation, 2017; GaBI Online – Generics and Biosimilars Initiative, 2017a). Biosimilars have significant potential for savings, with cost savings as high as 70% have been recorded with the use of biosimilars (GaBI Online – Generics and

Biosimilars Initiative, 2017b). This may translate into better patient access to high-cost biological therapies for various diseases including cancer, psoriasis, rheumatoid arthritis, asthma, Crohn's disease, diabetes and multiple sclerosis.

1.5 CONCLUSION

Many HCMs offer value over traditional medicines but they come with a high price tag. Countries across the globe are facing the challenges of significant increases in medicines spending and providing populations with affordable and equitable access to HCMs. Many healthcare systems are struggling with high out-of-pocket costs and restricted, delayed or denied access to HCMs. During the last decade, countries have witnessed and utilised a range of approaches that increase access to HCMs. This book covers accessibility and affordability issues related to HCMs in low-income, middle-income and high-income countries. Uganda is an example of a low-income country, whereas Portugal, Europe, Australia and New Zealand are examples of middle-income and high-income countries. Coverage and reimbursement decisions for HCMs should be based on scientific evidence and value-based pharmaco-economic evaluation with engagement of stakeholders in the process to account for patient and public preferences. With the proliferation of HCMs indicated for an increasing number of patients, it is important that countries share lessons learned in order to improve patient access to innovative care within finite budgets. The book aims to facilitate that exchange of knowledge and experience.

NOTE

Christine Y. Lu and Zaheer-Ud-Din Babar are co-senior authors on this work.

REFERENCES

Aggarwal, A., Fojo, T., Chamberlain, C., Davis, C., Sullivan, R., Aug 1, 2017. Do patient access schemes for high-cost cancer drugs deliver value to society? Lessons from the NHS Cancer Drugs Fund. Ann. Oncol. 28 (8), 1738–1750.

Bach, P.B., 2009. Limits on Medicare's ability to control rising spending on cancer drugs. N. Engl. J. Med. 360 (6), 626–633.

British Columbia. Pharmaceutical Services Act: drug price regulation. 2017. Available from: http://www.bclaws.ca/EPLibraries/bclaws_new/document/ID/freeside/344_2012.

Carlson, J.J., Garrison, Jr., L.P., Sullivan, S.D., Oct 2009. Paying for outcomes: innovative coverage and reimbursement schemes for pharmaceuticals. J. Manag. Care Pharm. 15 (8), 683–687.

Chambers, J.D., Thorat, T., Pyo, J., Chenoweth, M., Neumann, P.J., October 2014. Despite high costs, specialty drugs may offer value for money comparable to that of traditional drugs. Health Aff. (Millwood) 33 (10), 1751–1760.

Chan, K.K., Wong, B., Siu, L.L., Straus, S.E., Chang, J., Berry, S.R., 2012. Less than ideal: how oncologists practice with limited drug access. J. Oncol. Pract. 8 (3), 190–195.
Cheema, P.K., Gavura, S., Migus, M., Godman, B., Yeung, L., Trudeau, M.E., 2012. International variability in the reimbursement of cancer drugs by publically funded drug programs. Curr. Oncol. 19 (3), e165.
Crump, B.J., Panton, R., Drummond, M.F., Marchment, M., Hawkes, R.A., 1995. Transferring the costs of expensive treatments from secondary to primary care. BMJ 310 (6978), 509–512.
Dang, A., Mendon, S., Desireddy, P., 2016. Improving access to new treatments with value based pricing: an Indian perspective. PTB Rep. 2 (1), 1–5.
Davies, J.E., Neidle, S., Taylor, D.G., Jan 3, 2012. Developing and paying for medicines for orphan indications in oncology: utilitarian regulation vs equitable care? Br. J. Cancer 106 (1), 14–17.
Department of Health and Human Services, 2017. Office of inspector general. High-price drugs are increasing federal payments for Medicare part D catastrophic coverage. Available from: https://oig.hhs.gov/oei/reports/oei-02-16-00270.pdf.
European Medicines Agency: Epoetin Alfa Hexal, 2017. http://www.ema.europa.eu/ema/index.jsp?curl(pages/medicines/human/medicines/000726/human_med_000768.jsp&mid(WC0b01ac058001d125 (accessed 19.11.17).
Fendrick, M.A., Buxbaum, J., Westrich, K., 2014. Supporting Consumer Access to Specialty Medications through Value-Based Insurance Design. University of Michigan Center for Value-Based Insurance Design, Ann Arbor, MI, pp. 7–13.
First Biosimilar Drug Gets EU Market Authorisation, 2017. http://www.euractiv.com/health/biosimilar-drug-gets-eu-market-authorisation/article-154524 (accessed 19.11.17).
GaBI Online – Generics and Biosimilars Initiative, 2017. Biosimilars approved in Europe. http://www.gabionline.net/Biosimilars/General/Biosimilars-approved-in-Europe (accessed 19.11.17).
GaBI Online – Generics and Biosimilars Initiative, 2017. Huge discount on biosimilar infliximab in Norway. http://www.gabionline.net/Biosimilars/General/Huge-discount-on-biosimilar-infliximab-in-Norway (accessed 19.11.17).
Government of Western Australia Department of Health, 2014. WA statewide medicines formulary framework. Available from: http://www.watag.org.au/wasmf/docs/141124_SMF_Framework.pdf.
Howard, D.H.B.P., Berndt, E.R., Conti, R.M., 2015. Pricing in the market for anticancer drugs. J. Econ. Perspect. 29 (1), 139–162.
Lu, C.Y., Zhang, F., Golonski, N., Lupton, C., Jeffrey, P., Wagner, A.K., in press. State medicaid reimbursement for medications for chronic hepatitis C infection from 2012 through 2015, *Value Health*. Available from: http://dx.doi.org/10.1016/j.jval.2017.09.011.
Lu, C.Y., Lupton, C., Rakowsky, S., Babar, Z.U., Ross-Degnan, D., Wagner, A.K., 2015. Patient access schemes in Asia-Pacific markets: current experience and future potential. J. Pharm. Policy Pract. 8 (1), 6.
MacLeod, T.E., Harris, A.H., Mahal, A., June 2016. Stated and revealed preferences for funding new high-cost cancer drugs: a critical review of the evidence from patients, the public and payers. Patient 9 (3), 201–222.
McCormack, P., Quigley, J., Hansen, P., 2009. Review of access to high-cost, highly-specialised medicines in New Zealand, in Report to Minister of Health, Hon Tony Ryall. Wellington, p. 84.
McCormack, P., Quigley, J., Hansen, P., 2013. Report to Minister of Health, Hon Tony Ryall. Review of access to high cost, highly specialised medicines in New Zealand. Available from: http://img.scoop.co.nz/media/pdfs/1005/Review_of_Access_to_High_Cost_Highly_Specialised_Medicines_31_April_2010.pdf.
Müller, R., Renner, C., Gabay, C., Cassata, G., Lohri, A., Hasler, P., 2014 Jul 1. The advent of biosimilars: challenges and risks. Swiss. Med. Wkly. 144, w13980.

New South Wales Department of Health, 2004. Circular No. 2004/73. Funding arrangements for outpatient use of high cost drugs not funded by the Commonwealth. Available from: http://www1.health.nsw.gov.au/pds/ActivePDSDocuments/PD2005_395.pdf.

Pharmacy Benefit Management Institute, 2013. 2013 specialty drug benefit report. Plano (TX), The Institute.

Pharmacy Benefit Management Institute, 2014. 2014 specialty drug benefit report. Plano (TX), The Institute.

Poirier, T., Gianetti, V., 1995. Clinical and ethical principles on rationing high-cost drugs. Ann. Pharmacother. 29, 78–81.

Porter, M.E., Larsson, S., Lee, T.H., 2016. Standardizing patient outcomes measurement. N. Engl. J. Med. 374 (6), 504–506.

Powe, N.R., Eggers, P.W., Johnson, C.B., 1994. Early adoption of cyclosporine and recombinant human erythropoietin: clinical, economic, and policy issues with emergence of high-cost drugs. Am. J. Kidney Dis. 24 (1), 33–41.

Rickard, M., 2002. The Pharmaceutical Benefits Scheme: options for cost control. Available from: https://www.aph.gov.au/About_Parliament/Parliamentary_Departments/Parliamentary_Library/Publications_Archive/CIB/cib0102/02CIB12.

Souliotis, K., Papageorqiou, M., Politi, A., Loakeimidis, D., Sidiropoulos, P., 2014. Barriers to accessing biologic treatment for rheumatoid arthritis in Greece: the unseen impact of the fiscal crisis—the Health Outcomes Patient Environment (HOPE) study. Rheumatol. Int. 34 (1), 25–33.

South Australian Medicines Advisory Committee, 2013. Statewide formulary for high cost medicines. Available from: http://www.sahealth.sa.gov.au/wps/wcm/connect/ca647b-004890353c857ff57675638bd8/Directive_Statewide_Formulary_for_high_cost_Medicines_Aug11_final.pdf?MOD=AJPERES&CACHEID=ca647b004890353c857ff5767 5638bd8.

State Medicaid Alternative Reimbursement and Purchasing Test for High-Cost Drugs (SMART-D). High-cost specialty drugs and Medicaid. 2016. Available from: http://smart-d.org/high-cost-specialty-drugs-and-medicaid/.

Victorian Therapeutic Advisory Group VicTAG, 2004. Hospital Price and Resource Allocation Review: Good Practice Model for Controlling Medicines Costs in Hospitals. Victorian Therapeutics Advisory Group, Melbourne, pp. 1–52.

WHO, 2015. Access to new medicines in Europe: technical review of policy initiatives and opportunities for collaboration and research. Available from: http://www.euro.who.int/en/health-topics/Health-systems/medicines/publications2/2015/access-to-new-medicines-in-europe-technical-review-of-policy-initiatives-and-opportunities-for-collaboration-and-research.

WHO, 2017. Health technology assessment of medical devices. http://apps.who.int/iris/bitstream/10665/44564/1/9789241501361_eng.pdf (accessed 17.11.17).

WHO, 2017. Access to new medicines in Europe: technical review of policy initiatives and opportunities for collaboration and research. http://www.euro.who.int/__data/assets/pdf_file/0008/306179/Access-new-medicines-TR-PIO-collaboration-research.pdf?ua=1 (accessed 18.11.17).

Yazdany, J., Dudley, R.A., Chen, R., Lin, G.A., Tseng, C.W., Jun 2015. Coverage for high cost specialty drugs for rheumatoid arthritis in Medicare Part D. Arthritis Rheumatol. 67 (6), 1474–1480.

CHAPTER 2

Health Technology Assessment

Jennifer A. Whitty
Norwich Medical School, University of East Anglia, Norwich, United Kingdom

2.1 INTRODUCTION

This chapter provides an introductory overview of Health Technology Assessment (HTA) and its role in decision-making to support equitable access to healthcare, particularly as it applies to the public subsidy of high cost medicines. It therefore forms a foundation for some of the more detailed examples provided in later chapters in this book. Although HTA often feeds into the pricing of medicines and healthcare services, policies related to the pricing of technologies are outside the scope for this chapter; refer instead to Chapter 10 for a discussion around pricing.

2.2 WHAT IS HEALTH TECHNOLOGY ASSESSMENT (HTA)?

Healthcare expenditure has risen rapidly in most countries, both in absolute terms and as a proportion of Gross Domestic Product (GDP). Aging populations, the burden of chronic disease, consumer expectations around universal coverage, the provision and quality of healthcare, and the ongoing development of newer and often very expensive health technologies and advances in treatment have been cited as key cost drivers (AGPC, 2005).

In every health system there is a virtually unlimited list of potential uses for the somewhat more finite resources we have to spend on healthcare and often difficult decisions have to be made about how we can make the best use of the scarce resources that we have available for Health and Health Care. As a consequence, rationing decisions are made that may be perceived as denying treatment to some patients, resulting in 'winners' and 'losers'. Equitable access to sustainable healthcare is an important policy objective. Society needs an evidence-based, systematic, fair and reproducible mechanism for making these tough decisions.

HTA provides such a mechanism that can be used as a 'tool' to assist policy makers to effectively prioritise their health services, improve their quality, efficiency and responsiveness, and to reduce inappropriate variation in access. HTA is described by the International Network of Agencies

Equitable Access to High-Cost Pharmaceuticals
http://dx.doi.org/10.1016/B978-0-12-811945-7.00002-6

for Health Technology Assessment (INAHTA) as 'a *multidisciplinary* field of policy analysis. It studies the *medical, social, ethical, and economic implications* of development, diffusion, and use of health technology' (emphasis added) (INAHTA, 2013). Other similar definitions exist (Eddy, 2009). HTA has also been referred to as Comparative Effectiveness Research (CER), particularly in the United States (Chalkidou et al., 2009). HTA aims to make the evidence around these issues accessible and usable for policy decision-making purposes. In doing so, HTA has been described as a bridge between clinical research and health policy decision-making (Battista and Hodge, 1999).

Broadly, HTA involves an assessment of evidence related to the safety, efficacy, and effectiveness of a new technology, as well as other potential benefits such as those related to equity or patient preferences, and/or cost-effectiveness of a new technology (see Section 2.5 for further discussion of the evidence requirements for HTA). The assessment is often undertaken or at least critiqued by an independent group of individuals with relevant scientific expertise. This assessment is then used to inform the use of technology in the health system, commonly through marketing approval, reimbursement advice or the development of clinical guidelines (AGPC, 2005). The subsequent process by which the evidence from an HTA is appraised and considered within decision-making processes has been referred to as health technology *appraisal* (e.g. by the National Institute for Health and Care Excellence (NICE) in the UK).

The output of an appraisal is usually a recommendation regarding policy, access or funding. HTA processes can also sometimes include functions related to the early identification and evaluation of new and emerging technologies, referred to as horizon scanning, and to the ongoing monitoring and review of technologies after marketing and in clinical practice (AGPC, 2005). HTA can be used to inform decisions around the introduction of new technologies to the health system, or around disinvestment from existing technologies; that is, reallocation of resources away from ineffective healthcare practises towards those that offer greater efficiency (Elshaug et al., 2007; Pearson and Littlejohns, 2007).

The field of HTA has grown substantially since it was first conceptualised in the 1970s, alongside the development of the evidence-based medicine movement (Banta, 2003; Eddy, 2009). HTA processes are now extensive, and are undertaken in a range of countries globally; though the context of HTA remains crucial and specific to any one health system, and the jurisdiction's history, culture, values and preferences (Banta, 2003). HTA can occur at the national, provincial or state, and regional or institutional level in the health system; however, it appears to be most established—or at least most publicised—at the national level. Stafinski et al. (2011) compiled a list of health technology funding/coverage decision-making processes. Their review identified 21 national, four provincial/state and six regional/institutional level technology decision-making processes across 20 countries (Stafinski et al., 2011).

2.3 TECHNOLOGIES

HTA sits within policy frameworks related to accessing health technologies in the health system. For example, the Australian Government's vision for its HTA policy framework is that 'Australians have timely, equitable, and affordable access to the cost-effective health technologies needed to manage their health' (DHA, 2011). HTA is most strongly established for the assessment of pharmaceuticals, including vaccines and high cost medicines (Stafinski et al., 2011). As such, it feeds into broader governance frameworks related to National Medicines Policy. For example, Australia's National Medicine's Policy (2000) has four arms related to achieving universal access to medicines at a reasonable cost, appropriate standards for quality, safety and efficacy, the quality use of medicines, and encouraging a responsible and viable medicines industry (DHA, 1999). All four arms are relevant for Australia's HTA processes.

However, HTA is also commonly applied to health technologies other than pharmaceuticals such as diagnostic tests, devices and prostheses, medical procedures, and public health interventions (Stafinski et al., 2011). Indeed, a health technology can be broadly defined as 'The drugs, devices, and medical and surgical procedures used in health care, and the organisational and supportive systems within which such care is provided' (OTA, 1978). Therefore, HTA covers a wide scope, including assessment of services and systems such as Intensive Care Units, outpatient clinics, pre-admission clinics and the like (Banta, 2003).

2.4 PRINCIPLES UNDERPINNING HTA PROCESSES

The concepts of distributional and procedural justice are both relevant to HTA. Distributional justice concerns the fair allocation of health and healthcare in society. It is therefore related to the fairness of decisions and the criteria underpinning them. Procedural justice concerns fairness in the processes that lead to the allocation of resources. It is particularly important when it is difficult to agree on how health care should be distributed, such as when subsidy decisions might affect access to medicines and other health technologies. The importance of procedural justice has been highlighted in the context of HTA and related decision-making (Rawlins, 2005).

Daniels and Sabin's 'Accountability for Reasonableness' framework has been popularly cited as supporting fair decision-making around priority setting in healthcare, including in access to high cost medicines (Daniels and Sabin, 1997; Daniels, 2000; Daniels and Sabin, 2002; Hasman and Holm, 2005; Daniels and Sabin, 2008). Their framework is underpinned by four principles which if followed promote fair decision-making: publicity, reasons, appeals, and enforcement. The principles of procedural justice are often mirrored in the policy frameworks underpinning HTA. For example, according to the Australian Government, HTA processes in Australia are intended to be sustainable, transparent, accountable and independent, consultative and reflective of Australian community values, administratively efficient, flexible and fit for purpose, and informed by robust and relevant evidence (DHA, 2011).

However, achieving these principles in health technology decisions may be challenging in practice. Publicity is linked to transparency, which has been questioned, particularly where information and evidence underlying a decision may be commercial in confidence, as can be the case for processes involving pharmaceuticals (Stafinski et al., 2011). Appeals are possible, but often relate to the process and not the decision, and are not available in all jurisdictions (Stafinski et al., 2011). Appeal mechanisms have sometimes been criticised for not being independent from the decision-making authority (Stafinski et al., 2011).

Timeliness of the HTA process and/or limitations in the available evidence, which potentially lead to delays in access to technologies, has also created a challenge for policy makers (Stafinski et al., 2011). The average duration from lodgement to listing of a request to consider funding of a medical service in Australia has been reported to be as high as 30 months (range 19–48 months) (O'Malley, 2010), likely contributing to the rationale for a review of HTA processes in Australia (DHA, 2009). Access or Coverage with Evidence Development (AED or CED) and risk sharing schemes have been introduced in some HTA processes to provide interim funding with requirement for evidence development in an attempt to avoid delays in access (Owen et al., 2008; O'Malley, 2010). The former has most often been introduced to support decisions around non-pharmaceutical technologies, the latter for pharmaceuticals (Stafinski et al., 2011).

2.5 EVIDENCE-BASED DECISION-MAKING FOR THE SUBSIDY OF HEALTH TECHNOLOGIES

HTA sits within a broader evidence-based medicine framework. It uses 'scientific evidence to assess the [comparative] quality, safety, efficacy, effectiveness and cost effectiveness of health services' (DHA, 2009). Many health technology policy processes publish technical guidance on the evidence requirements to support their specific health technology decision processes, but the nature of the guidance varies. For example, NICE in the UK publish technical guidance that includes a prescriptive 'reference case' to promote consistency of methods (NICE, 2013). Whereas, the Australian Pharmaceutical Benefits Advisory Committee (PBAC) publishes detailed but less prescriptive guidance (PBAC, 2013), which arguably retains a greater level of flexibility in the evidence requirements but potentially threatens the consistency and therefore comparability of assessments between technologies.

Information describing the therapeutic claim, relevant patient populations, current standard management, evidence demonstrating safety, efficacy and clinical effectiveness, and a basic analysis of resource or cost implications appear to be universally required across all processes, regardless of jurisdiction or technology type (Stafinski et al., 2011). Many decision-making processes require economic evaluations to demonstrate cost-effectiveness (Stafinski et al., 2011). Approximately, two thirds of bodies making decisions for the subsidy of health technologies require a budget-impact analysis (Stafinski et al., 2011). The perspective of the economic analysis is variable, with some processes taking a payer and some a societal perspective (Stafinski et al., 2011).

2.5.1 Criteria Used to Inform Subsidy Decisions

The evidence-based requirements are aligned with the criteria that are used to make recommendations. As an example, the criteria that are applied to decisions by the PBAC and Medical Services Advisory Committee (MSAC) who make recommendations on the public reimbursement of pharmaceuticals and vaccines (PBAC) or medical services (MSAC) to the Minister for Health and Ageing in Australia according to their Guidelines are shown in Box 2.1 (MSAC, 2012; PBAC, 2013). The factors considered by NICE in making recommendations around the availability of health technologies in England and Wales according to their 'Guide to the methods of technology appraisals' are shown in Box 2.2 (NICE, 2013).

BOX 2.1 Decision-making criteria used by PBAC and MSAC in Australia (MSAC, 2012; PBAC, 2013).

- Comparative health gain (effectiveness, safety)
- Comparative cost effectiveness
- Financial implications for pharmaceutical benefits scheme and government health budget
- Severity of condition treated
- Presence of effective alternatives
- Ability to target therapy to those likely to benefit most
- Uncertainty
- Equity
- "Rule of Rescue"—may be favorable to recommending subsidy as a supplement to other considerations in exceptional circumstances, when:
  - No alternative treatment exists in Australia
  - Condition is severe, progressive, and expected to lead to premature death
  - Condition applies to only a very small number of patients

BOX 2.2 Factors considered by NICE Appraisal Committees when making recommendations (NICE, 2013)

- Broad balance between benefits and costs of providing health services or social care
- Degree of need for health services or social care
- Desirability of promoting innovation in providing health services or social care
- Clinical and cost-effectiveness
- Extent of uncertainty, including in the evidence
- 'Life-extending treatment at the end of life'
- Innovation
- Issues related to advancing equality and eliminating unlawful discrimination
- Social value judgements

Social values that are considered important by the society that is affected by the decision-making process are recognised as an important consideration in health technology decisions (Whitty and Littlejohns, 2015). It is clear that the general public value benefits from technologies that are much wider than health gain; for example, they value aspects of how a technology is delivered and to whom, convenience, and equity and fairness of distribution (Whitty et al., 2014a, b). Social value judgements are explicitly considered by approximately one fifth of health technology decision-making processes according to their technical guidance (Stafinski et al., 2011) including by NICE (Box 2.2). It seems likely they may be implicitly considered by others. Social value judgements may include factors such as fairness in distributing resource for health benefits, the impact of recommendations on health inequalities, special circumstances such as end of life care or criteria where a 'rule of rescue' might apply (Box 2.1), extra health benefits that might be relevant but not captured in the assessment of clinical or cost-effectiveness, or benefits related to innovation (NICE, 2008; Whitty and Littlejohns, 2015). However, exploration of the social values that are important has occurred to only a limited extent (Stafinski et al., 2011; Whitty, 2013; Whitty and Littlejohns, 2015). A notable exception to this is the establishment in 2002 of a Citizens' Council by NICE, consisting of 30 diverse members of the public, to provide NICE with a public perspective on the moral and ethical issues that are considered in NICE guidance and decision-making (Davies et al., 2005).

2.5.2 Threshold for Value for Money

The prominence of cost-effectiveness as a decision criterion in most jurisdictions is inextricably linked to the question of what is considered to be an acceptable cost to benefit ratio for a new health technology. That is, how much are the healthcare decision-makers willing to pay for an incremental health gain or other benefits for the population they serve? The quality-adjusted life year (QALY) is currently the prescribed (e.g. by NICE (NICE, 2013)) or preferred (e.g. by PBAC (PBAC, 2013)) outcome measure when economic evaluation is used to inform technology subsidy decisions. Few decision-making bodies have explicitly stated a threshold at which they are prepared to fund a technology. One exception though is NICE, who indicate a usual though not rigid maximum acceptable threshold range of £20,000–£30,000 per QALY (NICE, 2013). Most evidence strongly suggests that there is not a single threshold used by decision-makers, but rather that any judgement on cost-effectiveness is augmented by consideration of criteria and moderators that are not explicitly incorporated in a cost-utility analysis using the QALY as an outcome measure (e.g. George et al., 2001; Devlin and Parkin, 2004; Dakin et al., 2006; Harris et al., 2008; Whitty et al., 2011; Dakin et al., 2014).

2.5.3 Considering Multiple Criteria in Decision-making

The multiple criteria that are important for decisions requires a systematic and reproducible approach to considering their relative merits and impact for decisions around access to technologies such as high cost medicines. HTA decision-making processes often use deliberative approaches to consider the complex evidence and information that might be relevant for decision-making. However, the relative merits of deliberative approaches and those capable of weighting decision criteria have been discussed (Boaz et al., 2014; Whitty et al., 2014c). The integration of equity and social values into or alongside cost-effectiveness as decision criteria has been explored using quantifiable approaches such as equity weights and social welfare functions, mathematical programming, and multi-criteria decision analysis (MCDA) (Johri and Norheim, 2012). MCDA is recognised as a possible approach to underpin decisions around access to health technologies, in principle and potentially in practise (Jehu-Appiah et al., 2008; Devlin and Sussex, 2011; Tony et al., 2011; Thokala and Duenas, 2012; Youngkong et al., 2012; Marsh et al., 2016; Thokala et al., 2016).

2.6 WHO'S INVOLVED? STAKEHOLDERS AT THE TABLE

HTA is a multidisciplinary field, and the nature of the decisions mean that stakeholders include the healthcare and pharmaceutical industries, insurers, clinicians, researchers, patients and general public more widely (Banta, 2003). Stakeholders may be able to contribute to the HTA process by representation on the decision-making committee, presentation to the committee, attendance and participation in public meetings, and/or commenting on provisional recommendations (Stafinski et al., 2011). Patients and the public are recognised as stakeholders and their input to processes is invited by the majority of HTA bodies, though often through communication or consultation, rather than participatory methods (Whitty, 2013; Whitty and Littlejohns, 2015).

2.7 FUTURE DIRECTIONS IN HEALTH TECHNOLOGY ASSESSMENT FOR HIGH COST MEDICINES

The challenges that are associated with making decisions about the subsidy of high cost medicines are here to stay. Indeed, they may become heightened in a landscape of chronic disease, precision medicine and individualised care, rare diseases and orphan drugs, and enhanced consumer expectations and demands (World Health Organization (WHO), 2015; Harvey and de Boer, 2015). The importance of fair and transparent decision-making and the consideration of patients and public preferences around the availability of high cost medicines is likely to become increasingly prominent (Abelson et al., 2007; Bridges and Jones, 2007; Weale et al., 2016). The views of stakeholders around innovation and the importance for society of balancing the dual objectives of innovation and efficiency is likely to continue as a prominent debate around the funding of high cost medicines and other health technologies (Ciani and Jommi, 2014; World Health Organization (WHO), 2015). The extent to which harmonisation of HTA processes across countries or jurisdictions can be expanded is uncertain, and may be limited by political structures (Abbasi, 2016; Integlia and Mazzoni, 2017). Regardless, the spread and uptake of HTA processes to inform high cost medicine reimbursement decisions in both European and non-European countries is likely to continue (Yang, 2009; World Health Organization (WHO), 2015).

2.8 SUMMARY

HTA has become an important priority-setting process in many high income and increasingly in middle and lower income countries. This chapter has introduced the concept of HTA particularly as it applies to the assessment, appraisal and decision-making around access via public subsidy to high cost medicines. HTA is inherently an evidence-based process that adopts the principles of procedural justice and is used to inform policy and access decisions. Both scientific evidence and evidence on social values are relevant, and their joint consideration in health technology decision-making is both necessary and challenging.

REFERENCES

Abbasi, K., 2016. Drug approval and research assessment: arguments for reform. J. R. Soc. Med. 109 (9), 323.

Abelson, J., Giacomini, M., Lehoux, P., Gauvin, F.P., 2007. Bringing 'the public' into health technology assessment and coverage policy decisions: from principles to practice. Health Policy 82 (1), 37–50.

Australian Government Productivity Commission (AGPC), 2005. Impacts of advances in medical technology in Australia. Australian Government Productivity Commission, Melbourne, 604.

Banta, D., 2003. The development of health technology assessment. Health Policy 63 (2), 121–132.

Battista, R.N., Hodge, M.J., 1999. The evolving paradigm of health technology assessment: reflections for the millennium. CMAJ 160 (10), 1464–1467.

Boaz, A., Chambers, M., Stuttaford, M., 2014. Public participation: more than a method? Comment on "Harnessing the potential to quantify public preferences for healthcare priorities through citizens' juries". Int. J. Health Policy Manage. 3 (5), 291–293.

Bridges, J.F.P., Jones, C., 2007. Patient-based health technology assessment: a vision of the future. Int. J. Technol. Assess. Health Care 23 (1), 30–35.

Chalkidou, K., Tunis, S., Lopert, R., Rochaix, L., Sawicki, P.T., Nasser, M. et al., 2009. Comparative effectiveness research and evidence-based health policy: experience from four countries. Milbank Q. 87 (2), 339–367.

Ciani, O., Jommi, C., 2014. The role of health technology assessment bodies in shaping drug development. Drug Des. Dev. Ther. 8, 2273–2281.

Dakin, H.A., Devlin, N.J., Odeyemi, I.A., 2006. "Yes", "No" or "Yes, but"? Multinomial modelling of NICE decision-making. Health Policy 77 (3), 352–367.

Dakin, H., Devlin, N., Feng, Y., Rice, N., O'Neill, P., Parkin, D., 2014. The influence of cost-effectiveness and other factors on nice decisions. Health Econ. 24 (10), 1243–1388.

Daniels, N., 2000. Accountability for reasonableness: establishing a fair process for priority setting is easier than agreeing on principles. Brit. Med. J. 321, 1300–1301.

Daniels, N., Sabin, J., 1997. Limits to health care: fair procedures, democratic deliberation, and the legitimacy problem for insurers. Phil. Public Aff. 26 (4), 303–350.

Daniels, N., Sabin, J., 2002. Setting limits fairly: can we learn to share medical resources? Oxford University Press, New York, pp191.

Daniels, N., Sabin, J.E., 2008. Accountability for reasonableness: an update. BMJ 337, a1850.

Davies, C, Wetherell, M., Barnett, E., Seymour-Smith, S., 2005. Opening the box: Evaluating the citizens council of NICE. The Open University, Milton Keynes.

Department of Health and Ageing (DHA), National Medicines Policy 2000. 1999, Commonwealth of Australia: Canberra.

Department of Health and Ageing (DHA), Review of Health Technology Assessment in Australia. 2009, Australia Government: Canberra.

Department of Health and Ageing (DHA). HTA Policy Framework. Feb 2 2011 [cited 2013 Feb 14]; Available from: http://www.health.gov.au/internet/hta/publishing.nsf/Content/policy-1#vision.

Devlin, N., Parkin, D., 2004. Does NICE have a cost-effectiveness threshold and what other factors influence its decisions? A binary choice analysis. Health Econ. 13 (5), 437–452.

Devlin, N., Sussex, J., 2011. Incorporating multiple criteria in HTA: methods and processes. Office of Health Economics, London.

Eddy, D., 2009. Health technology assessment and evidence-based medicine: what are we talking about? Value Health. 12 (Suppl. 2), S6–S7.

Elshaug, A.G., Hiller, E., Tunis, R., Moss, R., 2007. Challenges in Australian policy processes for disinvestment from existing, ineffective health care practices. Aust. NZ. Health Policy 4 (1), 23.

George, B., Harris, A., Mitchell, A., 2001. Cost-effectiveness analysis and the consistency of decision making: evidence from pharmaceutical reimbursement in Australia (1991 to 1996). Pharmacoeconomics 19 (11), 1103–1109.

Harris, A.H, Hill, S.R, Chin, G., Li, J.J., Walkom, E., 2008. The role of value for money in public insurance coverage decisions for drugs in Australia: a retrospective analysis 1994–2004. Med. Decis. Making 28 (5), 713–722.

Harvey, R., de Boer, R., 7 Jan 2015. Growth in expenditure on high cost drugs in Australia [Research Paper], in Parliamentary Library Information Analysis Advice Research Paper Series, 2014–15. Parliament of Australia, Department of Parliamentary Services, Canberra.

Hasman, A., Holm, S., 2005. Accountability for reasonableness: opening the black box of process. Health Care Anal. 13 (4), 261–273.

International Network of Agencies for Health Technology Assessment (INAHTA). HTA Resources. [cited 2013 Apr 15]; Available from: http://www.inahta.net/.

Integlia, D., Mazzoni, E., 2017. Health technology assessment in the European Union state of art and future scenarios. In: de Empoli, S., Integlia, D. (Eds.), I-Com – Istituto per la Competitività, Rome, Italy.

Jehu-Appiah, C., Baltussen, R., Acquah, C., Aikins, M., Almeida, C, d'Almeida, S.A. et al., 2008. Balancing equity and efficiency in health priorities in Ghana: the use of multicriteria decision analysis. Value Health 11 (7), 1081–1087.
Johri, M., Norheim, O.F., 2012. Can cost-effectiveness analysis integrate concerns for equity? Systematic review. Int. J. Technol. Assess. Health Care (2), 125–132.
Marsh, K., Jzerman, M., Thokala, P., Baltussen, R., Boysen, M., Kaló, Z et al., 2016. Multiple criteria decision analysis for health care decision making--Emerging good practices: Report 2 of the ISPOR MCDA emerging good practices task force. Value Health 19 (2), 125–137.
Medical Services Advisory Committee, 2012. Overview of guidelines for the processes supporting the medical services advisory committee (Version, 1.0)., Draft for, consultation., Sept. Australian Government Department of Health and Ageing.
National Institute for Health and Care Excellence (NICE), 2013. Guide to the methods of technology appraisal. NICE, London.
National Institute for Health and Clinical Excellence (NICE), Social value judgements: principles for the development of NICE guidance. 2008, NICE: London.
Office of Technology Assessment (OTA). Assessing the efficacy and safety of medical technologies. 1978, Washington DC: U.S.: Government Printing Office.
O'Malley, S.P., 2010. Issues facing the Australian health technology assessment review of medical technology funding. Med. J. Aust. 193 (1), 30–33.
Owen, A., Spinks, J., Meehan, A., Hardy, M., Kwasha, D., Wlodarczyk, J. et al., 2008. A new model to evaluate the long-term cost effectiveness of orphan and highly specialised drugs following listing on the Australian Pharmaceutical Benefits Scheme: the Bosentan Patient Registry. J. Med. Econ. 11 (2), 235–243.
Pearson, S., Littlejohns, P., 2007. Reallocating resources: how should the National Institute for Health and Clinical Excellence guide disinvestment efforts in the National Health Service? J. Health Serv. Res. Policy 12 (3), 160–165.
Pharmaceutical Benefits Advisory Committee (PBAC), 2013. Guidelines for preparing submissions to the Pharmaceutical Benefits Advisory Committee (Version 4. 4). Australian Government Department of Health, Canberra.
Rawlins, M.D., 2005. Pharmacopolitics and deliberative democracy. Clin. Med. 5 (5), 471–475.
Stafinski, T., 2011. Health technology funding decision-making processes around the world: the same, yet different. Pharmacoeconomics 29 (6), 475–495.
Thokala, P., Duenas, A., 2012. Multiple criteria decision analysis for health technology assessment. Value Health 15 (8), 1172–1181.
Thokala, P., Devlin, N., Marsh, K., Baltussen, R., Boysen, M., Kalo, Z., 2016. Multiple criteria decision analysis for health care decision making--an introduction: Report 1 of the ISPOR MCDA emerging good practices task force. Value Health 19 (1), 1–13.
Tony, M., Wagner, M., Khoury, H., Rindress, D., Papastavros, T., Oh, P. et al., 2011. Bridging health technology assessment (HTA) with multicriteria decision analyses (MCDA): field testing of the EVIDEM framework for coverage decisions by a public payer in Canada. BMC Health Serv. Res. 11, 329.
Weale, A., Kieslich, K., Littlejohns, P., Tugendhaft, A., Tumilty, E., Weerasuriya, K. et al., 2016. Introduction: priority setting, equitable access and public involvement in health care. J. Health Organ. Manage. 30 (5), 736–750.
Whitty, J.A., 2013. An international survey of the public engagement practices of health technology assessment organizations. Value Health 16 (1), 155–163.
Whitty, J.A., Littlejohns, P., 2015. Social values and health priority setting in Australia: an analysis applied to the context of health technology assessment. Health Policy 119 (2), 127–136.
Whitty, J.A., Scuffham, P.A., Rundle-Thiele, S.R., 2011. Public and decision maker stated preferences for pharmaceutical subsidy decisions: a pilot study. Appl. Health Econ. Health Policy 9 (2), 73–79.

Whitty, J.A, Lancsar, E., Rixon, K., F J.A, Golenko, X., Ratcliffe, J., 2014a. A systematic review of stated preference studies reporting public preferences for healthcare priority setting. Patient 7 (4), 365–386.

Whitty, J.A., Ratcliffe, J., Chen, G., Scuffham, P.A., 2014b. Australian public preferences for the funding of new health technologies: A comparison of discrete choice and profile case best-worst scaling methods. Med. Decis. Making 34, 638–654.

Whitty, J.A., Burton, P., Kendall, E., Ratcliffe, J., Wilson, A, Littlejohns, P. et al., 2014c. Harnessing the potential to quantify public preferences for healthcare priorities through citizens' juries. Int. J. Health Policy Manage. 3 (2), 57–62.

World Health Organization (WHO), 2015. Access to new medicines in Europe: technical review of policy initiatives and opportunities for collaboration and research. WHO, Copenhagen, Denmark.

Yang, B.M., 2009. The future of health technology assessment in healthcare decision making in Asia. Pharmacoeconomics 27 (11), 891–901.

Youngkong, S., Baltussen, R., Tantivess, S., Mohara, A., Teerawattananon, Y., 2012. Multicriteria decision analysis for including health interventions in the universal health coverage benefit package in Thailand. Value Health 15 (6), 961–970.

CHAPTER 3

High-Cost Medicines in England

Darrin Baines
Bournemouth University, Bournemouth, Dorset, United Kingdom

3.1 INTRODUCTION

The Constitution of the UK's National Health Service (NHS) states that the health system will provide a comprehensive service, available to all, with access based upon clinical need and not individual ability to pay (DoH, 2015). At the same time, the system is committed to providing best value for taxpayers' money. The recent growth in the availability of 'high-cost medicines' has challenged the UK government's commitment to providing a comprehensive service, free at the point of delivery, when doing so has a substantial impact upon public expenditure. Most NHS services are funded through general taxation, with funds being allocated to providers primarily through the route of local contracting for services by Clinical Commissioning Groups (CCGs) (NHS England, 2017). Under the current arrangements, all medicines supplied by the NHS are reimbursed by the health system with funds initially provided by the Department of Health (DoH) on behalf of the UK government.

Prescribing spends in both primary and secondary cares are reimbursed nationally from money raised from general taxation and distributed by the DoH. Overall, NHS spending on medicines in 2015/2016 was £15.8 billion (NHS Digital, 2016). Hospital prescribing was 54.2% (£7.6 billion) of this total, with the rest (£9.0 billion) being spent in primary care. In recent years, there has been the rapid growth in spending on drugs by hospitals, which increased from £4.2 billion in 2010/2011 to £7.6 billion in 2015/2016, a rise of 81.8%. This growth was caused by the introduction of new and innovative medicines, as well as the greater use of specialist drugs. Positive technology appraisals by The National Institute for Health and Care Excellence (NICE) have also placed pressure on the nation's drugs bill. For instance, Adalimumab for auto-immune conditions cost the NHS £416.6 million in 2015/2016, with £391.1 million being spent in secondary care.

In 2016, the cost of prescription dispensed by community pharmacies in England was just over £9.20 billion (NHS Digital, 2016). The average cost

Equitable Access to High-Cost Pharmaceuticals
http://dx.doi.org/10.1016/B978-0-12-811945-7.00003-8

per item was £8.34 (£9,204,891,304/1,104,131,794 items). When receiving their medicines, some patients must pay a co-payment called the 'prescription charge' for each item dispensed (Baines, 2013a). Set at a rate of £8.60 from April 2017, the charge is slightly higher than the average cost per item dispensed. Although this seems like a positive balance, nearly 90% of all prescriptions are dispensed free of charge. In relation to high-cost medicines, patient age and the severity of illness means that most people receiving this class of drugs are usually exempt or choose to pre-paid the charge at a discounted rate. Even if patients are obliged to pay the fee, the amount does not increase with the price of the pharmaceuticals required. Therefore, the prescription charge does little to cover the costs of high-cost medicines supplied.

Prescriptions dispensed in the community are reimbursed by the Prescription Pricing Authority at agreed national rates (Baines, 2014a). In contrast, hospitals receive income for providing predefined packages of patient care that are reimbursed as part of the 'NHS tariff'. Drugs supplied in secondary care must be purchased and paid for by the hospitals themselves with the income generated providing patient services and payments received from NHS England. Consequently, the price for community-dispensed drugs is set nationally, whereas large variations in medicine prices between hospitals is common, particularly in relation to high-cost drugs. Both the variation and the growth of prices of high-cost drugs are issues of current concern to NHS policy-makers and the UK government.

The purpose of this chapter is to provide an overview of NHS policy to control public expenditure on high-cost drugs. As Scotland, Wales and Northern Ireland have devolved powers that cover the operation of their health services, the chapter will focus on policies and institutional structures in England. The chapter is written from the health service point of view, with an emphasis on existing measures designed to assist NHS decision-makers in dealing with pressures on its cash-limited hospital and primary care budgets. To analyse current policy, the following tasks are performed. First, background to the current policies for controlling high-cost drugs is provided. Second, arrangements and policies for controlling high-cost drugs are analysed. Third, the way ahead is discussed. The chapter closes with conclusions.

3.2 BACKGROUND

The NHS has been forced to manage ever-increasing drugs costs since the system was first introduced in 1948. This section discusses past and current approaches to prescribing cost control that affect the ways in which high-cost drugs are currently managed. These include: Policy in history; National arrangements; NICE guidance; The Carter Review.

3.2.1 Policy in History

Since its inception in 1948, the NHS has struggled to contain the nation's drugs bill. The introduction of healthcare, free at the point of delivery, stimulated an unprecedented demand for a wide range of available treatments, particularly medicines (Baines, 2013b). During the early years of the NHS, Regional Medical Officers would visit high-cost prescribers to discuss their medicines spends. Sanctions could only be applied if evidence suggested that over-prescribing had occurred at the level of an individual patient. Spending significant amounts on one product, or using high-cost drugs, were not grounds for investigation. This approach continued until the early-1990s, when the incumbent Conservative government introduced prescribing budgets into general practice (Baines et al., 1997a). From that time onwards, high-cost prescribing was defined in terms of total practice spends compared with local, regional and national averages. Spend was also judged in terms of out-turns against budgets set. Again, expenditure on individual or high-cost products was not a concern unless the result was significant overspends (Baines et al., 1997b). Not until very recently has the health service judged high-cost prescribing in terms of the price of individual medicines.

3.2.2 National Arrangements

In 2017/2018, planned spending for the DoH in England is approximately £123.7 billion (Charlesworth et al., 2017). The DoH leads the NHS by creating national policies and legislation, funding the service and assuring the delivery of services to Parliament. The DoH also leads on the Pharmaceutical Price Regulation Scheme (PPRS), which limits overall NHS spending on branded drugs (Baines, 2014b; DoH, 2016). This arrangement does not include special regulations for high-cost drugs and manufacturers are free to set their own prices. NHS England is an executive non-departmental pubic body of the DoH, which oversees the budget, planning, delivery and day-to-day operation of the NHS in England. Therefore, NHS England must deliver DoH policies on high-cost drugs. Within this framework, NICE appraises the clinical and cost-effectiveness of new drugs and recommends which should be routinely funded by the health service. NHS England assesses whether to approve funding for high-cost drugs and devices not approved by NICE. The DoH's Commercial Medicines Unit currently manages the frameworks for drug purchasing, whilst controlling demand for individual products is an NHS England responsibility.

3.2.3 NICE Guidance

The NICE Technology Appraisal process assesses the clinical and cost-effectiveness of new and existing medicines and provides guidance on their use by the NHS (Cowles et al., 2017). Three quarters of NICE technology appraisals affect provision by specialist services. Under current regulations, NHS bodies are legally required to fund NICE guidance within 90 days (NHS England Cancer Drugs Fund Team, 2016). Table 3.1 shows the cost implications of 20 recent NICE guidelines that have had the greatest impact on health service spends. As shown, the impact of a positive NHS appraisal on expenditure can be both rapid and significantly large. As the data suggests, NICE does not always consider affordability when approving high-cost drugs. However, the body adopted a more thoughtful approach for the introduction of a new Hepatitis C treatment by enabling NHS England to adopt a phased approach to its adoption (NHS England, 2015). In response, The Hepatitis C Trust has filed Court proceedings challenging the adoption of this delayed approach. In recent years, NICE recommendations have driven a substantial proportion of the annual uplift in spending by the NHS on specialist services. Once a NICE guideline is issued, all health service providers, including specialist teams, have a legal duty to follow its recommendations within three months. Therefore, NICE is a cost-driver that, in many instances, increases NHS spends on expensive medicines.

3.2.4 The Carter Review

Published in June 2015 and updated in February 2016, Lord Carter's review of efficiency in NHS acute hospitals in England found that significant improvements in productivity could be achieved, which could reduce the unwarranted variations in performance between providers (Lord Carter, 2016). In relations to medicines, the Carter Review found significant differences in total pharmacy and drug costs across acute trusts. Although some of the variance was related to teaching status or the provision of specialist services, Lord Carter found that savings of £800 million on medicines spends were available. To this end, the report recommended that hospital trusts should: (1) Through a Hospital Pharmacy Transformation Programme (HPTP), develop plans to ensure hospital pharmacies achieve specified productivity benchmarks; (2) ensure their HPTP plans include a review of services not

Table 3.1 Overall Top 20 Medicines by Estimated Prescribing Cost for Medicines Positively Appraised by NICE Prescribed or Issued in All Sectors in 2015/2016

Medicine	Most Recent TA	Condition	Sector Where Highest Cost is Incurred	Total Cost (£000's)
Adalimumab	TA383—February 2016	TNF–alpha inhibitors for ankylosing spondylitis and non-radiographic axial spondyloarthritis	Secondary care	416,647.8
Ranibizumab	TA298—November 2013	Choroidal neovascularisation associated with pathological Myopia	Secondary care	248,975.9
Etanercept	TA383—February 2016	TNF-alpha inhibitors for ankylosing spondylitis and non-radiographic axial spondyloarthritis	Secondary care	230,588.3
Aflibercept (solution for injection)	TA346—July 2015	Treating diabetic macular oedema	Secondary care	198,268.4
Infliximab	TA375—January 2016	Rheumatoid arthritis not previously treated with DMARDs or after conventional DMARDs only have failed	Secondary care	178,179.2
Rituximab	TA308—March 2014	Anti-neutrophil cytoplasmic antibody-associated vasculitis	Secondary care	155,893.3
Trastuzumab	TA208—November 2010	HER2-positive metastatic gastric cancer	Secondary care	152,037.6
Lenalidomide	TA322—September 2014	Treating myelodysplastic syndromes associated with an isolated deletion 5q cytogenetic abnormality	Secondary care	141,840.4
Rivaroxaban	TA335—March 2015	Preventing adverse outcomes after acute management of acute coronary syndrome	Primary care	106,586.8
Imatinib	TA326—November 2014	Adjuvant treatment of gastrointestinal stromal tumours	Secondary care	89,067.7

(*Continued*)

Table 3.1 Overall Top 20 Medicines by Estimated Prescribing Cost for Medicines Positively Appraised by NICE Prescribed or Issued in All Sectors in 2015/2016 (*cont.*)

Medicine	Most Recent TA	Condition	Sector Where Highest Cost is Incurred	Total Cost (£000's)
Enzalutamide	TA377—January 2016	Treating metastatic hormone-relapsed prostate cancer before chemotherapy is indicated	Secondary care	86,360.4
insulin glargine	TA053—December 2002	Type 1 and Type 2 Diabetes	Primary care	81,629.9
Ledipasvir-sofosbuvir	TA363—November 2015	Treating chronic hepatitis C	Secondary care	81,054.7
buprenorphine (excluding combination with naloxone)	TA114—January 2007	Drug misuse	Primary care	76,728.9
Abiraterone	TA259—June 2012	Treatment of castration-resistant metastatic prostate cancer previously treated with one docetaxel-containing regimen	Secondary care	74,148.7
Sofosbuvir	TA330—February 2015	Treating chronic hepatitis C	Secondary care	73,443.0
tacrolimus (immuno-suppression-oral)	TA099—April 2006	Renal Transplant	Secondary care	71,435.0
Docetaxel	TA109—September 2006	Breast cancer (early)	Secondary care	66,654.8
Dimethyl fumarate	TA320—August 2014	Treating relapsing remitting multiple sclerosis	Secondary care	64,178.5
Paclitaxel	TA55—January 2003	Treatment of ovarian cancer	Secondary care	61,298.3

Source: NHS Digital (2016). Provided under the terms of the Open Government Licence v3.0.

currently outsourced and have a plan in place for improving productivity and efficiency, including consideration of alternative supply routes, such as homecare providers or community pharmacies; (3) seek to reduce their medicines bill through best choices and from actively monitoring market developments, such as the launch of biosimilar products; (4) task their finance director, working with their chief pharmacist, to ensure that the coding of medicines, particularly high-cost drugs, are accurately recorded; and (5) identify the true value and scale of opportunities for rationalisation and integration of hospital pharmacy procurement and production. These recommendations set the requirements for medicines optimisation within English acute hospitals. They form the background against which current NHS policy for managing the use of high-cost drugs should be judged.

3.3 HIGH-COST DRUGS

Because of their nature, the initial decision to prescribe high-cost drugs is often made in secondary care, usually within specialist services and often funded by the NHS Cancer Fund. This section discusses these arrangements and provides an overview of current NHS policy for high-cost drugs, including an outline of a recent Commission for Quality and Innovation (CQUIN) payment for optimising the use of medicines in hospitals.

3.3.1 Specialised Services

Specialised services are provided in a small proportion of NHS hospitals for patients with rare conditions or individuals who need care from a specialised team (NHS England, 2016a). There are 146 services classified as 'specialised', which covers a wide range of complex interventions. These include treatments for long-term conditions (such as renal and mental health problems) to services for uncommon conditions such as rare cancers. Some specialised services (such as those for cystic fibrosis) cover all patient care. However, most specialised services only form a part of a patient's treatment pathway. A very small number of highly specialised services (including those for very rare diseases) are only provided in one or two centres across England. Others (such as chemotherapy services) are provided by most acute hospitals.

In April 2013, NHS England took responsibility for commissioning specialised services. Through its commissioning of these services, NHS England aims to: (1) Improve outcomes for patients; (2) ensure patients have equal access to services; and (3) improve productivity and efficiency. Like the objectives of the NHS Constitution, these commissioning aims for specialised services also embody a tension between the desire to provide patients with the effective medicines they need and the ability of cash-limited NHS budgets to supply them. Nowhere else in the health service is this conflict of aims more apparent than with high-cost drugs funded by specialised services. Budget out-turns since NHS England took over commissioning clearly tells the story. Between 2013/2014 and 2015/2016, the allocation for specialised services increased from £13 billion to £14.6 billion, an average annual increase of 6.3%. Over this period, the total NHS budget increased by 3.5% per average year. By 2020/2021, the allocation for specialist services is expected to rise to £18.8 billion, which will be 16% of the total NHS budget.

Even with a rapidly growing allocation, NHS England has found it challenging to live within its budget for specialised services. In 2013/2014, the overspend was £377 million. In 2014/2015, £214 million was overspent, with the Cancer Drugs Fund accounting for £136 million of this amount. In 2015/2016, high-cost drugs constituted about £3 billion of the total spend by NHS specialised services, and estimates for the future suggest that this amount will continue to grow. Given the current arrangements for managing high-cost drugs—such as NICE's role in recommending new treatments—NHS England has little control over the drivers of the rising spends on high-cost drugs by specialist providers.

3.3.2 Cancer Drugs Fund

Survival rates for cancer patients in England have generally been worse than those in other high-income countries in Europe, mainly because patients in England are diagnosed later and have poorer access to treatment (Grieve et al., 2016). The government set up the Cancer Drugs Fund in 2010 to improve access to cancer drugs. In the last five years, approximately 80,000 people received their medicines through the Fund, which grew from £175 million in 2012/2013 to £416 million in 2014/2015 (an increase of 138% over two years). In the years 2013/2014 and 2014/2015, NHS England overspent the Fund's £480 million budget by £167 million. NHS England did not act to control the growth in costs until November 2014, by which time 39 cancer drugs, covering 67 different licensed uses, were available through the Fund. Currently, there is general agreement that NHS England in consultation with NICE must improve the way in which the scheme is managed.

In January 2016, the House of Commons Committee of Public Accounts published a report on the operation of the Cancer Drugs Fund

(House of Commons Committee of Public Accounts, 2016). The report concluded that the DOH and NHS England: (1) Have not managed the Fund effectively; (2) are not using their buying power effectively to pay fair prices for cancer drugs; (3) do not have data to evaluate the impact of the Fund on outcomes for patients; (4) have not reduced regional variations to secure equal access between areas to the Fund; (5) have failed to support NICE develop its capacity to evaluate all new cancer drugs; and (6) have not improved survival rates for cancer patients to international standards. In response to these failings, the Public Accounts Committee recommended that: (1) NHS England should set clear objectives for the Fund, and be prepared to take tough decisions to ensure that the Fund does not overspend; (2) the DoH should outline how it ensures that fair prices for drugs are paid, and specify what lessons that can be drawn from the Fund's negotiations with pharmaceutical companies about drug pricing; (3) NHS England should provide data on the impact of the Fund on patient outcomes; (4) NHS England should analyse the extent of regional variation in access to the Fund, and outline plans to ensure that access is fair across the country; (5) NHS England should assess whether NICE has the capacity to appraise all new cancer drugs; and (6) NHS England should implement a clear plan to ensure that the NHS has sufficient diagnostic capacity, including appropriately trained staff, to improve early diagnosis of cancer. Currently, these recommendations are changing the ways in which the DoH and NHS England manage the Cancer Drugs Fund, which will soon have an impact on the commissioning (and spending) on high-cost drugs.

3.3.3 Hospital Medicines Optimisation

Throughout England, many NHS acute providers spend significantly on high-cost drugs. In response, the NHS recently launched a new CQUIN designed to support procedural and cultural changes in hospitals to fully optimise the use of medicines commissioned by specialised services (NHS England, 2016b). For instance, ensuring that hospitals have HPTP plans that reflect the NHS England priorities of improving value for money in medicines procurement and reducing unwarranted variation in high-cost drug spends. The CQUIN funds additional pharmacy staff to help achieve these end and to ensure that each HPTP plan is supported at Trust Board level. The funding assumes that one (whole time equivalent) pharmacist plus admin/analytical support is required for every £25 million of drugs expenditure. This extra staff time must be used to optimise the use of medicines and to help generate some of the savings identified by the Carter Review.

CQUIN funds are designed to deliver better outcomes in the following priority areas: (1) Faster adoption of best value medicines with a focus on generics and biologics; (2) significantly improved drugs data to include appropriate coding; (3) the consistent application of the lowest cost dispensing channels; and (4) compliance with policy/consensus guidelines to reduce variation and waste. The CQUIN is one of the first actions linked to the government's plans to rationalise medicines use and purchasing in NHS acute hospitals, particularly in relation to high-cost drugs.

3.4 THE WAY AHEAD

In July 2016, the House of Commons Committee of Public Accounts published a report on NHS specialised services. The report concluded that NHS England does not have a clear plan for configuring and delivering this type of NHS care. Moreover, a lack of transparency over NHS England's decision-making is undermining accountability to both patients and taxpayers. To add to its problems, NHS England has not overcome barriers to collaborative commissioning with CCGs and lacks information on costs, access and outcomes necessary to improve existing provision. In short, significant improvements are required. Importantly, many of the planned reforms of specialist services (the Cancer Drugs Fund) that will occur in coming years will have a direct impact on the accessibility to and spending on high-cost drugs. In particular, higher prices may be challenged, lower volumes prescribed and regional variations addressed.

The analysis performed in this chapter suggests that the NHS is at a turning point in the ways in which high-cost drugs are managed and funded. In recent years, costs have grown beyond what the Public Accounts Committee, the DoH and NHS England believe acceptable. The response will be a concerted attempt to produce joined-up policies that encourage acute hospitals and specialist service providers to optimise medicines use, whilst pursuing greater value for money in drug purchasing. Whilst NHS England is tasked with better managing specialist services and reducing high-cost drug spends, the question remains of what is achievable within the current framework. High-cost drugs are relatively expensive because of the high costs of developing and launching new clinical entities. Whilst some commentators believe that new medicine prices are not justifiable, high-cost drugs are, an international phenomenon. Beyond price negotiations with manufacturers, the only real solution to the extra expenditure that they generate is the rationing of access to the latest pharmaceutical technologies. In systems such as the NHS, high-cost drugs create a real tension between the objectives of meeting patient needs and securing value for money for tax-payers. Whatever policy initiatives are implemented, the conflict between need and affordability cannot be easily resolved. For real change to occur, either drug prices must drop significantly or a new remit may be required for NICE that focuses less on clinical and cost effectiveness and deals directly with affordability and budget out-turns. Whatever road is taken, high-cost drugs will remain a real challenge for NHS decision-makers, particularly as recent policy recommendations have yet to prove themselves in practice. In coming years, failure to control the growing spend on such medicines may eventually limit the ability of NHS England to fund care for patients outside of specialised services. Therefore, high-cost drugs is an issue of concern that directly challenges the viability of the NHS as currently constituted.

3.5 CONCLUSIONS

High-cost drugs are proving a challenge for many healthcare systems worldwide. Currently, arrangements for managing spends on these products are currently being reviewed and reformed for the NHS in England. With a clear focus on cost control, a consequence of ongoing policy changes may be reduced access to high-cost medicines. In coming years, close monitoring and objective evaluation will be required to analyse the effect of the current policy on patients and taxpayers, with an inevitable trade-off between spending and access driving the outcomes observed.

REFERENCES

Baines, D.L., Tolley, K.H., Whynes, D.K., 1997a. Prescribing, Budgets and Fundholding in General Practice. Office of Health Economics, London.

Baines, D.L., Whynes, D.K., Tolley, K.H., 1997b. General practitioner fundholding and prescribing expenditure control. Pharmacoeconomics 11 (4), 350–358.

Baines, D., 2013a. The prescription charge and Hinchcliffe Committee. Prescriber 24 (21), 40–42.

Baines, D., 2013b. From the NIS to the NHS via the floating sixpence. Prescriber 24 (19), 47–49.

Baines, D., 2014a. Pharmacists as dispensers and formation of the PPA. Prescriber 25 (1–2), 33–34.

Baines, D., 2014b. Drug budgets and the strengthening of the PPRS. Prescriber 25 (19), 20–23.

Charlesworth, A., Thorlby, R., Roberts, A., Gershlick, B., 2017. Election Briefing: NHS and Social Care Funding. The Health Foundation, London.

Cowles, E., Marsden, G., Cole, A., Devlin, N., 2017. A review of NICE methods and processes across health technology assessment programmes: why the differences and what is the impact? Appl. Health Econ. Health Policy 15, 1–9.

DoH, 2015. The NHS Constitution for England. DoH, London.
DoH, 2016. Pharmaceutical Price Regulation Scheme (PPRS): Payment Percentage Arrangements for 2017 and 2018. DoH, London.
Grieve, R., Abrams, K., Claxton, K.P., Goldacre, B., James, N., Nicholl, J., et al., 2016. Cancer drugs fund requires further reform. Br. Med. J. 354, i5090.
House of Commons Committee of Public Accounts, 2016. Cancer drugs fund twentieth report of session 2015–16. The Stationery Office, London.
Lord Carter, 2016. Operational Productivity and Performance in English NHS Acute Hospitals: Unwarranted Variations. DoH, London.
NHS England, 2016a. Manual for Prescribed Specialised Services 2016/17. NHS England, London.
NHS England, 2016b. CQUIN Schemes for Prescribed Specialised Services for April 2017 to March 2019. NHS England, London.
NHS England Cancer Drugs Fund Team, 2016. Appraisal and Funding of Cancer Drugs from July 2016 (including the new Cancer Drugs Fund)—A New Deal for Patients, Taxpayers and Industry. NHS England Cancer Drugs Fund Team, London.
NHS Digital, 2016. Prescribing Costs in Hospitals and the Community England 2015/16. Health and Social Care Information Centre, London.
NHS England, 2015. Treatment of Chronic Hepatitis C in Patients with Cirrhosis Interim Clinical Commissioning Policy Statement. NHS England, London.
NHS England, 2017. CCG Improvement and Assessment Framework 2016/17. NHS England, London/Leeds.

FURTHER READING

NHS Statistics and NHS Digital, 2017. Prescription Cost Analysis England. NHS Statistics and NHS Digital, London.

CHAPTER 4

Managed Entry Agreements and High Cost Medicines (European Perspective)

Claudio Jommi
Università del Piemonte Orientale, Novara, Italy; Cergas (Centre for Research on Health and Social Care Management), SDA Bocconi School of Management, Milano, Italy

4.1 RATIONALE FOR MEA

In most developed countries, public authorities and payers are putting increased attention on uncertainties around the impact of new drugs on health and health care budget.

On the one hand, clinical trials are essential to get marketing approval; however, they do not provide payers with complete evidence due to their experimental nature, the selection of patients in the trial, and the comparators—if any—used that do not necessarily correspond to drugs used in clinical practice (Toumi, 2017). The possible gap between the expected benefit and the actual benefit led payers (i) to be more demanding on the proof grounds for evidencing a new drug's value: the clinical efficacy demonstrated through pre-marketing studies, is considered a necessary but not sufficient condition to verify the value of a new product; (ii) to put greater emphasis on the post marketing evidence on the impact of new drugs on health and health care budget.

The diffusion of drugs for niche markets (target therapies, rare diseases, etc.) are pushing companies to require high prices for these drugs (Schey et al., 2011). The impact of these drugs on health care budget strongly depends on the actual number of patients treated and treatment duration: information on these two parameters is often incomplete when new drugs are launched into the market.

More generally, high cost drugs are putting pressure on healthcare budgets across the globe. High cost drugs include cancer drugs, immunologicals, biologicals and the newer anti-inflammatory agents. There are various

Equitable Access to High-Cost Pharmaceuticals
http://dx.doi.org/10.1016/B978-0-12-811945-7.00004-X

mechanisms in place to share the treatment costs and risk of failure to reduce the overall impact on healthcare expenditures. Managed Entry Agreement (MEA) is one such mechanism. Other mechanisms include value-based pricing at market launch, actions aimed at enhancing appropriate prescription, and—less frequently—co-payment.

MEA could be broadly defined as 'an agreement between two or more parties, who agree on the terms and conditions under which a product will get access to the market' (Toumi et al., 2016). MEA are aimed at managing uncertainty on the drugs risk-benefit profile, the drugs utilisation (identification of the eligible patients, adherence to treatment), and their financial impact (that depends on number of patients, treatment duration, number of doses per treatment).

MEA may be classified into two classes: financial agreements, which allow payers to sharing with the industry the post-marketing budget impact of new drugs; outcome-based agreements that link payers' commitment to the actual impact of the drugs on health (Carlson et al., 2010; Ferrario and Kanavos, 2013).

MEA bring important advantages for the industry and the payers.

Pharmaceutical companies use MEA to achieve drugs coverage, to improve their public image, their position into the competitive arena and the relationships with payers, due to the potential contribution of MEA to drugs sustainability. MEA are used by local affiliates of pharmaceutical companies to meet price cut requirements by payers, leaving list prices within the price corridor set by their parent companies (Jommi, 2012). These corridors avoid huge differences in list prices that may be exploited by payers through cross-reference pricing and/or the distribution system to take advantage from parallel trade (Gregson et al., 2005). Finally, MEA permit companies avoiding costlier alternative studies (e.g. pragmatic trials), and strengthening relationships with payers (Toumi et al., 2016).

Payers may show that through MEA they are caring for patients access to new drugs, for allocative efficiency and appropriate use of resources, thus managing pressure from patient associations, politicians and media. MEA could be also an opportunity to collect real world data, which could be useful for other products.

MEA may also allow for a flexible management of multiple indications. If prescription per indication is traced, MEA can be set per indication, depending on the relevant drugs' value (e.g. different discounts per indication) or the level of financial risk per indication.

4.2 DEFINITION AND TAXONOMY OF MEA

The origin of MEA can be traced to a paper by the health economist De Pouvourville (2006), who defined MEA as 'a contract between two parties, who agree to engage in a transaction in which there are uncertainties concerning its final value. Nevertheless, one party, the company, has sufficient confidence in its claims of either effectiveness or efficiency that it is ready to accept a reward or a penalty depending on the observed performance of its product'. In this definition, the author pointed out MEA key issues, that is, information asymmetry between the two agreement parties (producers and payers), that may turn into an advantage for the industry. Towse and Garrison (2010) defined MEA as 'agreements between a payer and a pharmaceutical company where the price level and/or revenue received are related to the future performance of the product in either a research or real-world environment'. The two authors further clarified the object of the agreement (its effects on unit prices and revenue) and that the post marketing impact could be measured in a research-based environment (e.g. through an observational study). Adamski and colleagues (Adamski et al., 2010) defined MEA as 'agreements concluded by payers and pharmaceutical companies to diminish the impact on the payer's budget of new and existing medicines brought about by either the uncertainty of the value of the medicine and/or the need to work within finite budgets', thus advocating for a wider perspective that includes also financial-based agreements and stressing the goal of MEA for managing budget constraints. The most comprehensive definition has been given by the HTAi Policy Forum and quoted by Morel and colleagues (Morel et al., 2013): 'MEA are arrangements between a (pharmaceutical) manufacturer and payer/provide that enables access to (coverage or reimbursement of) a health technology subject to specific conditions. These arrangements can use a variety of mechanisms to address uncertainty about the performance of technologies to maximise their effective use or limit their budget impact'. This definition incorporates any agreement addressed to 'manage' market access beyond deciding the reimbursement status and the unit price of a new drug.

As anticipated, MEA can be financial-based or outcome-based.

Financial agreements are commercial agreements between two or more parties entering a deal for goods acquisition (Toumi et al., 2016). Examples of financial-based MEA are:

- discounts over list prices, if the uncertainty concerns the value of the drug;
- price–volume agreements or spending cap per drug, if the risk is mostly generated by the uncertainty around the dimension of the target population;

- cost per patient capping or manufacturer funded treatment initiation, when the cost per patient is uncertain because of important variations in doses and number of cycles.

Outcome-based agreements are part of an insurance facility: the payer agrees to a price under the insurance that the product will deliver a pre-defined outcome.

In Performance-Linked-Reimbursement (PLR) or Payment for Performance (PfP) the outcome is measured for each individual patient: the payer is either refunded by the industry if the patient dies or discontinues treatment because of progression or side effects or it pays if the patient responds to treatment.

In a PLR agreement, payment is decided for each individual case, which will allow for minimising the possibility of paying for non-responders. PLR are more suited if (i) a clear and manageable indicator of patients' response is available, (ii) there is a consensus over this response indicator in the clinical community, (iii) impact of therapies could be observed in the short-term. Furthermore, PLR are better implemented for small population targets, due to the substantial administrative costs associated with monitoring patients' response to treatment. Otherwise, the administrative costs may offset savings derived from charging the industry with the failure.

Coverage with Evidence Development (CED) agreements allow conditional funding for new promising drugs, while more conclusive evidence is being gathered to address uncertainty regarding clinical or cost effectiveness at population level (NHS Quality Improvement Scotland, 2008). In fact, the whole population treated is observed for a certain period and if the expected benefit (or cost-benefit) profile is not confirmed, the industry is required to lower prices and possibly refund retrospectively the payment over the true value for money. The sums that are paid to the manufacturer during the period awaiting the final results of the agreed upon study, could be claimed as payback in case the performance of the drug does not meet the predefined expectations. The aim of CED agreements is to minimising the possibility of financing non-cost-effective drugs and maximising the likelihood that the manufacturer receives a price reflecting the drug's true value. While PLR are in principle long-term agreements, CED agreements are temporary agreements that are terminated, when evidence from a cohort of patients is produced. Their temporary nature allows for developing new evidence on real-life health outcomes and identifying elements, such as the duration of treatment, the appropriate dose, the target population.

Table 4.1 Taxonomy of Market Access Agreements

	Population Level	**Patient Level**
Financial based	Discounts, price–volume agreement, spending cap	Cost per patient cap, manufacturer funded treatment initiation
Outcome based	CED (coverage with evidence development)	PLR (performance-linked-reimbursement)

Table 4.1 summarises the taxonomy of MEA according to two parameters: financial vs. outcome based; individual vs. population impact measurement.

4.3 DIFFUSION OF MEA IN EUROPE

According to a rather recent survey (Ferrario and Kanavos, 2013) carried out on behalf of the European Commission DG Enterprise, there are many countries with MEA and a prevalence of financial-based contracts was found (40% were price volume agreements; 14% restricted access; 6% conditional continuation; 5% PLR; 5% discounts on doses, initial or general; 29% requirement for data collection, including drug utilisation studies and CED). In terms of therapeutic area, antineoplastic and immune-modulating agents represent 37% of all the agreements, followed by alimentary tract and metabolism (16.5%) and nervous system (9.8%).

A more recent review tracked published MEA from 1993 to 2016 counting 437 arrangements all over the world (41.9% were active), with different results from the previous survey, that is, a prevalence of outcome-based contracts including CED (34.1%), PLR (23.8%), conditional treatment continuation (17.8%), whereas financial or utilisation based (16.2%) and hybrid schemes (8.0%) were the minority (Carlson et al., 2017).

These contradictory results of the two studies are not surprising: many contracts, especially the financial-based ones, are not public and a survey on payers may provide more realistic results that reviews based on published evidence.

Other publications have been focused on cancer drugs (Pauwels et al., 2017) and orphan drugs (Morel et al., 2013) in some European Countries (Belgium, Czech Republic, France, England and Wales, Italy, The Netherlands, Scotland, Sweden, the former; Belgium, France, England and Wales, Germany, Italy, The Netherlands, Sweden the latter).

As already stated, the number of MEA could be underestimated, because many contracts, especially the financial-based ones, are not public. Confidentiality of financial details is the cornerstone of the application of MEA irrespective of the country where the MEA is applied. There are countries where the content of MEA is strictly confidential for all parties who are not involved in the negotiation (e.g. Belgium). In France, most of the price negotiations are concluded with price–volume agreements which are not public and not revealed to hospitals. Italian PLR on cancer drugs are mentioned in the Price & Reimbursement Decree (Determina of AIFA, the Italian National Drugs Agency), but the content of the scheme (endpoint used, follow-up duration) is not public.

The literature on MEA shows also a growing diffusion of these agreements with a big variability in schemes' implementation.

In Europe, Italy was the first country introducing PLR, thanks to existence of drugs registries and is still the country where MEA are more diffused for cancer drugs (Pauwels et al., 2017). The first contract was signed in 2006 and to date, 25 cancer drugs are subject to such contracts (Jommi, 2002; Jommi and Minghetti, 2015). If a cancer drug is approved for different indications, each indication may have its own PLR (e.g. bevacizumab was approved with five different contracts). Another example of PLR contracts is the response-based scheme implemented in England for bortezomib. In Spain, some regions (Comunidades Autonomas) have piloted MEA in some hospitals (three are reported in Granada, Ferrario and Kanavos, 2013). The Region of Catalonia has formalised guidelines on MEA in May 2014 (Mora-Ripoll et al., 2014).

CED was implemented in Belgium, the Netherlands, Portugal, Sweden, UK (only for drugs for Multiple Sclerosis) and more recently, France.

In Belgium, MEA were introduced in 2010 and are required to the pharmaceutical companies to get a temporary listing for drugs not intended to be reimbursed for insufficient evidence on their therapeutic added value and/or uncertainty related to the drugs budget impact. According to Morel and colleagues (Morel et al., 2013), 22 MEA have been negotiated in 2 years, but there are not official number on the drugs subject to CED or financial-based contracts, even if the same article reported that MEA on orphan drugs were financial-based (2 price–volume agreements, 1 discount and 1 cost capping).

The Swedish TLV (Dental and Pharmaceutical Benefits Agency), operating under the cost-effectiveness paradigm, does not recommend drugs with uncertain or high Incremental Cost Effectiveness Ration (ICER), depending on a specific disease threshold. TLV may approve for reimbursement in specific patient sub-groups (those in which the drug is most cost-effective) or stipulate an outcome-based agreement that provides a temporary coverage decision asking the manufacturer to collect real-world data on the effectiveness of the drug with the aim of resubmitting the cost-effectiveness model. Two examples are represented by CED on duodopa for Parkinson and rimonabant for Obesity (Toumi et al., 2016).

France was in the past reluctant to adopt outcome-based agreements, due to bias in real-world evidence and administrative burden. More recently both the Transparency Committee of the Haute Autorité de Santé (HAS), which oversees the evaluation of absolute and comparative risk-benefit profile and the pricing committee CEPS (Comité économique des produits de santé) signed a CED agreement on drugs. For example, the manufacturer of risperidone was asked to perform a 1 year study aimed at showing the reduction in the rate of hospitalisations for patients treated with this drug as compared to other antipsychotics (HAS, 2010[1]). The drug was charged the cheapest comparator, but the company was given a premium price with the difference would be deposited as public funds in the Caisse des Dépôts et Consignations until results from the study were available. The results showed reduction in hospitalisation rate and money has been transferred to the company and the premium price maintained (Jarosławski and Toumi, 2011; Garrison et al., 2013). Another CED was signed by the Transparency Committee and CEPS and the producers of the anti-diabetic drugs glitazones (pioglitazone and rosiglitazone) in type 2 diabetes. They have agreed to carry out a 2 year observational study to support (or invalidate) the manufacturers' claim of a superior real-life efficacy (i.e. drugs would delay escalation to insulin therapy) as compared to what was previously observed in clinical trials. The observational study did not support the manufacturer's claim for rosiglitazone (Jarosławski and Toumi, 2011). Consequently, CEPS cut the drug's price by 30% and requested rebates for the drugs that were already purchased. The reimbursement level also dropped from 65% to 35%. In 2006, the launch of omalizumab in France was conditional upon conducting a study that should demonstrate a positive impact in terms of severe asthma exacerbations (Pax Study). The Pax Study confirmed minor improvement in benefit and did not support the request by the company of a moderate added value (Grimaldi-Bensouda et al., 2013). A CED has been

[1] https://www.has-sante.fr/portail/upload/docs/application/pdf/2010-06/risperdalconsta_-_ct-7257.pdf (last access, 30th of July 2017).

recently signed also for a cancer drug for multiple myeloma (pomalidomide; Pauwels et al., 2017).

In the Netherlands, CED agreements were introduced in 2006 on a voluntary basis to have access to hospitals' dedicated budget for orphan and very expensive drugs. In the period 2006–12, the industry applied for 36 drugs (10 orphans and 23 with important budget impact) (Morel et al., 2013). Since 2012 CED contracts have become compulsory for drugs with an important impact on hospital budget (more than 2.5 million €) and with a high uncertainty on their benefits and cost-benefit profile. The relevant drugs are provisionally included in the positive list and re-assessed after 4 years. However, the system is now under reform to only apply financial agreements in the future (Pauwels et al., 2017).

In Portugal CED agreements are less common and offer temporary coverage, which can become permanent if the manufacturer provides additional data supporting the drug's effectiveness at the end of the 2 year conditional reimbursement period (Ferrario and Kanavos, 2013).

Despite the increasing role of outcome-based agreements, in most countries financial-based agreements are by far the most numerous, according to many references: for example, in Sweden MEA for cancer drugs are in form of utilisation/dose cap (Pauwels et al., 2017).

Financial-based contracts have been prevailing in France (in the form of price–volume agreements), Spain (with a prevalence of hidden discounts) and England (and Scotland). In England, MEA are named Patient Access Scheme (PAS): there are currently 122 PAS, with only one response-scheme based (bortezomib) and the other are financial-based (86% of them are simple discounts, 11% are manufacturer funded treatment initiation, 3% are cost per patient cap)[2]. PAS, together with the Cancer Drugs Fund and higher cost-effectiveness thresholds for the end-of-life treatments, have been introduced to make drugs with a high cost-effectiveness accessible (Jommi, 2015). Financial-based agreements are also diffused in Italy (with different schemes ranging from total spending cap, cost per patient cap), where also multiple MEA are negotiated: for example, vemurafenib, approved for the treatment of advanced and inoperable melanoma in BRAF-mutated patients, has been approved with a PLR, a spending cap of 36 million Euros for 2 years, and the promise by Roche to provide the relevant biomarker free at the point of delivery[3].

[2] https://www.nice.org.uk/about/what-we-do/patient-access-schemes-liaison-unit/list-of-technologies-with-approved-patient-access-schemes (last access, 30th of July, 2017).

[3] http://www.gazzettaufficiale.it/eli/id/2013/06/04/13A04712/sg (last access, 3rd of August, 2017).

In Germany, the Statutory Health Insurance providers (Krankenkass) have been allowed to negotiate discounts and rebates with the industry (Morel et al., 2013). Hence, MEA have been diffusing at Regional or local levels. A mix of methods (price–volume, outcome-based, etc.) has been reported (Adamski et al., 2010). They have been increasingly used also by private insurers which cover patients who have opted out the social insurance system. However, the use of MEA has been reduced since 2011, when companies have been obliged, according to the AMNOG system, to negotiate a discount over list prices, freely set at market launch, on the grounds of added therapeutic value[4].

4.4 IMPACT EVALUATION AND FUTURE PERSPECTIVES

In principle MEA, should be evaluated on different perspectives: organisational and economic impact, contribution in reducing uncertainty, improvement in drugs market uptake, impact on innovation process.

Design and evaluation of outcome-based MEA were discussed for the first time by McCabe and colleagues (McCabe et al., 2010) and Menon and colleagues (Menon et al., 2010). However, most of these first proposals have been systematically analysed by the Ispor Task Force for Performance Based Risk Sharing Arrangements (PBRSA, i.e. outcome-based agreements), with a focus on CED (Garrison et al., 2013).

The Ispor Task Force identified requirements for implementation, governance and evaluation of CED. The Task Force on outcome-based MEA report indicates that evaluation should rely on process indicators for the scheme's success. 'It will be an important part of the design of any Performance Based Risk Sharing Arrangements ... to define the metrics by which the success of that scheme can be assessed' (Garrison et al., 2013). The Task Force identified questions to seize process indicators of success. These questions include: were the intended outcome measures collected? Was uncertainty in associated parameter estimation reduced for the outcomes that were the focus of the scheme? Did the scheme keep within budget? Was the integrity of the design/estimation maintained? Did the governance arrangements work? Did the process to underpin a decision with further evidence work? According to the Task Force 'The appropriate decision-making will require the ability to show that the agreed outcome

[4] http://www.english.g-ba.de/benefitassessment/information/ (last access, 30th of July, 2017).

adjustments were made to guarantee the cost-effectiveness of the intervention.'

The Task Force has pointed out that a good implementation of CED can be favoured if (i) outcomes are clinically robust, plausible, appropriate and monitorable; (ii) costs of the schemes are acceptable to the health care system and proportionate to the potential gains; (iii) the time horizon is realistic and timeline adequately pre-planned, considering the changing clinical practice and technological advancement. It has also been suggested to provide for (i) a clear provision for funding arrangements and an agreement on responsibility for data collection and analysis; (ii) an agreement on the economic consequences of the CED. These consequences can be defined in advance or left to negotiation between parties; (iii) an exit strategy, in case the agreements cannot be carried out anymore.

The governance of MEA may range from very simple bilateral negotiation for most financial-based contracts to very complex structures for CED, where (i) different stakeholders beyond the industry and payers are involved (researchers, clinicians, patients), and in some instances (ii) steering and scientific committees are usually created to supervise the agreement implementation and its scientific content, respectively.

Transparency is also advocated for reporting in outcome-based agreements, especially for CED carried out only 'in research', where coverage is restricted to patients receiving the drug as part of a clinical study or registry (Carlson et al., 2010). The rationale for the publication of the results of an outcome-based MEA is the public nature of these data.

More in general, outcome-based MEA should not involve appreciable administrative burden: for example, already available information systems, such as patients' registries, could be customised to implement PLR agreements. Furthermore, parties involved should take into consideration possible changes which may impact the agreement, such as new drugs launch or changes in therapeutic guidelines.

The most prominent example of problems arising from governance issues in CED agreements is the risk sharing agreement for β interferons and glatiramer in the treatment of Multiple Sclerosis in UK. In its initial appraisal, the NICE refused to fund these drugs on clinical and cost-effectiveness grounds (McCabe et al., 2010). In 2002, the Government established a CED with the four relevant manufacturers, where a cohort of approximately 5000 patients in 72 centres would be followed for 10 years with the maximum cost of drugs funded of £35,000/QALY. The interim analysis, expected after 2 years, was published only in 2009 (Boggild et al., 2009), due to problems in recruiting patients. It was observed that the results were not positive with an actual benefit (measured with the Expanded Disability Status Scale) lower that the expected one and the untreated comparator dataset. However, the authors declared that 'It was too early to reach any conclusion about the cost effectiveness of disease modifying treatments from this first interim analysis. Important methodological issues, including the need for additional comparator datasets, the potential bias from missing data, and the impact of the 'no improvement' rule, will need to be addressed and long-term follow-up of all patients is essential to secure meaningful results' (Boggild et al., 2009). Many researchers advocated for stopping the experiment (among them McCabe et al., 2010; Raftery, 2010) or criticised the way the study was designed: for example, Sudlow and Counsell (2003) were very critical for having companies as co-funder and would have preferred a fully independent study. The risks of not having available these treatments anymore within the scheme and a switch of patients to new more expensive drugs, convinced the parties involved continuing the scheme, thus revealing a difference of opinion in the scientific community. Furthermore, the scheme was criticised (Adamski et al., 2010; Towse et al., 2012) because of the delays in patients' recruitment, contract's incompleteness, doubts over independence of the Scientific Advisory Group and because hospitals did not receive additional funding for the extensive follow-up consultations and the insufficient infrastructure required including specialist nurses. A new study was initiated with a new natural history dataset and an improved cost-effectiveness model (Palace et al., 2014) and results on 6 years evidence were published in 2015 (Palace et al., 2015).

Despite the recommendation by the Ispor Task Force, impact evaluation of MEA is quite rare. Except for studies referring to the UK Multiple Sclerosis CED, other studies included only qualitative discussions of costs and benefits, without evaluating the overall economic impact of the scheme (Puig-Peiró et al., 2011). In the survey conducted by Ferrario and Kanavos (2013) financial and administrative burden estimates, required to responders, were rarely reported, and, if reported, the information was often incomplete. For example, in Italy, only people working on drugs registries in AIFA were reported, but the administrative burden is mostly driven by the time spent by the end-users of registries in hospitals (Garattini et al., 2015). Some studies have provided evidence on (i) administrative costs of PAS in England (Williamson, 2010), (ii) reduction in prices due to discontinuation rate of bosentan in Australia (Wlodarczyk et al., 2011), (iii) speeder access of cancer drugs subject to PLR in Italy (Russo et al., 2010), but with a limited application of payback for non-responders (Navarria et al., 2015). Despite the confidentiality nature of the agreements, a higher level of transparency has been advocated at least on their impacts. For example, it has been stressed that, despite the availability of drugs registries in Italy, there are no published report on the actual impact of new drugs except for a summary report in 2007 (Garattini and Casadei, 2011).

The impact on the industry has been investigated only theoretically. On the one side, more predictability of price has been considered as a factor that could encourage innovation (Cook et al., 2008; Stafinski et al., 2010), but this may have an impact on the overall investments in Research and Development and not on the location of these investments. In fact, recent evidence shows that cost-containment policies (including unexpected price cut) are not a driver of investments location by the companies (Eger and Mahlich, 2014). On the other hand, reallocation of the costs of failures and uncertainty about future income stream (McCabe et al., 2010) might act as a disincentive for the industry.

Notwithstanding the limited evidence on their impacts, MEA have being growing in the last decade and this has facilitated patients access to drugs characterised by an important uncertainty around their clinical and financial impacts. MEA extension to other health technologies is moving its first steps (e.g. medical devices, Fuchs et al., 2017) or is under discussion (e.g. vaccines, Baron-Papillon et al., 2014).

Financial-based contracts are still more frequent than outcome-based contracts, due to their easier management, the prominent importance of the financial impact of new drugs, and the frequent high uncertainty around the target population, which is an important component of the financial impact of high-cost drugs. Among outcome-based contracts most countries have adopted a CED approach, with the relevant exception of Italy, where PLR have been extensively used for cancer drugs. It is unlikely that many countries will adopt a PLR approach, due to the need of a drugs registry.

Future perspectives of MEA (especially outcome-based) depend on the convenience of stipulating them and their ability to face uncertainty issues.

The industry will support MEA if they favour market access. However, the larger the MEA are used by payers the more the industry will incorporate in their price proposals the expected impact of these contracts.

Payers will support MEA if their pros (reducing the financial impact of new drugs, allowing market access, collecting real world data) will compensate the cons (asymmetric information at contract sign, management costs, increase in prices requests). Health care professionals and patients will take advantage of drugs availability, but the professionals will be required additional burden to manage these agreements.

More specifically MEA could be considered in the future, for new treatments in a high priority disease area with an expected net health gain, but with important uncertainty about their effects.

Hence, it is not excluded that MEA might experience further evolution in the coming years, due to the increasing pressure for better health and right price, and the growing dynamics of interrelated drug markets.

REFERENCES

Adamski, J., Godman, B., Ofierska-Sujkowska, G., et al., 2010. Risk sharing arrangements for pharmaceuticals: potential considerations and recommendations for European payers. BMC Health Serv. Res. 10, 153.

Baron-Papillon, F., Easley, C., Saint Sardos, C., Lucas, F., 2014. Managed-entry agreements: possible options for vaccines? Value Health. 17 (7), A686.

Boggild, M., Palace, J., Barton, P., et al., 2009. Multiple sclerosis risk sharing scheme: two-year results of clinical cohort study with historical comparator. Br. Med. J. 339, b4677.

Carlson, J.J., Chen, S., Garrison, Jr, L.P., 2017. Performance-based risk-sharing arrangements: an updated international review. Pharmacoeconomics 35, 1063–1072.

Carlson, J.J., Sullivan, S.D., Garrison, L.P., et al., 2010. Linking payment to health outcomes: a taxonomy and examination of performance-based reimbursement schemes between healthcare payers and manufacturers. Health Policy 96 (3), 179–190.

Cook, J.P., Vernon, J.A., Manning, R., 2008. Pharmaceutical risk-sharing agreements. Pharmacoeconomics 26 (7), 551–556.

De Pouvourville, G., 2006. Risk-sharing agreements for innovative drugs: a new solution to old problems? Eur. J. Health Econ. 7 (3), 155–157.

Eger, S., Mahlich, J.C., 2014. Pharmaceutical regulation in Europe and its impact on corporate R&D. Health Econ. Rev. 4 (1), 23.

Ferrario, A., Kanavos, P., 2013. Managed entry agreements for pharmaceuticals: the European experience. EMiNet, Brussels, Belgium, (http://eprints.lse.ac.uk/50513/, last access 29th of July 2017).

Fuchs, S., Olberg, B., Panteli, D., et al., 2017. HTA of medical devices: challenges and ideas for the future from a European perspective. Health Policy 121 (3), 215–229.

Garattini, L., Casadei, G., 2011. Risk sharing agreements: what lessons from Italy? Int. J. Technol. Assess Health Care 27 (2), 169–172.

Garattini, L., Curto, A., Van de Vooren, K., 2015. Italian risk-sharing agreements on drugs: are they worthwhile? Eur. J. Health Econ. 16 (1), 1–3.

Garrison, Jr., L.P., Towse, A., Briggs, A., et al., 2013. Performance-based risk-sharing arrangements-good practices for design, implementation, and evaluation: report of the ISPOR good practices for performance-based risk-sharing arrangements task force. Value Health 16 (5), 703–719.

Gregson, N., Sparrowhawk, K., Mauskopf, J., Paul, J., 2005. Pricing medicines: theory and practice, challenges and opportunities. Nat. Rev. Drug Discov. 4 (2), 121–130.

Grimaldi-Bensouda, L., Zureik, M., Aubier, M., et al., 2013. Does omalizumab make a difference to the real-life treatment of asthma exacerbations? Results from a large cohort of patients with severe uncontrolled asthma. Chest 143 (2), 398–405.

Jarosławski, S., Toumi, M., 2011. Market access agreements for pharmaceuticals in Europe: diversity of approaches and underlying concepts. BMC Health Serv. Res. 11, 259.

Jommi, C., 2012. Managed market entry (risk-sharing) agreements: rationale for the NHS and future directions. Pharmacoecon. Italian Res. Articles 14 (Sup1), 38–43.
Jommi, C., 2015. Innovation and drugs price and reimbursement: a comparison between Italy and the other major EU countries. Glob. Region. Health Technol. Assess. 2 (3), 117–162.
Jommi, C., Minghetti, P., 2015. Pharmaceutical pricing policies in Italy. In: Babar, Z.U.D. (Ed.), Pharmaceutical Prices in the 21st Century. Springer, London, pp. 131–151.
McCabe, C.J., Stafinski, T., Edlin, R., et al., 2010. AED summit. Access with evidence development schemes: a framework for description and evaluation. Pharmacoeconomics 28 (2), 143–152.
Menon, D., McCabe, C.J., Stafinski, T., Edlin, R., 2010. Principles of design of access with evidence development approaches: a consensus statement from the Banff Summit. Pharmacoeconomics 28 (2), 109–111.
Mora-Ripoll, R., Gilabert-Perramon, A., Espinosa-Tome, C., et al., 2014. Guidance for risk sharing agreements/pay per: results. Value Health 17 (7), A447.
Morel, T., Arickx, F., Befrits, G., et al., 2013. Reconciling uncertainty of costs and outcomes with the need for access to orphan medicinal products: a comparative study of managed entry agreements across seven European countries. Orphanet. J. Rare Dis. 8, 198.
Navarria, A., Drago, V., Gozzo, L., et al., 2015. Do the current performance-based schemes in Italy really work? "Success fee": a novel measure for cost-containment of drug expenditure. Value Health 18 (1), 131–136.
NHS Quality Improvement Scotland 2008. Coverage with evidence development in NHS. Scotland: discussion paper. Coverage with evidence development workshop; 19 Sep 2008; Glasgow. (http://www.healthcareimprovementscotland.org/previous_resources/hta_report/evidence_development.aspx (accessed 30.07.2017).
Palace, J., Bregenzer, T., Tremlett, H., et al., 2014. UK multiple sclerosis risk-sharing scheme: a new natural history dataset and an improved Markov model. Br. Med. J. Open. 4 (1), e004073.
Palace, J., Duddy, M., Bregenzer, T., et al., 2015. Effectiveness and cost-effectiveness of interferon beta and glatiramer acetate in the UK multiple sclerosis risk sharing scheme at 6 years: a clinical cohort study with natural history comparator. Lancet Neurol. 14 (5), 497–505.
Pauwels, K., Huys, I., Vogler, S., et al., 2017. Managed entry agreements for oncology drugs: lessons from the European experience to inform the future. Front Pharmacol. 8, 171.
Puig-Peiró R, Mestre-Ferrandiz J, Sussex J, Towse A. Literature review on patient access schemes, flexible pricing schemes and risk sharing agreements for medicines. PPRI Conference 29–30 September 2011. https://www.ohe.org/sites/default/files/old-wp/498.pdf (accessed 30.07.2017).
Raftery, J., 2010. Multiple sclerosis risk sharing scheme: a costly failure. Br. Med. J. 340, c1672.
Russo, P., Mennini, F.S., Siviero, P.D., Rasi, G., 2010. Time to market and patient access to new oncology products in Italy: a multistep pathway from European context to regional health care providers. Ann. Oncol. 21 (10), 2081–2087.
Schey, C., Milanova, T., Hutchings, A., et al., 2011. Estimating the budget impact of orphan medicines in Europe: 2010–2020. Orphanet J. Rare Dis. 6, 62.
Stafinski, T., McCabe, C.J., Menon, D., 2010. Funding the unfundable: mechanisms for managing uncertainty in decisions on the introduction of new and innovative technologies into healthcare systems. Pharmacoeconomics 28 (2), 113–142.
Sudlow, C.L., Counsell, C.E., 2003. Problems with UK government's risk sharing scheme for assessing drugs for multiple sclerosis. Br. Med. J. 326 (7385), 388–392.
Toumi, M., 2017. Introduction to Market Access for Pharmaceuticals. CRC Press, Taylor & Francis, Florida.
Toumi, M., Zard, J., Abdallah, I.B., et al., 2016. An overview of market access agreements. In: Ethgen, O., Staginnus, O. (Eds.), The Future of Health Economics. Routledge, London, pp. 75–108.

Towse, A., Garrison, Jr., L.P., 2010. Can't get no satisfaction? Will pay for performance help? Toward an economic framework for understanding performance-based risk-sharing agreements for innovative medical products. Pharmacoeconomics 28 (2), 93–102.

Towse, A., Garrison, L., Puig-Peiro, R. The Use of Pay for Performance for Drugs: Can it Improve Incentives for Innovation? Occasional Paper 11/05. Office of Health Economics. 2012.

Williamson, S., 2010. Patient access schemes for high-cost cancer medicines. Lancet Oncol. 11 (2), 111–112.

Wlodarczyk, J., Reid, C.M., Pater, G., 2011. Funding linked to on going research: impact of the bosentan patient registry on pricing in Australia. Value Health 14 (6), 961–963.

CHAPTER 5

Setting a Public Health Agenda to Support Access to High-Cost Medicines

Inthira Yamabhai
International Trade and Health Programme, International Health Policy Program, Ministry of Public Health, Nonthaburi, Thailand

5.1 INTRODUCTION

The right to health and the right to share in the benefits of scientific advancements are a global priority, acknowledged since the creation of the Charter of the United Nations in 1945 (Secretary-General, 2016). Today, improving health outcomes remains a top priority—evidenced by the adoption of the 2030 Agenda for Sustainable Development and its Sustainable Development Goals (SDGs) by 193 member states in September 2015.

Goal 3 of the SDGs, which countries committed to achieving in 2030, is to ensure healthy lives and to promote well-being of all people of all ages. With respect to access to medicine, one target is to achieve universal health coverage, including financial risk protection, access to essential health-care services and access to essential medicines and vaccines for all. In addition, the SDGs also aim to end the epidemics of AIDS, tuberculosis, malaria and neglected tropical diseases, as well as to combat hepatitis, water-borne diseases and other communicable diseases (World Health Organization, 2016a).

Yet even as public attention has turned to the difficulties of securing affordable medicines, access to medicines problems have proliferated. With significant improvement in infrastructure and health technologies that has been seen over the past decades, global life expectancy at birth has increased from 66.4 years in 2000 to 71.4 years in 2015 (Life expectancy, 2016). As people grow older, the disease burden has shifted towards non-communicable diseases, including cancer, which often requires lengthy, expensive treatments with expensive medicines. In high-income countries, mortality rate of cancer has been decreasing because patients have access to better screening programs and new and effective treatments. In lower-income countries, however, access is often non-existent, mainly because

Equitable Access to High-Cost Pharmaceuticals
http://dx.doi.org/10.1016/B978-0-12-811945-7.00005-1

new anti-cancer medicines can be priced at more than 100,000 USD per course of treatment (Siddiqui and Rajkumar, 2012).

Major progress has been made on increasing access to medicines to treat HIV/AIDS and hepatitis C (World Health Organization, 2014, 2016a). Yet more effort is needed to fully eradicate a wide range of diseases and address many different persistent and emerging health issues. Affordable pricing of essential medicines is necessary to attain universal health coverage and to expand access to needed therapies. All too often, high prices for medicines impede access to life-saving or health-supporting drugs, exposing individuals and families to unnecessary financial hardship, and strain national health resources. At the same time, low prices may jeopardise the continuity of supply, drive manufacturers out of the market and reduce investment into needed research. Under the current approach, countries do not appear likely to achieve their 2030 goals (Afdhal et al., 2014). The Goal 3 will be reviewed in depth at the high-level political forum in July 2017 (United Nations, 2017).

5.2 THE EMERGING SIGNIFICANCE OF THE IMPACT OF HIGH-COST MEDICINES

Concerns with high prices for essential medicines have been seen in low- and middle- income countries for decades. Recently, those prices have become a salient political issue in high-income countries as well, including in the United States. In the recent presidential election, both U.S. candidates drew attention to the problems associated with high prices. Hillary Clinton excoriated drug companies that

'*sell the same drug all over the world at a much lower price to everybody else. Now, I am proud that our drug companies invent drugs to cure terrible diseases and treat chronic diseases. I'm proud of that. But let's be clear, your tax dollars help support the research that is used to create those drugs in the first place. Your tax dollars support the Food and Drug Administration [FDA] that tests those drugs to determine whether or not they are safe and effective to be able to go to market. And then we end up in America paying the highest price for those drugs that we have helped to create. We have got to take this on. And we can do it without hurting research, and discovery and new drugs and new devices*' (Jaffe, 2016).

At a Republican debate in March, Donald Trump proposed using price negotiations to reduce spending on prescription drugs. He said '*We will save $300 billion a year if we properly negotiate*'.

High priced medicines have increasingly come to the forefront of media coverage. For example, ledipasvir-sofosbuvir, a direct-acting antiretroviral combination showing a sustained virological response rate of up to 99% after 12 week of treatment (Afdhal et al., 2014), was a significant innovation with a significant price tag—with initial list prices as a high as US$94000 per treatment in 2014. Medicines for rare diseases, some of which have had historically affordable prices as generics, have been subject to substantial price hikes in recent years. In the United States (Rosenthal, 2014), the price per unit of digoxin rose 100-fold from US0.11 to US$1.10 between 2012 and 2014; the price per unit of doxycycline rose from US$0.04 to US$3.7 between 2013 and 2014. These hikes have been blamed on low levels of generic competition, leading to monopolistic behaviours from participating pharmaceutical companies.

In other cases, some pharmaceutical companies have adopted strategies to buy old neglected drugs and later turning them into high-priced specialty drugs (Pollack, 2015). The price per unit of pyrimethamine, a generic product used to treat toxoplasmosis and cystoisosporiasis, rose overnight from US$13.50 to US$750 after Turing Pharmaceuticals acquired its marketing rights from Impax Laboratories in August 2015 (Lorenzetti, 2015). Price hikes of this degree raise the annual cost of treatment of some patients to unaffordable levels, reducing overall availability of the product in health systems and forcing clinical substitution of potentially less efficacious products (Pollack, 2015).

Other low-volume orphan medicines also present with high-list prices because of government incentives to develop products for patients with rare diseases. EU and US legislation has helped bring to market upwards of 200 therapies for rare diseases since 2000, with or without orphan status (Abd El Rihim et al., 2013; Eurordis, 2016); however, critics argue that the legislation may allow companies to repurpose existing products and 'salami slice', or identify small patient populations to gain orphan drug approval with all the associated patent extensions, government benefits and subsidies—allowing exploitation of a system intended for new drug development and potentially increasing prices (Daniel et al., 2016).

5.3 EUROPEAN COOPERATION

Countries have begun to cooperate to find a solution to the problem of high-cost medicines, in 2016, the Belgian Healthcare Knowledge Centre (KCE) and Zorginstituut Nederland (Dutch Health Care Institute, ZIN) took the first step to conduct a study titled **Future scenarios about drug development and drug pricing** (Vandenbroeck et al., 2016). This

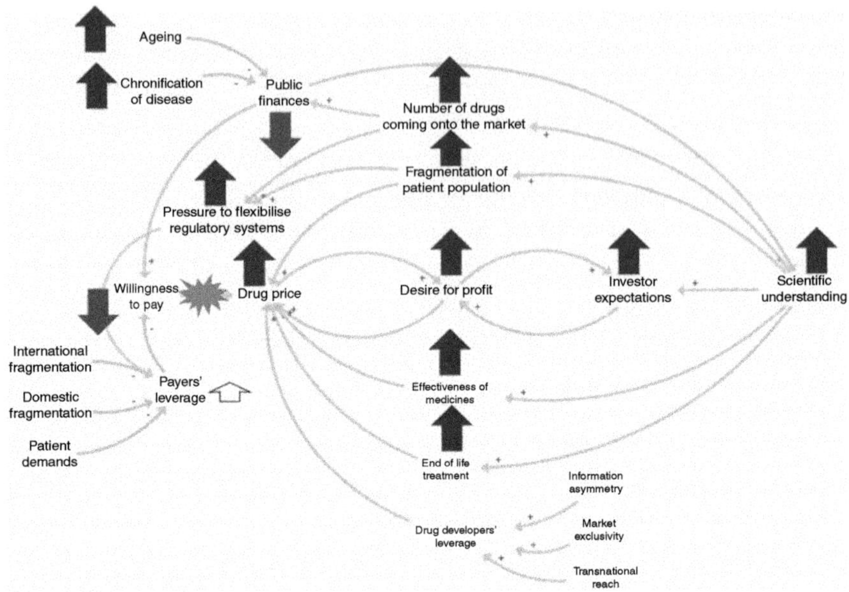

Figure 5.1 The factors that contribute to high prices, including governments' current willingness to pay those prices. Keys drivers include fragmentation of patient population, developers' profit motive, higher investments to get the more effective medicine, demand for end-of-life medicines and price negotiation. The factors that influence payers, including changes in demographic and epidemiology, the new and highly effective medicines and health technologies coming onto the market, and the leverage that payers have to negotiate prices. This figure was used to generate discussion among stakeholders to identify the key drivers of high-priced medicines.

initiative held workshops with international stakeholders including patient groups, pharmaceutical industry, academics, not-for-profit research organisations, regulators, payers, government representatives from Europe and the US and international organisations. This initiative developed the diagram showing the complex system of pharmaceutical industry, as shown in Fig. 5.1.

Through several stakeholder workshops held in 2016 for the Future scenarios about drug development and drug pricing study, KCE/ZIN tasked its group of experts and stakeholders from Europe and North America to develop seed scenarios based on functional building blocks for alternative drug development and pricing mechanisms determined through literature review and stakeholder in-depth interviews.

From the two 2-day deliberative workshops in Amsterdam in March and April 2016, four scenarios (Table 5.1) were proposed. They offer possible

Table 5.1 Results from the workshop

Scenarios	**Brief Information**
Needs-oriented public–private partnership	Public actors and drug developers are tackling public health priorities in vigorous and pragmatic partnerships. The public actor identifies indications representing high public health needs; specifies criteria for the performance levels of drugs to be developed for those indications; and indicates his willingness to pay. Through procurements with enforceable contractual commitments, the public actor enters into a partnership with drug developers to find solutions for these needs. Developers are prepared to enter into the partnership and to give price concessions for a pre-negotiated fixed agreement on price and volume, which reduces their development risk.
Parallel drug development trace	EU member states have set up a parallel, not-for-profit drug development track that exists alongside, but independent of, the pharmaceutical and biotechnological industry. The aim of the parallel track is to develop cheaper drugs without compromising safety and effectiveness.
Pay for patents	A consortium of European countries has joined forces and has established a 'Public Fund for Affordable Drugs'. Each of the participating countries deposits a fixed annual percentage of what they currently spend on drugs into the Fund. Private payers (including insurance companies) can also join the Fund.
Public good from A to Z	Drug development is essentially a public enterprise, and has been radically reoriented from serving private profits towards serving the public interest and the needs of patients. In a drug development system that is essentially a public enterprise; private drug companies still have a role, albeit with a completely different business model. They mainly manufacture drugs and deliver services to the public provider on a competitive basis. With drugs and other health technologies being essentially public goods, there is no role for patents or monopolistic prices.

innovative approaches to replace the current drug development and pricing system. All scenarios are framed around the principles of basic human rights and the public interest. The initiative recommends these scenarios as a starting point for countries to start the global dialogue.

Governments across the EU have also prioritised actions to address high-priced medicines. Malta, which took over the rotating presidency of the EU in 2017, stated that its EU presidency will focus on accessibility and affordability of medicines by promoting agenda items that improve transparency during government negotiation with pharmaceutical companies (Michalopoulos, 2016). Due to confidentiality clauses, rebates and discounts obtained in national procurement arrangements are often not disclosed—neither in Europe nor the rest of the world. When true prices are disclosed, negotiations can bring down the price of medicines and make them more affordable to health systems and ultimately patients.

Some European member states have also begun regional and joint procurement mechanisms to strengthen purchasing power and obtain fairer prices for their regions. Notably, in 2015, Luxembourg joined Belgium and the Netherlands in their cooperation on joint negotiation for orphan drugs (Ministre des Affaires Aociales et de la Santé publique, 2015). Australia has joined in 2016 and the pharmaceutical policy collaboration is called 'BeNeLuxA' (KCE, 2017). Under the collaboration, it will allow the countries to exchange data, share registries, coordinate assessment methodologies, conduct horizon scanning activities and jointly negotiate with pharmaceutical companies to obtain lower prices on orphan products by aggregating demand. By participating in the joint negotiation activities, pharmaceutical companies will only need to provide one dossier for assessment and will be granted access to larger patient populations. Similar arrangements been made between Malta, Cyprus, Greece, Italy, Spain and Portugal (i.e. Valleta Declaration) and between Bulgaria, Romania, Croatia and Lithuania (i.e. Visegrad +2) (Michalopoulos, 2017).

5.4 G7 AND G20

High drug prices are also receiving attention before the G7 and G20. France has been instrumental at putting the issue on the agenda. Former President Francois Hollande has called for 'fighting soaring medicine prices' and cooperation between countries on international pricing system (Lagrange, 2016), and the former French Health Minister, Marisol Touraine, told RMC radio that high prices have made the system unsustainable. Instead of negotiating with companies individually, she argued, countries should band together and insist on transparency, while at the same time assuring that manufacturers receive a fair award for developing new medicines (Medical Xpress, 2016).

In March, France pushed medicine prices onto the agenda of the G7, held in Japan in May 2016, as well as the G20, held in China in September same year (Hollande, 2016). The G7 nations are the world's leading economies[1] and also home to many leading pharmaceutical companies (Blamont and Vey, 2016). France raised the issue at both meetings and, according to the communiqué of the G20, discussion focused mostly on trade and economic development (University of Toronto, 2016). Members recognised that pricing practices is a public health challenge for all countries that have set their goals to reach the universal health coverage as committed to SDGs. (Ministère des Affaires étrangères, 2016) The G7's official statement, however, focused only on questions pertaining to antimicrobial resistance, not to access to medicines more generally. The price discussion was shelved for a discussion held among G7 health ministers in September 2016.

When those ministers met, they were joined by the World Health Organisation (WHO), the UN Office for the Coordination of Humanitarian Affairs (UNOCHA), the Organisation for Economic Co-operation and Development (OECD), and the World Bank as well as the Ministers from Lao People's Democratic Republic, Myanmar, Singapore and Thailand. Unfortunately, the issue of high price was not explicitly discussed, according to the meeting report. (Ministry of Health Labour and Welfare, 2016) It only says

> *In light of rising health care costs, we reaffirm that investments to strengthen health systems, through evidence-based and transparent prioritization methodologies, particularly health technology assessment are crucial in the decision-making process toward UHC. Economic evaluation of interventions is essential for the efficient and sustainable allocation of finite resources within health systems, and we encourage research and improved information sharing on this matter.*

The G7 Health Ministers meeting report mentioned that the members recognised the issues of promoting R&D, access to medicines, ensuring the sustainability of health systems and encouraged the collective actions to achieve these goals. It mentioned in the report that OECD is working on this issue and would hold the OECD Health Ministerial Meeting in January 2017. Minister Touraine informed the health ministers that OECD would conduct a research on evaluation the sustainability of pharmaceutical expenditure in the medium term, with a specific focus on cancer, Alzheimer's disease, diabetes, HIV, and hepatitis C. In addition, the OECD will set up an expert group and consult with industry, patient groups, research institutes and NGOs to provide approaches for sustainable access to

[1] Canada, France, Germany, Italy, Japan, the United Kingdom, the United States and the European Commissioner.

medicines (Bietry, 2016). It is expected that the report will be published in December 2017. At the time of writing, the report has not been released.

5.5 THE UN HIGH-LEVEL PANEL ON ACCESS TO MEDICINES

When Member States adopted the 2030 Agenda for Sustainable Development, the High-Level Panel on Access to Medicines was convened in November 2015. The role of the Panel was to 'to review and assess proposals and recommend solutions for remedying the policy incoherence between the justifiable rights of inventors, international human rights law, trade rules and public health in the context of health technologies'. The Panel was co-chaired by Ruth Dreifuss, the former President of the Swiss Confederation, and Festus Gontebanye Mogae, the former President of the Republic of Botswana. Panel members consisted of experts in areas of trade, public health, human rights and legal issues associated with innovation of, and access to medicines.

After the first meeting of the High-Level Panel in New York, the Panel put out a call for contributions on how best to promote innovation and access to medicines, vaccines and diagnostics. Hearings and global dialogues were held in London and South Africa in March 2016, and a final report was then distributed publicly in September 2016.

The report provides recommendations to relevant stakeholders, including industry, civil society, governments and international organisations. The report addresses issues surrounding the relationship between incentives for research and development (R&D) through intellectual property protection and access to health technologies.

The report concludes that the current incentive system has failed to foster research into new antibiotics and into medicines to treat neglected diseases. The system also rewards manufacturers that set exorbitant prices for their medicines. In response to the high prices, the report suggests that governments to re-design national laws and regulations, including intellectual property law, competition law, medicine regulatory laws and government procurement regulations, to satisfy national public health objectives. The co-chair of the Panel stated that

'Policy incoherencies arise when legitimate economic, social and political interests and priorities are misaligned or in conflict with the right to health. On the one hand, governments seek the economic benefits of increased trade. On the other, the imperative to respect patents on health technologies could, in certain instances, create obstacles to the public health objectives and the right to health'. President Ruth Dreifuss, 2016.

In particular, the report encourages Member States to use TRIPS flexibilities to increase access to medicines. In the past, not many countries have used TRIPS flexibilities, partly because they fear political and economic repercussions from certain states. In the Panel's view, states that bring pressure others to discourage the use of TRIPS flexibilities violate human rights and undermine the legitimacy of the Doha Declaration. The report also suggests governments form a working group to establish a standard of negotiation procedure and create Code of Principles for Biomedical R&D.

Throughout, the report addresses issues of transparency. The report recommends that governments demand the disclosure of R&D costs to assure that the price for medicines reflect the resources put into the innovation. As it stands, reliable data on R&D costs are unavailable.

To introduce transparency, the Panel report suggests that WHO should establish and update a public database of prices of patented and generic medicines, as well as biosimilars in the private and public sectors of all countries, if the medicines are registered. The report also encourages WIPO to develop an international, easily searchable database which should including international names, application date, and patent status (granted or expired).

The Panel also recommends that the UN General Assembly hold a Special Session on health technology innovation and access before 2018. The Session is to have an agreement on strategies and accountability framework ensuring sustainable access to medicine and promoting innovation to reach the Goal 3 under the 2030 SDG Agenda.

In response to the UNHLP, in March 2016 GlaxoSmithKline (GSK) moved to address criticisms about its pricing strategies. GSK announced that it would adopt a graduated approach to filing and enforcing patents depending on countries' income levels. This means that GSK will not file for patents for its medicine in least developed countries and low-income countries. For low- and middle-income countries, the company will provide low-cost licenses to generic manufacturers to supply in LMICs for 10 years. Also, GSK will continue working with the Medicines Patent Pool to cover more anticancer medicines (GSK, 2016). In response to requests for the disclosure of patent information, GSK will also make its patent portfolio publicly available.

5.6 WHO FAIR PRICING FORUM

Medicine prices affect access along two dimensions. As mentioned previously, while high prices have been observed, in particular, for cancer medicines, orphan medicines and most recently the new treatments for hepatitis

C, some older and off-patent medicines are not attractive to the generic pharmaceutical industry because either demand for those medicines might be insufficiently strong (World Health Organization, 2016b) or the return on investment is not sufficient. Two clear examples of this phenomenon are Benzathine penicillin, the antibiotic of choice for certain bacterial infections and methotrexate, used to treat arthritis, psoriasis, and certain cancers. Although these products are still needed and often prescribed, they are frequently unavailable in lower-income health systems.

These recent trends represent a two-fold setback: on the one hand, new medicines are out of reach of even the wealthiest countries, and on the other, older medicines are in great shortage. The WHO recognises this problem and has called for a global discussion on how to assure a fair price for essential medicines (Silverman, 2016). New approaches and new partnerships are needed to refresh the discussion on medicine pricing and to find workable solutions.

5.6.1 What Is a Fair Price? And How Is Such a Fair Price to Be Achieved?

The questions of what a fair price is and how a fair price can be achieved are easier asked than answered, and raise difficult questions at the intersection of ethics, politics and public health. What seems fair to sellers may appear unfair to buyers, and vice-versa. The economic concepts of consumer and producer surplus may offer traction on the question. If the consumer gets a medicine at a lower price than what it is being sold, the difference is consumer surplus for buyers. In contrary, if the product owner sells the product higher than their cost, that gain is producer surplus.

The discussion of a fair price around economic surplus enables the disaggregation of two questions. First, what is the size of the surplus that exists in the pharmaceutical industry? Because researching, developing, manufacturing and distributing medicines are costly; drug manufacturers often suggest that the surplus is small. Critics point to data on R&D and production costs and to the large profits in the pharmaceutical industry to cast doubt on that assertion.

However, there is a notable lack of robust data on R&D costs. Estimates of average drug development costs are range from \$180 million to \$2.6 billion—a ten-fold difference. In part, the difference reflects methodological differences between studies. Some of the highest estimates of R&D costs, for example, focus only on the costs of developing new chemical entities, which account for only about one-quarter of drug approvals. Costs will generally be lower to develop a variant on an older drug—perhaps a different mode of administration (e.g. oral versus injection) or a combination product. Similarly, some of the lowest estimates of drug development costs come from product development partnerships that target neglected diseases. It may be cheaper to develop a drug for a long-neglected disease than for diseases that have been subject to intensive research.

In the absence of better information from the pharmaceutical industry, the WHO's most recent figures may offer a realistic starting point. In connection with the R&D pipeline for drugs to treat emerging pathogens with epidemic potential, the WHO has estimated that R&D costs range from $58.4 million (for a repurposed drug that can immediately begin Phase II trials) to $743 million (for new chemical entities to treat poorly understood diseases) (World Health Organization, 2016c). These estimates exclude the capital costs of investing in R&D instead of pursuing alternative investments; if those costs were included, the WHO figures would be considerably higher.

At a minimum, a fair price for a medicine cannot fall to a level below which manufacturers will not supply it. It is important to know what it costs to manufacture, develop and register medicines. Most of the essential medicines are no longer patented; for those drugs, manufacturers need not be compensated for the cost of (R&D). The major cost driver, instead, is the expense of manufacturing—most significantly, the costs of synthesising the active pharmaceutical ingredient (API). For example, it is estimated to cost $68–136 to secure enough API for one course of treatment of sofosbuvir (Hill et al., 2014). The costs of formulating the drug, packaging it and a 10% profit, would raise the price to $75–150—a trivial fraction of the $84,000 list price for the drug.

Second, how should any surplus be allocated between consumers and producers? The nature of medical need means that demand for medicines is relatively inelastic. As a result, manufacturers will often have market power to set high prices for essential medicines—implying that manufacturers acquire a large share of any surplus. On ethical and human rights grounds, however, there is a strong case that the surplus should be allocated to buyers through price reductions, which would in turn improve access to needed medicines.

The lack of price transparency surrounding drugs is also a significant problem. Although the advertised 'list price' for a drug often does not reflect its actual price, particularly given the global proliferation of rebates over the past two decades, manufacturers rarely share good data about the true price at which they sell their medicines. Indeed, many of the most prominent drug-price databases include only the list price and therefore offer a misleading picture. Countries engaging in external reference pricing activities will find that their baselines for comparison are not reflective of the actual prices paid by reference countries, artificially inflating prices. The obscurity of drug prices also hinders national efforts to negotiate effectively with manufacturers, which is an especially acute problem for national programs that operate on constrained budgets. Indeed, lack of transparency is a concern even in the market for generic medicines, where many government procurers appear to pay well above the cost of production. They do so partly because they lack good information about what other countries pay. Price transparency could therefore reduce the burden of high generic prices, especially in low- and middle-income countries.

At the same time, recent drug shortages of essential and generic medications illustrate that prices can be too low as well as too high. With thin profit margins, multiple manufacturers may be unwilling to produce a generic drug. Consolidation in the generic pharmaceutical industry exacerbates the problem. Without multiple competitors, relatively minor shocks—manufacturing problems, unexpected spikes in demand, and problems in the supply chain—can lead to shortages.

Thus, where do we go from here?

5.6.2 Towards the Fair Pricing System

Recognising both the urgency and the complexity of the task, Department of Essential Medicine and Health Products (EMP), WHO convened a global forum with the aim of the fairer price setting system (Kieny, 2016) in May 2017. In partnership with the Dutch Ministry of Health, Welfare and Sport, WHO gathered stakeholders from government, industry, academia and non-governmental organisations to explore strategies for establishing fair prices of essential medicines. The underlying approach was to identify the most promising options and strategies to expand access to new medicines while ensuring that sufficient incentives remain for research and innovation, and that generic medicines also remain on the market.

The Forum provided a platform for the initial discussions and consultation to later develop consensus with all stakeholders on an approach to setting prices of new medicines that are sustainable for health systems and for innovation and to define strategies that address the ethical considerations related to use of products in short supply due to inadequate price.

Specifically related to the problems around high-priced medicines, stakeholders discussed the issues surrounding the current value-based pricing (VBP) system used by the pharmaceutical industry. VBP may be a reasonable mechanism for prioritising treatments within a health system, but it could be problematic when used as a basis for price setting. VBP does not explicitly consider the costs to health systems, nor does it account for affordability to either patients or payers.

Similarly, stakeholders discussed delinkage from the price of products from R&D and production costs as a strategy to lower prices of medicines. The delinkage proposal suggests that current high-prices of medicines and patent-related monopolies exist to recoup the costs of bringing a product to market and incentivising further investment into R&D. Government funding with cash prize incentives to researchers and successful drug developers reduces the risk burden on individual companies involved in drug development, therefore removing the need for high-prices on the final product. Competition among firms involved in drug development replaces the need for legal monopolies, which also lowers the price of products and ultimately expands access to patients. The effectiveness of delinkage was illustrated by the Drugs for Neglected Diseases Initiative (DNDi), which has produced six new treatments and 12 new chemical entities in 10 years for less than €183 million (Balasegaram, 2009). Stakeholders noted that delinkage models are effective, but require commitments by governments to function.

Among the most important themes identified at the Forum was the need for transparency to give evidence for future action. Without transparency on the cost of production, spending on clinical trials, the cost of R&D, who bears the cost of R&D and the true price of medicines, stakeholders will not fully understand the environment or actual causes of high-prices nor will they be to effectively target interventions. WHO aims to keep advocating for a fairer pricing system that is sustainable for health systems and for innovation.

5.7 CONCLUSION

More high-income countries are now echoing the concerns that many LMICs and international NGOs have raised over the past decade and a half: that today's medical R&D system, which incentivises innovation primarily through patents, creates significant barriers to access for millions of people. Policy discussions are escalating to global forums; the United Nations, the

WHO, the European Union, and the G7 are each considering innovation and access challenges with renewed interest.

The status quo is no longer working—if indeed it has ever worked—to assure global access to essential medicines. Many dialogues have been initiated at national, regional and global level suggesting a huge demand to reform of price setting system to make medicines more affordable for all. This agenda has been extended, from countries to groups of countries. The medicine price issue is now a matter of global concern and discussion. Global action will be needed to assure sustainable access to essential medicines.

ACKNOWLEDGEMENTS

I gratefully acknowledge the support and helpful input from Andrew Rintoul and Swathi Iyengar, Innovation Access and Use, Department of Essential Medicines and Health Products, World Health Organization. I also have received useful feedback from Prof Nicholas Bagley, University of Michigan Law School. I would like to thank Andrew, Swathi and Prof Nicholas for their feedback and invaluable comments.

REFERENCES

Abd El Rihim, A.Y., Omar, R.F., Fathalah, W., El Attar, I., Hafez, H.A., Ibrahim, W., 2013. Role of fibroscan and APRI in detection of liver fibrosis: a systematic review and meta-analysis. Arab J. Gastroenterol. 14 (2), 44–50.

Afdhal, N., Reddy, K.R., Nelson, D.R., Lawitz, E., Gordon, S.C., Schiff, E., et al., 2014. Ledipasvir and sofosbuvir for previously treated HCV genotype 1 infection. N. Eng. J. Med. 370 (16), 1483–1493.

Balasegaram m. Best science for the most neglected: what can we learn from the dndi modelAt 10 years? 2009; available from: https://www.dndi.org/wp-content/ Uploads/2009/03/manicabalasegaram_lessonsfrom10yearsdndi.pdf.

Bietry g. Stirrings of international cooperation on drug prices at g7 health meeting. Apmhealtheurope.com; 2016 [9 December 2016]; available from: http://www.apmhealtheurope.com/stirrings-of-international-cooperation-on-drug-prices-at-g7-Health-meeting-fs_49509.html.

Blamont, M., Vey, J.B., 2016. France gets G7 to discuss global regulation of medicine prices. Reuters, 2016 May 3.

Daniel, M.G., Pawlik, T.M., Fader, A.N., Esnaola, N.F., Makary, M.A., 2016. The Orphan Drug Act: restoring the mission to rare diseases. Am. J. Clin. Oncol. 39 (2), 210–213.

Eurordis. Eurordis welcomes dutch eu presidency's conclusions on strengthening the Balance in the eu pharmaceutical system but identifies major challenges. 2016; available from: http://www.eurordis.org/sites/default/files/dutchcouncil_eurordis-pressrelease_final.pdf.

Gsk. Gsk expands graduated approach to patents and intellectual property to widen access to Medicines in the world's poorest countries. 2016 [9 December 2016]; available from: http://www.gsk.com/en-gb/media/press-releases/2016/gsk-expands-graduated-approach-to-patentsand-Intellectual-property-to-widen-access-to-medicines-in-the-world-s-poorest-countries/.

Hill, A., Khoo, S., Fortunak, J., Simmons, B., Ford, N., 2014. Minimum costs for producing Hepatitis C Direct Acting Antivirals, for use in large-scale treatment access programs in developing countries. Clin. Infect. Dis. 58 (7), 928–936, 2014 JANUARY 6.

Hollande, F., 2016. Towards a global agenda on health security. Lancet 10034 (387), 2173–2174.

Jaffe, S., 2016. US presidential candidates' proposals to reduce drug prices. Lancet 388, 855–856.

Kce. Horizon scanning for pharmaceuticals: proposal for the beneluxa collaboration: Kce2017.

Kieny, M.P., 2016. A comprehensive and fair solution to the price of medicines. Huffington Post, 2016 June 28.

Lagrange c. France's hollande to seek regulation of medicine prices at g7, g20 summits. Reuters; 2016 [9 December]; available from: france's hollande to seek regulation of medicine prices at g7, g20 Summits.

Life expectancy [database on the internet]2016 [cited 6 December 2016]. Available from: http://www.who.int/Gho/Mortality_Burden_Disease/Life_Tables/Situation_Trends/En/

Lorenzetti, L., 2015. This 62-year-old drug just got 5,000% more expensive. Fortune.

Medical Xpress. France to call for lower drug prices at g7. Medical Xpress. 2016.

Michalopoulos, S., 2016. Health minister: drugs pricing will top Malta's EU presidency. Euractiv.

Michalopoulos, S., 2017. Southern EU states present unified front in drug talks. Euractiv 10.

Ministère des affaires étrangères. Official speeches and statements of June 03, 2016. 2016 [9 December 2016]; available from: http://basedoc.diplomatie.gouv.fr/exldoc/France-diplomatie/pdf/baen2016-06-03.pdf.

Ministre des affaires sociales et de la santé publique. The grand duchy of luxemburg joins Belgium-Netherlands initiative on orphan drugs. 2015.

Ministry of Health Labour and Welfare, 2016. Kobe Communiqué, G7 Health Ministers' Meeting, 11-12 September 2016. 2016 [9 December 2016]; Available from: http://www.mhlw.go.jp/seisakunitsuite/bunya/hokabunya/kokusai/g7kobe/en/KobeCommunique_en.pdf.

Pollack a. Drug goes from $13.50 a tablet to $750, overnight. The New York Times. 2015 20 September 2015.

Rosenthal, E., 2014. Officials Question the Rising Costs of Generic Drugs, The New York Times; 2014 [6 May 2017]; Available from: https://www.nytimes.com/2014/10/08/business/officials-question-the-rising-costs-of-generic-drugs.html.

Secretary-general u. The united nations secretary-general's high-level panel on access to Medicines report: promoting innovation and access to health technologies. 2016.

Siddiqui, M., Rajkumar, S.V., 2012. The high cost of cancer drugs and what we can do about it. Mayo Clin. Proc. 87 (10), 935–943.

Silverman, E., July 2016. Q&A: why the World Health Organization plans a fair pricing model for drugs. Pharmalot 7.

United Nations., 2017. High-level political forum, [5 December 2016]; Available from: https://sustainabledevelopment.un.org/hlpf.

University of Toronto., 2016. G20 leaders' communiqué: Hangzhou Summit, 2016 [9 December 2016]; Available from: http://www.g20.utoronto.ca/2016/160905-communique.html.

Vandenbroeck, P., Raeymakers, P., Wickert, R., Becher, K., Goossens, J., Cleemput, I., et al., 2016. Future scenarios about drug development and drug pricing.

World Health Organization., 2014. Increasing access to HIV treatment in middle-income countries: key data on prices, regulatory status, tariffs and the intellectual property situation. Geneva: World Health Organ.

World Health Organization., 2016a. World Health Statistics 2016: monitoring health for the SDGS sustainable development goals. World Health Organ.

World Health Organization., 2016b. Addressing the global shortages of medicines, and the safety and accessibility of children's medication. Sixty-Ninth World Health Assembly, Geneva.
World Health Organization., 2016c. An R&D blueprint for action to prevent epidemics: funding and coordination models for preparedness and response. Geneva: World Health Organ.

CHAPTER 6

Human Rights and Intellectual Property for Universal Access to New Essential Medicines

Katrina Perehudoff*, Ellen 't Hoen**
*University Medical Center Groningen, Department of Health Sciences - Global Health Unit, University of Groningen, Groningen, The Netherlands
**University of Groningen, University Medical Center Groningen, Global Health Unit, Groningen, The Netherlands

6.1 INTRODUCTION

The 19th edition of WHO's Model List of Essential Medicines, published in 2015, contains several important medicines including for the treatment of cancer, tuberculosis and hepatitis C that are widely patented and highly priced (WHO, 2015). When WHO labels a medicine as essential this means that it must be made available and affordable to all. Such a label imposes human rights obligations on governments and industry to act to ensure access to essential medicines. The Essential Medicines List is therefore a tool for the practical implementation of the internationally agreed principle that intellectual property (IP) should not stand in the way of measures to promote the human right to health and access to essential medicines as a component of that right (WTO, 2001).

Yet, when a medicine is patented, unless licenses are available for patents related to the product, it will likely remain out of reach for many. The tension between finite health budgets and the human rights imperative to provide essential medicines is now felt by low-, middle- and high-income countries alike (Ploumen and Schippers, 2016). So, *how can governments with limited public health budgets ensure access to expensive, essential medicines in line with the right to health?*

This chapter illustrates how human rights principles can help governments, even those with the most modest budgets, take all possible action to ensure universal access to essential medicines. The key message is that governments have legally binding obligations to immediately take steps to provide essential medicines. These obligations arise from the right to health in international law and its authoritative interpretation by human rights experts on the Committee on Economic, Social and Cultural

Equitable Access to High-Cost Pharmaceuticals
http://dx.doi.org/10.1016/B978-0-12-811945-7.00006-3

Rights. These steps include making a maximum of public resources available to finance essential medicines, particularly for the vulnerable and marginalised, and using those resources efficiently. Crucially, controlling medicines prices to ensure access to essential medicines is aligned with governments' duties under the right to health. In the case of high-priced patented medicines the TRIPS flexibilities can be effective tools to access lower priced generic medicines. Moreover, the right to health imposes duties on the international community of States and the pharmaceutical industry to respect and protect access to essential medicines (UN CESCR, 2000; Khosla and Hunt, 2008).

6.2 ACCESS TO ESSENTIAL MEDICINES IN THE ERA OF INTELLECTUAL PROPERTY AND HUMAN RIGHTS

6.2.1 The WTO TRIPS Agreement—Globalising Intellectual Property Rules

On 1 January 1995, the World Trade Organization (WTO) Agreement on Trade-Related Aspects of Intellectual Property Rights (TRIPS) came into being. TRIPS were part of a set of international treaties agreed upon at the end of the Uruguay Round of trade negotiations which established the WTO (Uruguay Round, 1986). The TRIPS Agreement globalised intellectual property (IP) requirements that had only recently been adopted by rich nations. When the Uruguay Round of multilateral trade negotiations was launched in 1986, 49 of the 98 members of the Paris Convention excluded pharmaceutical products from patent protection, 10 excluded pharmaceutical processes and 22 excluded chemical processes (World Intellectual Property Organization, 1988). Countries varied in the periods of protection granted and/or set out conditions that restricted patent holders' rights (Dutfield, 2003).

Before TRIPS, pharmaceutical patent law, policies and practices differed among countries, particularly between developed and developing countries. As a result, developing countries had for many years been able to rely on countries such as India, Egypt, Israel, Jordan, Brazil and Argentina for their supply of affordable medicines. ('t Hoen, 2009) India's 1970 Patents Act, for example, provided for process patents but not product patents for medicines; this law encouraged the development of a generic pharmaceutical industry that reverse-engineered its own versions of new medicines that were often patented in other countries (Waning et al., 2010).

TRIPS signalled a fundamental change in that, for the first time, global minimum requirements for the creation and protection of IP were enforceable through the WTO (World Trade Organization, 1994). The TRIPS Agreement requires WTO Members to make patents available for any inventions, whether products or processes, in all fields of technology without discrimination (subject to the normal tests of novelty, inventiveness and industrial applicability) with a minimum duration of 20 years. A patent is the right granted to an inventor by a State, or by regional office acting for several States, to exclude others from commercially exploiting his invention for a certain period of time (World Intellectual Property Organization, 2017a). It is also required that patents be available and patent rights enjoyable without discrimination as to the place of invention and whether products are imported or locally produced. TRIPS imposed the new IP norms globally around the same time the HIV/AIDS epidemic took hold in the world and the call for access to AIDS treatment in the developing world had become loud.

6.2.2 HIV and the Drive for Change in Intellectual Property

In the late 1990s, the magnitude of the AIDS crisis drew attention to the fact that millions of people in the developing world did not have access to the medicines they needed to treat disease or alleviate suffering.

The high cost of HIV medicines focused attention on the relationship between patents and drug prices. The difficulties that developing countries experienced in paying for new essential medicines that were needed to treat the millions of people that were dying of AIDS raised concerns about medical patents. In 2000, only one in a thousand people living with HIV in Africa had access to treatment (Gellman, 2000). Highly active antiretroviral (ARV) treatment was available in wealthy countries and had changed AIDS from a death sentence into a manageable chronic disease. But the ARV medicines were available only from originator companies, who controlled the patents. They produced small quantities carrying paralysing price tags—US$10,000 to US$15,000 per person per year (Perez-Casas et al., 2001).

The generic industry, mainly from India played an important role in changing the course of HIV treatment. The 1970 Indian Patents Act, which then still excluded pharmaceutical product patents, provided the legal framework for large scale generic production of ARVs including innovative fixed-dose combinations (FDCs) and paediatric formulations ('t Hoen, 2016).

The establishment of the early AIDS treatment programs in developing countries such as Brazil and Thailand in the late nineties and early 2000 were possible, in part, because key pharmaceuticals, primarily '1st line' HIV drugs were not patent-protected and could be produced locally at much lower costs ('t Hoen, 2016).

However, in many other countries, there were patent barriers to the supply of generic ARVs. And a number of patent related trade and legal disputes broke out. A much publicised dispute was the legal case mounted by 39 drug companies in 1998 against South Africa over changes to the Medicines Act aimed at facilitating the import and use of lower priced medicines claiming the changes were unconstitutional and in violation of South Africa's obligations under TRIPS (Pharmaceutical Manufacturers, 1998). The legal action by the companies caused global outrage and confronted with a global public-relations disaster coupled with a weak legal case the companies dropped the suit in 2001. However, these events had propelled the issue of access to medicines and patents onto the international political agenda including at the WTO where African countries had put the topic on the agenda of the TRIPS Council ('t Hoen, 2002).

6.2.3 The Emergence of Access to Essential Medicines in the Right to Health

Global disparities in access to expensive and lifesaving ARVs were met with calls from activists for equal access to treatment as a human right. Ensuing political arguments embraced a human rights approach to push for reform and to negotiate affordable prices (Wirtz et al., 2016). A human rights perspective centres on the value and dignity of each person. Certain inalienable, basic rights—namely the right to the highest attainable standard of health—must be guaranteed out of respect for one's dignity and worth. A right to health does not convey a right to a healthy life; instead, it establishes that all people are entitled to an equal opportunity to achieve the highest attainable standard of health (Daniels et al., 2015).

The right to health first emerged as a social right in the World Health Organization (WHO) Constitution and the Universal Declaration of Human Rights (World Health Organization, 1948). However, one of the most important affirmations of the right to health is in the binding global agreement, the International Covenant on Economic, Social and Cultural Rights (ICESCR) of 1966. The ICESCR recognised the right to health and directed governments to take measures to prevent and treat diseases, and ensure to all access to medical services in the event of illness. Over 165 countries have ratified the ICESCR and, as a result, those governments (called States parties) are now legally obliged to protect and promote the Covenant rights in their national context (United Nations Office of the High Commissioner for Human Rights, 2017). In some cases, the right to health in international law can also be enforced in domestic courts (Hogerzeil et al., 2006). In 2013, the ICESCR Optional Protocol entered into force, allows individuals to submit complaints that allege a violation of their social rights, including the right to health (United Nations General Assembly, 2008). This landmark instrument creates the first-ever forum for individuals to claim their health rights before an international tribunal empowered to issue decisions on national governments (Forman, 2016). However, State commitment to the Optional Protocol is voluntary and only claimants in the 22 ratifying countries (to date) may submit a complaint, which limits the global applicability of this instrument and its potential to advance the enjoyment of health rights (United Nations Office, 2017).

It was not until 2000 that the content and meaning of the right to health was further defined to include essential medicines. At the height of the HIV/AIDS pandemic, the Committee on Economic, Social, and Cultural Rights (CESCR), a collection of human rights experts and scholars, interpreted the scope of the right to health in the seminal General Comment No. 14. This authoritative guidance document operationalises the right to health by outlining how States parties can implement and report on this right, and ultimately fulfil their responsibilities under international law (UN CESCR, 2000). General Comment No. 14 signals several fundamental 'core obligations' of States parties. Core obligations indicate the basic minimum aspects of the right to health that must be achieved in order to give meaning to the right (UN CESCR, 1990). Unsurprisingly, the provision of essential medicines defined by WHO appears here as a core duty (see UN CESCR, 2000). Additionally, State parties have the core obligations to ensure non-discriminatory access to and equitable distribution of health facilities, goods and services (UN CESCR, 2000). When read together, General Comment No. 14 compels State parties to provide essential medicines equitably with attention to the needs of the worst-off, including vulnerable and marginalised groups, free of discrimination. In summary, the Committee's interpretation obliges States to guarantee access to essential medicines without discrimination, and that they violate the right to health when they reduce the level of access to essential medicines (Perehudoff et al., 2016).

While General Comment No. 14 brought greater recognition to essential medicines as part of the right to health, important ethical and economic questions remained. *How can governments with limited public health budgets ensure access to expensive, essential medicines in line with the right to health?* The human rights approach does not automatically create an immediate right for everyone to treatment at any cost. The subsequent sections of this chapter will illuminate how the right to health implores governments.

6.2.4 Doha Declaration on TRIPS and Public Health

The struggle to assure access to affordable antiretroviral medicines for the treatment of HIV/AIDS was instrumental in the adoption of the Doha Declaration on TRIPS and Public Health by the World Trade Organisation ministerial meeting in 2001 ('t Hoen et al., 2011). The Doha Declaration recognised the effect of intellectual property protection on medicines prices. It affirmed the sovereign right of governments to take measures to protect public health, including, but not limited through the use of compulsory licensing and parallel importation (see Doha Declaration, 2017). See Box 6.1 for examples of TRIPS flexibilities most relevant for access to medicines.

BOX 6.1

Examples of TRIPS flexibilities most relevant for access to medicines (World Intellectual Property Organization, 2010)

Compulsory Licenses and Public non-commercial use (Government use)

Provision that allows third parties including the government to make use of a patent without the consent of the patent holder. For example, countries have used this provision to allow importation or production of lower priced generic medicines after price negotiations with the patent holder failed and in procurement of antiretrovirals. A recent example is from the US State of Louisiana where the cost of purchasing new antivirals such as sofosbuvir and ledipasvir + sofosbuvir for its 35,000 uninsured and Medicaid-dependent residents with Hepatitis C is unaffordable at a price of $764 million. In 2017 the State health authorities proposed issuing government-use licenses to purchase lower-cost generic forms of these antivirals (Tribble, 2017).

An amendment to the TRIPS Agreement adopted on 23 January 2017 provides for special compulsory licensing to produce and export generic medicines to countries that lack sufficient local pharmaceutical production capacity (World Trade Organization, 2017) to make effective use of compulsory licensing. These provisions existed as a temporary waiver since August 30, 2003.

Exclusion from patentability

While excluding an entire field of technology such as medicines or food is not possible anymore since the adoption of the TRIPS Agreement, the agreement does allow that certain inventions are excluded from patentability under certain conditions, including protection of human health.

Exhaustion of rights (parallel import)

International exhaustion of patent rights, permitted under TRIPS, means that the patent holder cannot use the patent to control subsequent dealings with the product once he/she put a product on the market. This provides countries with the possibility to shop around globally for the best priced medicine of that supplier. This is also known as 'parallel import or 'parallel trade' and countries are fee to determine the exhaustion regime. The European Union for example has regional exhaustion allowing parallel trade within the Union (European Union, 1957).

Regulatory review exemption

A generic manufacturers use this exemption to conduct the necessary research to prepare the registration dossier to apply for marketing authorisation of the generic product before patent expiry of the product. This enables swift generic market entry upon patent expiry. This is also known as the 'Bolar' exception ('t Hoen, 2016).

Research exemption

Allows the use of patented material for scientific research so as to not hamper scientific progress.

Transition periods

TRIPS provided for different implementation deadlines for the TRIPS Agreement or certain provisions of TRIPS for developing and least-developed countries. Most of these transition periods have now expired with the exception of those for LDCs. Today LDCs benefit from the broadest transition flexibility because they are not required to be TRIPS compliant until 2021. A separate LDC pharmaceutical waiver, resulting from the Doha Declaration on TRIPS and Public Health in 2001 allows them not to grant and/or not to enforce existing IP rights on pharmaceutical products. This waiver will be in place until at least 2033 (World Trade Organization, 2013).

Paragraph 4 of the Doha Declaration on TRIPS and Public Health establishes primacy of public health when implementing the TRIPS Agreement. It reads:

> *We agree that the TRIPS Agreement does not and should not prevent Members from taking measures to protect public health. Accordingly, while reiterating our commitment to the TRIPS Agreement, we affirm that the Agreement can and should be interpreted and implemented in a manner supportive of WTO Members' right to protect public health and, in particular, to promote access to medicines for all. In this connection, we reaffirm the right of WTO Members to use, to the full, the provisions in the TRIPS Agreement, which provide flexibility for this purpose.*

The declaration further extended the deadline of the transition period for least developed countries (LDCs). Members for the implementation of pharmaceutical product patents and the protection of undisclosed test data from 2006 to at least 2016 (Council for Trade-Related Aspects of Intellectual Property Rights, 2015). It also waived the obligation to enforce such rights until at least 2016 (Council for Trade-Related Aspects of Intellectual Property Rights, 2015). This waiver was important because many LDCs had already granted patent protection for medicines. In 2015 the LDC waivers were extended to 2021 for the TRIPS implementation waiver and 2033 for the pharmaceutical waiver (Council for Trade-Related Aspects of Intellectual Property Rights, 2015). The Ministerial meeting further promised a solution to the restriction TRIPS puts on the effective use of compulsory licensing by limiting it to the supply 'predominantly for the domestic market' (see Doha Declaration, 2017). This restriction caused problems for countries without (sufficient) production capacity that rely on importation for their supply of medicines to make effective use of compulsory licensing. Solving this problem became subject to a separate process at the TRIPS Council which adopted in 2003 the so called 'August 30 decision' setting out rules for compulsory licensing for export purposes. This temporary waiver was adopted as an amendment (Art.31*bis*) to the TRIPS Agreement in 2005 and came into force on 23 January 2017 (WTO, 2017).

6.2.5 Patents and New Essential Medicines

The patent disputes around HIV medicines, the offer of the Indian drug manufacturer Cipla of a triple first line ARV treatment of less than a dollar a day, the global mobilisation around HIV and the plans for a global financing mechanism to pay for the treatment of HIV in low and middle-income countries caused a qualification program, established in 2003 provided the necessary regulatory framework to allow smooth international trade in generic ARVs[1] ('t Hoen et al., 2014).

However, such mechanisms for other new and patented essential medicines only now begin to emerge. The 19th edition of WHO's Essential Medicines List (2015) contains several important medicines including for the treatment of cancer, tuberculosis (TB) and hepatitis C (HCV) that are widely patented and highly priced (see World Health Organization, 2015). The robust generic competition that brought down prices of early HIV medicines has become harder to achieve, both for newer HIV medicines

[1] In 2017 the WHO launched a pilot project for prequalifying biosimilar medicines to expand access to these expensive cancer treatments in low- and middle-income countries. The pilot concerns rituximab for non-Hodgkin's lymphoma and chronic lymphocytic leukaemia, and trastuzumab to treat breast cancer.

in countries that cannot benefit from the licenses of the Medicines Patent Pool and for medicines to treat other diseases that have a major impact on global public health—notably hepatitis C, cancer and tuberculosis, all of which can be better treated with the effective, and unfortunately highly-priced, new medicines added to the EML in 2015.

The high prices of the new essential medicines illustrate the challenges to access in the post-TRIPS era. Governments must act to ensure availability of essential medicines (Gray et al., 2015). Yet, mandatory patenting of new essential medicines has entrenched price-setting power within the commercial industry, reducing the effective authority of governments. Monopoly pricing of medicines routinely precludes wide access to people in need while tying the hands of the government to intervene. This now has become a global issue. The continued rise of the prices of cancer medications is of particular concern. In the UK NICE has recommended against making the breast cancer medicines trastuzumab emtansine available through the National Health Service because of the high price while recognising that the medicine is effective (NICE, 2016). In the US around a quarter of cancer patients cannot afford their care of those, 18% do not comply with their prescription medication (Crow, 2017).

There is an embedded conflict between government obligations under IP law and obligations under human rights law that will need to be resolved to ensure that public authorities can take effective actions to ensure access to new essential medicines. To this end, the Committee on Economic, Social and Cultural Rights instructs governments to balance an inventor's right to benefit from his scientific innovations against other human rights, including the right to health and the public interest in broad access to health-related products (UN CESCR, 2006).

In 2015, the UN Secretary-General established a High-Level Panel on access to medicines (UNHLP) specifically to recommend solutions for the problems resulting from the incoherence between the justifiable rights of inventors, international human rights law, trade rules and public health in the context of health technologies (United Nations Secretary-General, 2017). The Panel's recommendations, which were published in September 2016, seemed to indicate that a better balance between protecting human rights and the rights of inventors is possible within the current TRIPS framework. In contrast, the UNHLP's predecessor, The Commission on HIV and the Law, had recommended that the WTO urgently suspend TRIPS obligations with regards to essential pharmaceutical products for low and middle-income countries pending the outcome of a review of TRIPS by the UN.

The Commission also suggested new innovation systems including a R&D treaty for pharmaceuticals (Global Commission on HIV and the Law, 2012). In the same vein, the UNHLP report did indeed recommend the start of negotiations for a global agreement on the coordination, financing and development of health technologies including a binding R&D agreement that delinks the cost of R&D from end prices. Such an agreement could become an alternative to the current market exclusivity-based pharmaceutical innovation model that makes it difficult to escape high medicines prices.

The following sections of this chapter will explore the human rights imperative for governments to ensure access to essential medicines and concrete government action to uphold their human rights responsibilities.

6.3 HUMAN RIGHTS OBLIGATIONS OF GOVERNMENTS

6.3.1 Maximum Available Resources

Governments have a primary legal obligation to take steps to realise health rights by continuously increasing health budgets through domestic sources. The obligation to move as expeditiously and effectively towards the full realisation of health rights implies governments should finance therapies which offer best health value for money (UN CESCR, 1990). Efficient resource allocation requires governments to prioritise medicines for public financing and to take steps to reduce the cost of essential medicines. The vital influence of medicines prices on their ranking means that reducing the price of an effective medicine may trigger its reimbursement.

Although States hold primary responsibility to realise their core obligations, this duty is shared by the international community of foreign governments and other actors, which can supplement domestic pharmaceutical funding. This assistance can be a valuable step to afford a universal basic package of essential medicines in low- and lower-middle-income countries where public spending on medicines is demonstrably insufficient (see Wirtz et al., 2016; General Comment, 2000).

Health systems are depleted and patients suffer when governments fail to uphold these tenants of the right to health. Faced with few avenues to acquire expensive medicines, patients seek government-funded access through their national courts. Much of the medicines litigation in the early-2000s was driven by HIV/AIDS patients pursuing State-financed access to high-cost, lifesaving anti-retrovirals. Since then court claims have drastically increased in number, particularly in Latin America (Biehl et al., 2012; Norheim and Wilson, 2014).

In recent years, trastuzumab has been at the centre of such court claims that arose from the unfortunate combination of high prices commanded by the manufacturer and insufficient government budget. For example, in 2006 New Zealand's Health Technology Assessment Agency, Pharmac, concluded that a 12-month regimen of trastuzumab would be effective for early stage HER2-positive breast cancer; however, it would increase the budget for cancer treatments in public hospitals by 45%, causing Pharmac to recommend against its reimbursement largely on financial grounds (Manning, 2014). Such legitimate resource limitations do not absolve States of their human rights responsibilities to take further steps to augment the available resources through international cooperation and to use the range tools at their disposal to lower the costs of medicines.

6.3.2 Efficient Use of Government Resources

Trends in global pharmaceutical spending suggest that inefficiencies exist and they may inhibit progress towards universal access to essential medicines. The Lancet Commission on Essential Medicines Policies estimates that providing a basket of essential medicines in low and middle-income countries would cost between US$77.4 and 152.0 billion annually (Wirtz et al., 2016). This range is shadowed by the total global pharmaceutical sales, which are forecasted to reach $1.4 trillion in 2020 (Wirtz et al., 2016). In other words, the global community has sufficient funds to purchase basic essential medicines for all; however, realising that goal relies on political will and cost-efficient investments based on solidarity between nations.

6.3.3 Prioritising Medicines for Reimbursement

Progressive realisation justifies ranking treatments for reimbursement, with more cost-effective treatments being financed first (Perehudoff et al., 2016). The ranking system ensures that available resources are used as effectively as possible, thereby progressively realising the right to health for the largest number of people at the lowest possible cost (Perehudoff et al., 2016). Besides progressive realisation, a fair priority setting process should conform to human rights principles of transparency, consultation and accountability. The Accountability for Reasonableness framework for rationing healthcare fairly is a useful tool (Daniels and Sabin, 2008). It requires a fully transparent process that offers transparency will allow for meaningful consultation of consumers and patients, as well as a heightened understanding of the trade-offs (Vitry et al., 2016). A balanced representation of stakeholders can ensure societal values are represented in the decision-making process while guarding against the involvement of a few vocal advocates representing only a fraction of patients in need of therapies (Hogerzeil, 2006).

6.3.4 Use of Price Control Mechanisms and TRIPs Flexibilities

Exerting control over medicines prices is in line with States' duty to provide an environment that facilitates the discharge of human rights obligations of the private business sector (see UN CESCR, 2000). In other words, the right to health empowers governments to take steps to structure and regulate medicines prices in order to ensure all essential medicines are available at a price that the health system and patient can afford ('t Hoen et al., 2016). Moreover, General Comment No. 17 addresses States' obligations to assure authors' rights to the material benefits of their inventions when there is an overarching public interest in broad access to health innovations. The Committee on Economic, Social and Cultural Rights has explicitly affirmed that private interests should not impede States parties ability to realise their minimum core obligations to the right to health (UN CESCR, 2006). The Committee notes that 'States parties thus have a duty to prevent unreasonably high costs for access to essential medicines,... from undermining the rights of large segments of the population to health...' (UN CESCR, 2006).

A government's tool box holds multiple instruments to regulate medicines prices. However, the introduction of price regulation is only as effective as its proper enforcement by the government.

When price control measures fail to yield affordable essential medicines, governments have the core obligation to use all means to provide essential medicines, including TRIPS flexibilities. Such use should include issuing of compulsory licenses and public non-commercial use by the government ('Government use' or 'Crown use') of a patent, not-granting or enforcing of medicines product patents by LDCs and other flexibilities that are contained in the TRIPS Agreement and the Doha Declaration on TRIPS and Public Health (World Intellectual Property Organization, 2017b) (see Box 6.1 for other examples of TRIPS flexibilities). The use of the TRIPS flexibilities is not optional when failing to do so means that people suffer or die from lack of essential medicines. A government faced with having to deny access to essential medicines that could be made available if licenses were issued does not fulfil its obligations under human rights law.

6.4 PROTECTING ACCESS TO MEDICINES IN INTERNATIONAL FORA

States should prevent third parties, including the pharmaceutical industry, from violating or impeding others from fulfilling their obligations towards the right to health in other countries (UN CESCR, 2000). They should ensure that their actions as members of international organisations take due account of the right to health, specifically by ensuring that international agreements do not adversely impact the right to health (UN CESCR, 2000). However, evidence from international and bilateral agreements shows that some governments have failed to heed these human rights obligations in practice.

The trend in regional and bilateral trade agreements and in accession agreements with new WTO members to include TRIPS-plus provisions roll back much of the positive momentum represented by the Doha Declaration. TRIPS-plus provisions limit the instruments countries have at their disposal to realise the human right to access to essential medicines (Sell, 2007). The trend in international norm setting for patents reflects the IP agenda of large corporations that seek expansion of their monopoly positions in the market through patents and through other market exclusivity mechanisms.

Further, Investor to State Dispute Settlement (ISDS) mechanisms, often contained in trade agreements, are being used by the pharmaceutical industry to contest decisions by national patent offices and courts and as such have a chilling effect on any government's considerations to use the TRIPS flexibilities and on health regulation (Crouch, 2015). ISDS allows corporations to take legal action against countries to seek compensation for regulation that allegedly has negatively affected their investments. Concerns over the inclusion of ISDS in trade agreements are not imaginary. The drug company Eli Lilly relied on the investment chapter of the North American Free Trade Agreement (NAFTA) to sue the Canadian government over losses resulting from the invalidation of secondary patents related to atomoxetine (Strattera) and olanzapine (Zyprexa), medicines used to treat attention deficit hyperactivity disorder, schizophrenia and bipolar disorder (Public Citizen, 2015). In March 2017 the NAFTA Tribunal dismissed the case (Government of Canada, 2017).

ISDS can also be used as a tool to pressure governments to desist from using TRIPS flexibilities. In 2017, amid an ongoing debate about the high price of imatinib in Colombia, evidence has emerged that the manufacturer, Novartis, threatened the Colombian authorities with international investment arbitration to allege that granting a compulsory license is a violation of the Swiss-Colombian bilateral investment treaty. Public Eye claims that this threat may have influenced the Colombian health authorities 'to stop short of pursuing a compulsory license' and instead use other price controls (Public Eye, 2017).

The United Nations Conference on Trade and Development (UNCTAD) maintains a database of ISDS cases, which counts over 600 cases (UNCTAD, 2017). In its 2015 World Investment Report, UNCTAD notes that developing countries 'bear the brunt of these claims' and that most claimants (i.e., the companies) come from developed countries (UNCTAD, 2015). UNCTAD adds that claims against developed country governments are on the rise.

TRIPS meant to protect against TRIPS-plus demands (see Box 6.2 for examples of TRIPS-plus demands.) TRIPS Article 1.1 states that countries are free but not obliged to implement more extensive IP protection than is required by TRIPS. One could call Article 1.1 of TRIPS the 'anti-TRIPS-plus clause'. While countries are free to adopt more stringent IP protection than TRIPS requires, by agreeing to the TRIPS standards they expected to

BOX 6.2

Examples of provisions that require more stringent IP standards than those contained in TRIPS or that limit flexibilities inherent in TRIPS ('TRIPS-plus') pursued in trade agreements by the US or EU that can delay the introduction of generic medicines and thereby affect access to medicines ('t Hoen, 2016):

Patent linkage: Prohibits granting of marketing approval by drug regulatory authorities during the patent term without the consent of the patent holder. These provisions effectively create a new function for medicines regulatory agencies in the enforcement of patents on medicines.

Data exclusivity: Prohibits for a certain period of time the use of pharmaceutical test data for drug regulatory purposes, which will delay the registration and thereby the marketing of generic medicines and bio products, regardless of the patent status of the product.

Extension of the patent term for pharmaceuticals beyond the 20 years required by the TRIPS Agreement, which will further delay generic competition (European Commission, 2012).

Extension of the scope of patent protection to allow known substances to be patented for each 'new use'.

Restrictions on the grounds for compulsory licensing.

Restrictions to parallel importation.

have struck a bargain that would protect them from pressures to further expand national levels of IP protection. These expectations were re-enforced when World Trade Organisation (WTO) members adopted the Doha Declaration on TRIPS and Public Health.

That bargain has been broken by the plethora of trade agreements containing TRIPS-plus provisions that have been concluded in the last decade, including after the adoption of the Doha Declaration on TRIPS and Public Health. The US and the EU are systematically seeking higher levels of IP protection in agreements with other countries that affect access to medicines and seriously hamper the full implementation of the Doha Declaration. TRIPS-plus law in the European Union, for example the EU's data exclusivity rules and the EU's opting out of the WTO August 30 decision in 2003 have rendered some key flexibilities useless. TRIPS-plus provisions are also found in WTO accession agreements with new WTO Members, including with LDCs (Abbott and Correa, 2007).

Governments that pursue a trade policy aimed at further limiting the TRIPS flexibilities are actively undermining the instruments that are indispensable for governments to realise their core obligation to provide essential medicines under the right to health. The Human Rights Council has affirmed that TRIPS-plus measures in trade agreements directly contravene General Comment No. 14 (Human Rights Council, 2017).

6.4.1 Human Rights Obligations of the Pharmaceutical Industry

While the fulfilment of basic human rights is primarily a state obligation, in the case of patented medicines one also has to recognise the responsibility of the patent holding pharmaceutical company. After all, with patenting of essential medicines now more widespread, the power to determine who has access to such medicines has shifted to the private sector.

Major progress to establish the human rights obligations of the business sector, and the pharmaceutical industry, in particular, has been made by key human rights experts. During his term as UN Special Rapporteur on the Right to Health (2002–2008), Paul Hunt submitted a report to the UN General Assembly on guidelines for the pharmaceutical industry in relation to access to medicines. These include refraining from actions that limit accessibility, such as pursing stronger intellectual property protection, and also taking all reasonable steps to make new medicine accessible to those who need them.

UN special rapporteur on the right to health, Paul Hunt:

> *Society has legitimate expectations of a company holding the patent on a life-saving medicine. In relation to such a patent, the right-to-health framework helps to clarify what these terms, and expectations, are. Because of its critical social function, a patent on a life-saving medicine places important right-to-health responsibilities on the patent holder. These responsibilities are reinforced when the patented life-saving medicine benefited from research and development undertaken in publicly funded laboratories. (Paul Hunt, 2009)*

The right-to-health standards offer a normative framework against which companies can be held accountable, which is useful for monitoring companies' policies and actions. The Access to Medicines Index ranks pharmaceutical companies using this right-to-health framework to assess pharmaceutical companies' policies and behaviours with regards to access to medicines (Access to Medicines Index, 2017).

The Guiding Principles on Business and Human Rights (the 'Ruggie Principles') were endorsed by the Human Rights Council in 2009, and as such, are somewhat more forceful than Hunt's guidelines (Guiding Principles on Business and Human Rights, 2011). Business actors 'should avoid infringing on the human rights of others' and they should 'address the adverse human rights impacts with which they are involved' (Guiding Principles on Business and Human Rights, 2011).

Enforcement mechanisms to ensure that companies indeed act on their responsibility for human rights are lacking. Anand Grover, who followed Paul Hunt as Special Rapporteur on the Right to Health, sought to give the normative framework developed by Hunt teeth. He suggested establishing direct legal obligations for pharmaceutical companies at the international level and holding pharmaceutical companies directly accountable under international human rights law, including through direct compensation to victims and the granting of compulsory licenses (Grover et al., 2012).

6.5 CONCLUSION

The human rights framework defines clear 'core obligations' of national governments and the international community to provide essential medicines to all who need them. The principle of progressive realisation of the right to health implies that States should use the maximum of their available resources to ensure that services are provided expeditiously and on the basis of non-discrimination, while taking deliberate, concrete and targeted steps towards full realisation. States must allocate sufficient financing to provide a universal package of essential medicines. Foreign governments have a shared responsibility to assist States lacking the resources to meet their core obligations in this area.

Adequate public financing alone will not necessarily yield universal access, particularly to expensive essential medicines. The obligation to use resources efficiently implores governments to prioritise medicines for public financing in a non-discriminatory, transparent and accountable manner. The need for efficiency implies that governments should not accept high prices of new medicines when the consequence of that high price is that proven effective medicines are not available to patients who need them. In such cases they should employ the legal and policy tools available to reduce them, including price control mechanisms and TRIPS flexibilities in case of patented medicines. The proposals for better international rules underpinning new ways of financing pharmaceutical innovation offer opportunities for reform in the global IP based pharmaceutical innovation architecture that currently relies on high pricing as its main resource mobilisation. In particular, the recommendation by the UNHLP and others to start negotiations for a treaty on pharmaceutical innovation based on the principles of delinkage would halt this reliance on high medicines prices for the financing of R&D should be followed up.

Human rights arguments for access to essential medicines should not only direct government and industry action, but should also be enforceable on these actors such as through the Optional Protocol to the ICESCR or an enforcement mechanism for the pharmaceutical industry. The international community has a shared responsibility to assist governments lacking adequate resources and to ensure international agreements are compatible with the right to health and do not infringe on access to essential medicines. Pharmaceutical companies have a duty under human rights law to ensure that the fruits of science are made available and affordable to all who need them.

REFERENCES

't Hoen, E., 2002. Public health and international law: TRIPS, pharmaceutical patents, and access to essential medicines: a long way from Seattle to Doha. Chic. J. Int. Law 3, 27–48.

't Hoen, E., 2009. The Global Politics of Pharmaceutical Monopoly Power. AMB Publishers, Diemen, the Netherlands, pg. 6.

't Hoen, E., 2016. Private Patents and Public Health. Changing Intellectual Property Rules for Access to Medicines. AMB Press, Diemen.

't Hoen, E., Hogerzeil, H.V., Quick, J.D., Sillo, H.B., 2014. A quiet revolution in global public health: The World Health Organization's Prequalification of Medicines Programme. J. Pub. Health Policy 35 (2), 137–161.

't Hoen E., Berger, J., Calmy, A., Moon, S., et al., 2011. Driving a decade of change: HIV/AIDS, patents and access to medicines for all. J. Int. AIDS Soc. 14 (1), 15.

Abbott, F., Correa, C., 2007. World Trade Organization Agreements: Intellectual Property Issues. Quaker United Nations Office, Geneva, Switzerland, <http://quno.org/sites/default/files/resources/QUNO%2BWTO%2Baccession%2BIP.pdf>.

Access to Medicines Index. <http://accesstomedicineindex.org/> [accessed 28.02.17].

Biehl, J., Amon, J.J., Socal, M.P., Petryna, A., 2012. Between the court and the clinic: lawsuits for medicines and the right to health in Brazil. Health Hum. Rights 14 (1), E36–E52.

World Intellectual Property Organization, Committee on Development and Intellectual Property. Patent related flexibilities in the multilateral legal framework and their legislative implementation at the national and regional levels.<http://www.wipo.int/edocs/mdocs/mdocs/en/cdip_5/cdip_5_4_rev-main1.pdf>; 2010. [accessed 21.02.17] For exceptions to patent rights see: Garrison C, Exceptions to Patents Rights in Developing Countries, UNCTAD-ICSTD, issue paper No. 17 <http://unctad.org/en/docs/iteipc200612_en.pdf> [accessed 21.02.17].

Constitution of the World Health Organization, 1946 (1948), preamble. Universal Declaration of Human Rights (UDHR), G.A. Res. c, Social and Cultural Rights. United Nations General Assembly Resolution 2200A (XXI) Art. 12. 1966. <http://www.ohchr.org/EN/ProfessionalInterest/Pages/CESCR.aspx>, [accessed 03.11.15].

Council for Trade-Related Aspects of Intellectual Property Rights. Document IP/C/73. Extension of the transition period under article 66.1 of the TRIPS agreement for least developed country members for certain obligations with respect to pharmaceutical products decisions of the council for TRIPS. 6 November 2015.

Crouch, D., 2015. Million Dollar Mistake? The Cost of Limiting or Canceling IP Rights. Patently-O, <http://patentlyo.com/patent/2015/03/million-limiting-canceling.html>; [accessed 21.02.17].

Crow D. Cancer pill costs soar as drug companies retain pricing power. Financial Times <https://www.ft.com/content/935e6ebe-29a1-11e7-9ec8-168383da43b7> 30 April 2017. [accessed 30.04.17]

Daniels, N., Sabin, J.E., 2008. Accountability for reasonableness: an update. Br. Med. J. 337, a1850.

Daniels, N., Charvel, S., Gelpi, A.H., Porteny, T., Urrutia, J., 2015. Role of the courts in the progressive realization of the right to health: between the threat and the promise of judicialization in Mexico. Health Syst. Reform 1 (3), 229–234.

United Nations Committee on Economic. Social and Cultural Rights (CESCR). Document E/C.12/2000/4. General Comment No 14 (2000). The right to the highest attainable standard of health (article 12 of the International Covenant on Economic, Social and Cultural Rights). Paragraph 6. Twenty-second Session of the Committee on Economic, Social and Cultural Rights, Geneva, 25 April–12 May 2000. <http://www.ohchr.org/Documents/Issues/Women/WRGS/Health/GC14.pdf> [accessed 20.09.16].

World Trade Organization, Document WT/MIN(01)/DEC/2. Declaration on the TRIPS agreement and public health [Doha Declaration]. In: World Trade Organization Ministerial Meeting 2001, Doha, 20 November 2001. <https://www.wto.org/english/thewto_e/minist_e/min01_e/mindecl_trips_e.htm> [accessed 17.06.17].

Dutfield, G., 2003. Intellectual Property Rights and the Life Science Industries: A Twentieth Century History (Globalisation and Law). Ashgate Publishing, Hampshire, England.

European Commission, "Protection of Intellectual Property in Free Trade Agreements," Brussels, October 2012. <http://trade.ec.europa.eu/doclib/docs/2012/november/tradoc_150081.pdf>.

European Union, Treaty Establishing the European Community (Consolidated Version), Rome Treaty, Art. 30, 25 March 1957, available at: http://www.refworld.org/docid/3ae6b39c0.html [accessed 19 June 2017].

Forman, L., 2016. Can minimum core obligations survive a reasonableness standard of review under the optional protocol to the international covenant on economic, social and cultural rights? Ottawa Law Rev. 47 (2), 557–573.

Gellman, B., 2000. An Unequal Calculus of Life and Death; As Millions Perished in Pandemic, Firms Debated Access to Drugs; Players in the Debate Over Drug Availability and Pricing. The Washington Post, (A01).

Global Commission on HIV and the Law. Risks, Rights, and Health. <http://hivlawcommission.org/resources/report/Executive-Summary-GCHL-EN.pdf>; July 2012. [accessed 28.02.17].

Government of Canada. Eli Lilly and Company v. Government of Canada. <http://www.international.gc.ca/trade-agreements-accords-commerciaux/topics-domaines/disp-diff/eli.aspx?lang=eng> [accessed 09.05.17].

Gray, A.L., Wirtz, V.J., 't Hoen, E., Reich, M.R., Hogerzeil, H.V., 2015. Essential medicines are still essential. Lancet 386 (10004), 1601–1603.

Grover, A., Citro, B., Mankad, M., Lander, F., 2012. Pharmaceutical companies and global lack of access to medicines: strengthening accountability under the right to health. J. Law Med. Ethics. 40 (2), 234–250.

Guiding Principles on Business and Human Rights. Geneva: UN Office of the High Commissioner; 2011. <http://www.ohchr.org/Documents/Publications/GuidingPrinciplesBusinessHR_EN.pdf> [accessed 10.05.16].

't Hoen E, Toebes B, Perehudoff K, Abbott FM on behalf of the Global Health Law Committee of the International Law Association. Submission to the UN High Level Panel on Access to Medicines. February 2016. <http://www.rug.nl/research/groningen-centre-for-law-and-governance/onderzoekscentra/ghlg/ila-ghlc-proposal1-hlp-process.pdf> [accessed 17.06.17].

Hogerzeil, H.V., 2006. Essential medicines and human rights: what can they learn from each other? Bull. World Health Organ. 84 (5), 371–375.

Hogerzeil, H.V., Samson, M., Casanovas, J.V., Rahmani-Ocora, L., 2006. Is access to essential medicines as part of the fulfilment of the right to health enforceable through the courts? Lancet 368 (9532), 305–311, http://dx.doi.org/10.1016/S0140-6736(06)69076-4.

Human Rights Council, Access to medicines in the context of the right of everyone to the enjoyment of the highest attainable standard of physical and mental health. Resolution A/HRC/C/L.23/Rev.1. <http://www.un.org/ga/search/view_doc.asp?symbol=A/HRC/32/L.23/Rev.1>; 2016. [accessed 21.02.17].

United Nations General Assembly, International Covenant on Economic, Social and Cultural Rights Optional Protocol. Resolution A/RES/63/117. 2008. <http://www.ohchr.org/Documents/HRBodies/CESCR/OProtocol_en.pdf>, [accessed 21.02.17].

Khosla, R., Hunt, P., 2008. Human Rights Guidelines for Pharmaceutical Companies in Relation to Access to Medicines. The Sexual and Reproductive Health Context. University of Essex Human Rights Centre, Colchester.

Manning, J., 2014. Litigating a right to healthcare in New Zealand. In: Flood, C.M., Gross, A. (Eds.), The Right to Health at the Public/Private Divide: A Global Comparative Study. Cambridge University Press.

NICE. Kadcyla too expensive for routine funding on NHS. <https://www.nice.org.uk/news/article/kadcyla-too-expensive-for-routine-funding-on-nhs>29 Dec 2016. [accessed 09.05.17].

Norheim, O., Wilson, B., 2014. Health rights litigation and access to medicines: priority classification of successful cases from Costa Rica's constitutional chamber of the Supreme Court. Health Hum. Rights 16 (2), 47–61.

Paul Hunt, Report of the Special Rapporteur on the Right of Everyone to the Enjoyment of the Highest Attainable Standard of Health, Annex: Mission to GlaxoSmithKline, UN Doc. No. A/HRC/11/12/Add.2, 5 May 2009, <http://www.who.int/medicines/areas/human_rights/A_HRC_11_12_Add_2.pdf>.

Perehudoff, K., Toebes, B., Hogerzeil, H., 2016. A human rights-based approach to the reimbursement of expensive medicines. Bull. World Health Organ. 94 (12), 935, http://dx.doi.org/10.2471/BLT.15.166371.

Perez-Casas, C., Mace, C., Berman, D., Double, J., 2001. Accessing ARVs: Untangling the Web of Antiretroviral Price Reductions, First ed. Medecins Sans Frontieres/Campaign for Access to Essential Medicines, Geneva.

Pharmaceutical Manufacturers' Association of South Africa v President of the Republic of South Africa, Case No 4183/98 (filed Feb 18, 1998).

Ploumen, L., Schippers, E., 2016. Better life through medicine—let's leave no one behind. Lancet, http://dx.doi.org/10.1016/S0140-6736(16)31905-5.

Public Citizen, Investor-State Attacks on Public Interest Policies: Access to Medicines; ISDS: Enforcer for Big Pharma Wish List Health at Stake, Washington, DC: Public Citizen, 30 March 2015. <http://www.citizen.org/documents/tpp-investment-chapter-and-access-to-medicines.pdf>.

Public Eye, 2017. Compulsory Licensing in Colombia—Leaked Documents Show Aggressive Lobbying by Novartis. <https://www.publiceye.ch/en/media/press-release/compulsory_licensing_in_colombia_leaked_documents_show_aggressive_lobbying_by_novartis/>; [accessed 09.05.17].

Sell, S.K., 2007. TRIPS-plus free trade agreements and access to medicines. Liverp. Law Rev. 28 (1), 41–75, Gray J. Lilly ramps up NAFTA fight over loss of patents. <http://www.theglobeandmail.com/report-on-business/international-business/us-business/lilly-ramps-up-nafta-fight-over-loss-of-patents/article13223813/>; 2013. [accessed 21.02.17].

Trade-Related Aspects of Intellectual Property Rights, including Trade in Counterfeit Goods [Uruguay Round]. In: Ministerial meeting of the contracting parties to the general agreement on Tariffs and Trade (GATTs), Punta del Este, Uruguay, 20 September 1986.

Tribble SJ. Louisiana proposes tapping a century-old patent law to cut hepatitis C drug prices. Washington Post. <https://www.washingtonpost.com/national/health-science/louisiana-proposes-tapping-a-century-old-patent-law-to-cut-hepatitis-c-drug-prices/2017/05/02/fc611990-2f76-11e7-9534-00e4656c22aa_story.html?tid=ss_tw&utm_term=.a5c3d9734fbd>; 2017. [accessed 09.05.17]

UNCTAD, *World Investment Report 2015: Reforming International Investment Governance,* Switzerland, 2015, <http://unctad.org/en/PublicationsLibrary/wir2015_en.pdf>.

UNCTAD, Database of Investor-State Dispute Settlement. <http://unctad.org/en/Pages/DIAE/ISDS.aspx> [accessed 21.02.17].

United Nations Committee on Economic. Social and Cultural Rights (CESCR). Document E/1991/23 General Comment No 3: The Nature of States Parties' Obligations (Art. 2, Para. 1, of the Covenant). Fifth Session of the Committee on Economic, Social and Cultural Rights, on 14 December 1990.

United Nations Committee on Economic. Social and Cultural Rights (CESCR). Document E/C.12/GC/17 General Comment No 17: The Right of Everyone to Benefit from the Protection of the Moral and Material Interests Resulting from any Scientific, Literary or Artistic Production of Which He or She is the Author (Art. 15, Para. 1 (c) of the Covenant), Paragraphs 35 and 39(e). Discussed at the thirty-fifth session of the Committee of Economic, Social, and Cultural Rights. Adopted on 12 January 2006.

United Nations Office of the High Commissioner for Human Rights. Status of the ratification of the ICESCR Optional Protocol <http://indicators.ohchr.org/>; 2017 [accessed 02.20.17].

United Nations Office of the High Commissioner for Human Rights. Status of the ratification of the ICESCR <http://indicators.ohchr.org/>; 2017 [accessed 02.20.17].

United Nations Secretary-General's High-Level Panel on Access to Medicines. The Process. <http://www.unsgaccessmeds.org/the-process/>. [accessed 28.02.17].

Vitry, A., Mintzes, B., Lipworth, W., 2016. Access to new cancer medicines in Australia: dispelling the myths and informing a public debate. J. Pharm. Policy Pract. 9 (1), 1.
Waning, B., Diedrichsen, E., Moon, S., 2010. A lifeline to treatment: the role of Indian generic manufacturers in supplying antiretroviral medicines to developing countries. J. Int. AIDS Soc. 13, 35.
World Health Organization. WHO moves to improve access to lifesaving medicines for hepatitis C, drug-resistant TB and cancers <http://who.int/mediacentre/news/releases/2015/new-essential-medicines-list/en/>; 2015 [accessed 20.02.17].
Wirtz, V.J., Hogerzeil, H.V., Gray, A.L., Bigdeli, M., de Joncheere, C.P., Ewen, M.A., et al., 2016. Essential medicines for universal health coverage. Lancet, http://dx.doi.org/10.1016/S0140-6736(16)31599-9.
WHO, 2015. 19th WHO Model List of Essential Medicines (April 2015), Geneva: World Health Organization. Available from: http://www.who.int/medicines/publications/essentialmedicines/EML2015_8-May-15.pdf.
World Intellectual Property Organization, Negotiating Group on Trade-Related Aspects of Intellectual Property Rights, including Trade in Counterfeit Goods, "Existence, scope and form of generally internationally accepted and applied standards/norms for the protection of intellectual property," *Note prepared by the International Bureau of WIPO*, Revision 15 September 1988 (Original published 5 May 1988), MTN.GNG/NG11/W/24/Rev.1.
World Intellectual Property Organization. Frequently asked questions: Patents. <http://www.wipo.int/patents/en/faq_patents.html> [accessed 28.02.17].
World Intellectual Property Organization. Flexibilities in the Intellectual Property System. <http://www.wipo.int/ip-development/en/agenda/flexibilities/> [accessed 21.02.17].
Agreement on Trade-Related Aspects of Intellectual Property Rights (TRIPS Agreement). Geneva: World Trade Organization; 1994. <https://www.wto.org/english/tratop_e/trips_e/t_agm0_e.htm> [accessed 06.10.16].
World Trade Organization, 2013. Responding to Least Developed Countries' Special Needs in Intellectual Property. <https://www.wto.org/english/tratop_e/trips_e/ldc_e.htm>; [accessed 21.02.17].
World Trade Organization, 2017. WTO IP Rules Amended to Ease Poor Countries' Access to Affordable Medicines. <https://www.wto.org/english/news_e/news17_e/trip_23jan17_e.htm> [accessed 21.02.2017].

FURTHER READING

Rachel Z and Jesse P, Drug Industry, AIDS Community Is Jolted by Cipla AIDS-Drug Offer. (2001) Wall Street Journal, February 8. Also see 't Hoen et al. 2011.
Nguyen, T.A., Knight, R., Roughead, E.E., Brooks, G., Mant, A., 2015. Policy options for pharmaceutical pricing and purchasing: issues for low-and middle-income countries. Health Policy Plan. 30 (2), 267–280.
United Nations General Assembly, Report of the Special Rapporteur on the right of everyone to the enjoyment of the highest attainable standard of physical and mental health: Report of Paul Hunt. U.N. General Assembly, 63rd Session, Agenda Item 67(b). U.N. Doc. A/63/263, <http://www.who.int/medicines/areas/human_rights/A63_263.pdf>.

CHAPTER 7

Access to High Price Medicines in Portugal

Filipa Alves da Costa*,, Ana Paula Martins**,†**

*Centro de Estudos Interdisciplinar Egas Moniz (CiiEM), Instituto Universitário Egas Moniz (IUEM), Campus Universitário, Quinta da Granja, Monte da Caparica, Portugal
**Portuguese Pharmaceutical Society, Rua da Sociedade Farmacêutica, Lisboa, Portugal
†Research Institute for Medicines (iMED.ULisboa), Universidade de Lisboa, Lisboa, Portugal

7.1 HEALTHCARE IN PORTUGAL

Access to health is considered a universal right, deeply embedded into the Humans Rights. However, as perfectly described by Weale, the inconsistent triad refers to the inability of most health care systems, if not all, to simultaneously ensure that comprehensive and high quality care is available to all citizens, regardless of the individuals' financial capacity (Weale, 1998). This leads to different approaches taken by different health systems across the world, either choosing to be less comprehensive, either compromising quality or finally opting not to be universal. In the European Union, governments have been focusing on universal and equitable access to healthcare and all policy has been driven to ensure these. However, in the current global context, this principle seems to fail if one considers for instance the large disparity set in medicines' prices across member states (Vogler, 2016).

In Portugal, the Constitution states that access to health care is universal and, depending on the financial capacity of the individual, tends to be free at the point of delivery. This last point in fact means that the citizen pays a user fee whenever the public health care service is used, and this value varies according to the classification of care [e.g. urgent care pays more (18€) than planned primary care. (4.5€) (Portaria No. 234/2015; values updated for 2016)]; but depending on the citizens' income, exemption may apply (Constituição da República Portuguesa, 2005). In Portugal, there is a universal health care service, entitled *Serviço Nacional de Saúde* (SNS), which stands for Portuguese National Health Service (PNHS) and follows the basic principles of all Beveridge systems. Health care is state organised and financed by taxes and co-payments (Martins et al.,,2015). Citizens may have a professional insurance (subschemes) or opt for voluntary health insurance. Having health insurance enables citizens to have easier access to private

Equitable Access to High-Cost Pharmaceuticals
http://dx.doi.org/10.1016/B978-0-12-811945-7.00007-5

health care, paid at the point of delivery, which may ultimately favour inequality in access to care.

The PNHS spent on average 924€/inhabitant in 2015, averaged at 6% of Gross Domestic Product (GDP). Private expenditure equals 3% of GDP. The proportion of GDP applied to health has been for the past 4 years, around 9%–9.5%, a value lower than the OECD average or the world average (WorldBank, 2014; Eurostat, 2016; OECD Health Statistics, 2016; Pordata, 2017). However, where differences with other European countries are more striking is on the out-of-pocket payments, being considerably higher in Portugal, mostly following the economic crisis and the adoption of Austerity measures, and continuously rising (European Observatory of Health Systems, 2017).

A recent study conducted in Portugal, following the peak of the financial crisis indicated over 27% of patients reported problems using health care in the previous year for financial reasons. 'Private medical appointments' were where barriers were more frequently encountered, followed by dentist appointments and purchase of glasses, hearing aids and other devices. This study also showed that even public services, including primary care appointments and hospital emergency visits had barriers to access perceived by over 20% of patients (Costa et al., 2016). It has indeed later been confirmed that user fees seem to be a factor of inequality and as a result, the proportion of citizens given exemption has continued rising in 2017. For example, patients referred by Saúde 24 (a telephone triage line), the national emergency service (INEM) or by primary care units have become exempt from emergency services users fee; and other referral pathways also now grant exemption.

The provision of care is structured in three layers, where primary care is located within communities and focuses mainly on prevention and treatment of long term conditions. Primary care is provided in Family Health Units (since 2007) or in Primary Healthcare Centre Groups (since 2008), with progressively increasing efficiency as these are organised to provide integrated care. Community pharmacies are also often used as first point of care for minor ailments (Coelho and Costa, 2014), but with care still not integrated in the PNHS.

Secondary care is provided in hospitals, intended mainly for specialised care, emergency treatment and conditions that require hospitalisation. For each 100,000 inhabitants, there are 21 hospitals and 340 beds (206 within the PNHS). Roughly 20% of hospitals are specialised (FIP, 2015; Pordata, 2017). Unlike primary care, hospital reorganisation long planned has not yet been accomplished.

Tertiary care is mainly targeted at dependent citizens and includes units for long, medium and short-term care requiring hospitalisation, but also units that may serve the citizen in the ambulatory setting (RNCCI, 2017). The functioning of these units is regulated by law and currently have the capacity to serve over 14,000 inhabitants (Portaria n.° 50/2017 de 2 de fevereiro).

In Portugal, for every 100,000 inhabitants, there are on average 468 physicians, 85 dentists, 654 nurses and 117 pharmacists, where a constant rise has been observed for all professions (FIP, 2015; Pordata, 2017). The number of programmed medical appointments has been progressively rising, whereas the number of urgent care appointments is diminishing (Pordata, 2017). Many efforts have been developed in the recent years to favour a more rational use of scarce resources, namely the creation of triage systems intended to correctly identify patients and signpost them to the most appropriate care (*e.g.* Manchester system), but the overuse of the accident and emergency units for unurgent situations is still a reality to be solved. The information system has been evolving and currently there is a portal where patients can have access to waiting times within the PNHS.

7.2 ACCESS TO MEDICINES IN PORTUGAL

When a medicine enters the market, the pharmaceutical industry needs to demonstrate the new drug is safer and more efficacious than the already existing ones. The dossier is submitted to INFARMED, the National drug regulatory agency, or to the European Commission (EMA), if a centralised procedure is used.

However, there will be a second phase to decide on reimbursement, where additionally, the proposed drug needs to demonstrate therapeutic added-value, always to be judged by INFARMED. Some of the roles of this agency are to ensure that medicines on the market meet quality standards, are safe and accessible to patients.In Portugal, medicines are classified in two main categories: prescription medicines (PM) and non-prescription medicines (NPM). NPM are fully paid out-of-pocket. All medicines in Portugal are subject to value-added taxes (VAT) of 6% regardless of their legal category. Additionally, a sales tax of 0.4% is applied to the net Pharmacy Retail Price, known as the INFARMED tax (Teixeira and Vieira, 2008; Decreto-Lei 282/95). Some medicinal products not classified as medicines but as alimentary supplements, have an additional VAT of 23%. Prescription medicines are subdivided, depending on their accessibility to the citizen. The majority is classified as 'standard prescription medicines', available in the outpatient setting through community pharmacies, and their price is partly paid by the patient and partly by the PNHS, according to the reimbursement category the medicine falls into (Portaria n.° 195-D/2015); these categories vary from 15% to 90% of co-payment attributable to the PNHS, where the higher co-payments are attributable to medicines considered to have a higher added therapeutic value. These values are higher for pensioners having a monthly income below the minimum salary (set at 530€ in 2016). All prescription medicines in Portugal have their price regulated. Dispensing of medicines is restricted to physicians and other entities where potential conflict of interests may arise. Prescribing in Portugal uses the international non-proprietary name (INN) and the pharmacist should offer patients a choice of three generics with price set lower than the reference price (introduced in 2003). The international referencing system uses three countries in Europe to establish the price, which are annually reviewed. In 2018, these are Spain, France, and Italy (Portaria n.° 359/2017). The patient may opt for a more expensive medicine (exceptions include medicines with narrow therapeutic margins), paying the difference out-of-pocket (Portaria n° 137-A/2012). In 2014, the regulatory agency launched an app for citizens to identify the lowest priced generic, empowering citizens' choice. Since 2012 that prescription is done electronically, becoming fully implemented in 2016 (Lei 11/2012). Use of generic medicines has been promoted in the past decade and has been constantly rising, although market share (47.4% in units; INFARMED, 2016a, 2016b, 2016c, 2016d, 2016e) is still below the set goals (European Commission, 2012).

The 'Special Prescription Medicines' are available both in outpatient and inpatient settings, which are subject to a control mechanism given their tendency for abuse (*e.g.* morphine). The 'Restricted Access Prescription Medicines' are exclusive to treatments provided in hospital and require a special prescription (DL n.° 195/2006); the list is long and supported by various decrees and subsequent updates, including most oncolytics, immunomodulators, antiretrovirals, specific antivirals (*e.g.* Hepatitis C), orphan drugs, drugs used in renal transplant and chronic renal insufficiency, tumour necrosis factor alpha inhibitors (TNFα-in) and other biological medicines.

Only medicines approved by the National Pharmaceutical and Therapeutic Committee to be included in the National Formulary based on economic evaluations may be used within the public hospital sector and financing is totally supported by the PNHS. Medicines outside this list may not be purchased by public hospitals. Within hospital, prescribing is made by INN, but a formulary policy enables specific drugs or formulations to be made available, a decision made annually by the hospital's Pharmaceutical and Therapeutic Committee (a parity commission comprising physicians and pharmacists). Drugs prescribed outside this formulary need justification and are only made available upon the commission's approval.

Nearly all hospitals in Portugal have a hospital pharmacy, and one of the pharmacist's major role is ensuring patients' access to medicines, mostly in-patients, but also outpatients in the case of specific disease areas. Hospital medicines are in most cases purchased directly to the pharmaceutical industry, although also possible to purchase to wholesalers and annually negotiated by the hospitals.

Medicines prices are regulated and are available through official price lists. However, this list is merely indicative because the actual price results from a two-phase tender process. During the first stage, the price is negotiated between the central administration of health systems (ACSS, 2017) and the manufacturer, leading to the establishment of the maximum and official price. The second phase then results from direct negotiations established between the individual hospital (hospital group) and the manufacturer (Caldeira et al., 2010).

The citizens' access to medicines depends mainly on two factors: availability and affordability. In the case of Portugal, a few relevant changes in the last years have strongly influenced availability to medicines, namely the pharmacy sector crisis, and the establishment of intense parallel exports, that impacted on the availability of medicines in Portugal (OPSS, 2014). However, these are relevant mostly for the outpatient sector, where no high-cost medicines are available and will, therefore, not be detailed. Financial crisis in Europe, with its peak in 2011, led Portugal, to adopt several austerity measures to contain costs, being described as the country where most measures have been adopted (Leopold et al., 2014). These measures were diverse; some focused on access to health care, whilst others were specific for the pharmaceutical market (Costa et al., 2016; Panteli et al., 2016). Most of the reductions witnessed were through the reduction of public spending on medicines, which apply both to the hospital and the ambulatory setting (Sakellarides et al., 2014). However, cost reduction has been most successful for the outpatient setting (OPSS, 2014). Fig. 7.1 shows the evolution of hospital costs with medicines within the PNHS, highlighting an increase of 8% in the last year. Worth noticing that these

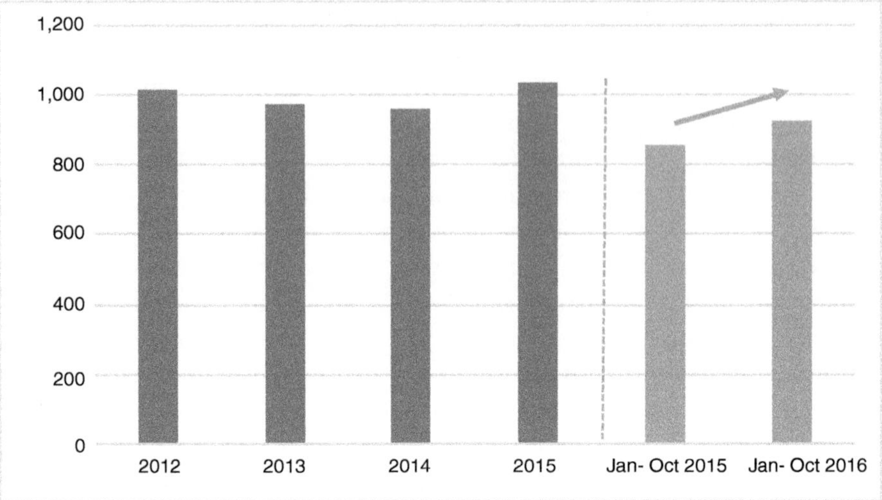

Figure 7.1 ***Annual evolution of costs (M€) with medicines within the hospitals of the PNHS (2012–2016).*** *Source, INFARMED, 2016a, 2016b, 2016c, 2016d, 2016e.*

costs do not include hepatitis C treatments, given the current financing system.

The ability that the patients have to pay for their medicines will ultimately impact on their decision to take the medicine. However, when the payer is the PNHS, the impact of the medicine cost on the state budget may also be considered to influence affordability of medicines, even if the payer is not the patient. The fact that a given medicine is unaffordable to the state budget, even if highly cost-effective, may ultimately determine the inability to include it in the hospital formulary, and, therefore, depriving citizens to have access to it. If the price of a medicine is too high for a government, the medicine can be considered unaffordable to the national health budget (Hawlik and Devalière, 2016).

Recently, cost-sharing agreements have becoming possible to establish between the pharmaceutical industry and INFARMED. There are different variants of such agreements, but the core idea is that the risk of different effectiveness from what has been reported in the clinical trial is shared. These agreements demand for the ability to evaluate real-world effectiveness of medicines and in a timely manner, a task highly dependent on the existence of patient registries. These agreements evolved from the adaptive pathways proposed by Eichler et al. (2012), which should lead patients to have early access to medicines, while creating a debate platform for all stakeholders.

7.3 FINANCING OF HIGH-COST MEDICINES

In Portugal, there is not a specific framework for financing high-cost medicines. There is a State Budget which is annually approved (Lei n.° 42/2016), which includes a prediction for the 4 subsequent years (the current one is for 2017–2020). However, some of the sections comprised fall short of planning; for example, we know how much will be assigned to health in 2017 (8.125 M€), but in 2018 we only know the subtotal of the group where the health budget falls into. Analysing in retrospect, we know that for instance in 2015, 12.7% of the total state budget was spent on health (social protection accounted for 37.8% and education for 12.4%, Eurostat (2016)). What falls into this group includes various small groups, namely: disease prevention, day-to-day costs, vertical programmes created by the health directorate, priority programmes and specific investment. Most of the money goes to what is considered 'day-to-day costs', which is something that always needs to be ensured for people to have care (particularly, functioning hospitals). Medicines fall into this sack. So, what this means is that when more expensive medicines are needed, additional resources need to be sought elsewhere, for example, saving on other medicines (lowering their prices or co-payments) or saving, for example, on prevention; in the ultimate resource, the ministry of health will have to negotiate with other ministers to have more money assigned to health and less to other ministries.

7.4 ACCESS TO HIGH COST MEDICINES IN PORTUGAL

Despite the fact that the concept of 'high-cost' medicine has not yet been clearly defined internationally, we have adopted a suggested definition, which assumes these to be those that for the patient to complete therapy over a one-year will exceed 10,000€, assuming this cost to be reimbursed by a public payer (WHO, 2015a). Considering this definition, all current ambulatory treatments fall out of the scope of this chapter. The therapeutic groups representing higher costs for the PNHS were in 2015, the immunomodulators and antivirals, followed by cytotoxic drugs (OPSS, 2016). These three classes only are responsible for 61% of the overall costs (INFARMED, 2016a, 2016b, 2016c, 2016d, 2016e). The scenario until October 2016 did not change much, and is illustrated on Fig. 7.2, referring to the top 5 of groups representing higher costs to the PNHS.

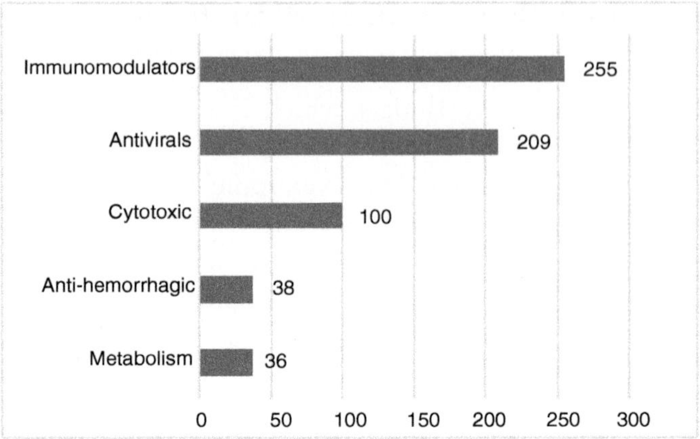

Figure 7.2 ***Top 5 of costs by pharmacotherapeutic group (January–October 2016), presented in M€.*** *Source: INFARMED, 2016a, 2016b, 2016c, 2016d, 2016e.*

7.5 CANCER DRUGS

Medicines used in cancer include immunomodulators and cytotoxic. A recent study comparing prices of cancer drugs, has shown wide variability among 31 EMA-approved drugs. In this analysis, Portugal was highlighted for absence of price data for 19 medicines (61.3%) (Vogler, 2016). For the remaining medicines analysed, the percent difference between the cost registered in Portugal and registered in the highest and lowest cost country is presented in Table 7.1. The percent difference was calculated assuming the

Table 7.1 Percent difference between the cost reported for Portugal and the countries where the highest and lowest costs have been reported (adapted from Vogler, 2016)

Substance	Difference % to Lowest Priced	Difference % to Highest Priced
Abiraterone acetate	109.9	75.0
Bevacizumab	124.6	82.1
Bortezomib	133.6	83.7
Erlotinib	130.7	80.9
Gefitinib	219.1	80.5
Imatinib	116.4	73.7
Interferon alpha 2b	126.2	47.8
Lapatinib	129.2	74.7
Pemetrexed	112.3	48.4
Temsirolimus	125.7	82.1
Trastuzumab	171.2	96.9
Zoledronic acid	201.0	78.3

comparator (either the highest or lowest priced) to correspond to 100%, in which case the percent presented refers to the observed for Portugal.

The country where the lowest prices were registered was more frequently Greece (n = 7; 58.3%), a country with a lower GDP than Portugal. However, for three of these substances (25.0%) the lowest price was found in the UK, with a GDP nearly 13 times higher than Portugal (International Monetary Fund World Economic Outlook, October 2016), and in one substance the lowest price was observed in Norway. This apparent contradiction may be assumed to result from the fact that in these countries, the number of patients accessing the drugs is likely to be larger and hence the rebates and discounts may also be higher.

In various types of cancer, immunotherapy is still considered second or third line therapy, whereas cytotoxic medicines are often used as first line (Direção Geral de Saúde (DGS), 2013). This class represents the third with higher costs, where the major responsible is imatinib (Fig. 7.3).

Patients can gain access to medicines mainly in two phases: pre-approval, through their participation in clinical trials or after the medicine has reached the market (post-approval). A report issued in 2013 showed that Portugal is one of the countries in Europe with a lower rate clinical trial per inhabitant (PWC, 2013). The number of patients recruited, at this time was also diminishing, with the lowest number reached in 2012, when less

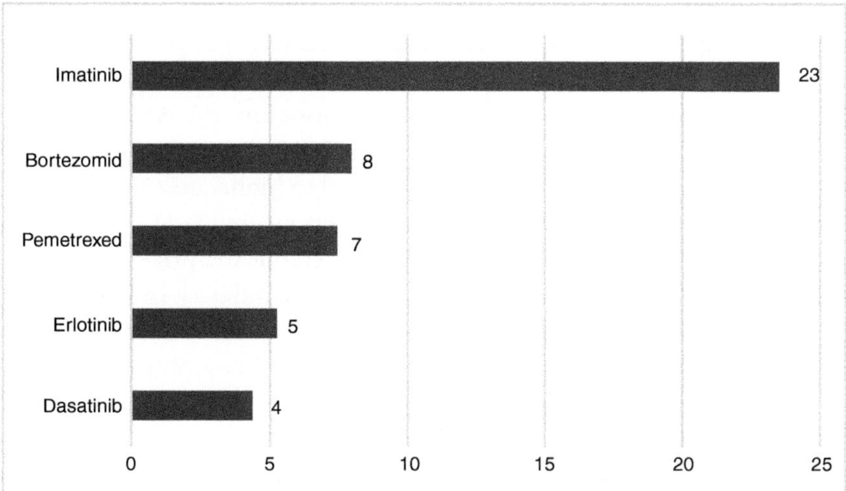

Figure 7.3 ***Top 5 of substances representing higher costs within the PNHS hospitals (January–October 2016), presented in M€.*** *Source: INFARMED, 2016a, 2016b, 2016c, 2016d, 2016e.*

than 1000 patients were recruited. Since then, the number of submitted and of authorised clinical trials has been increasing, with 123 trials approved in 2015, aside with an increased number of recruited patients. It is estimated that on-going trials in Portugal are expected to involve up to 12 million people, which means there are citizens participating in more than one trial (Portugal has roughly 10.5 million inhabitants). Most medicines being tested are for oncology.

In recent years, following the development of different mechanisms for early approval, including adaptive pathways, the Programmes of Precocious Access (PPA) have become an alternative to collect additional evidence and to accelerate access (Eichler et al., 2011; Eichler et al., 2012). Adaptive pathways have been defined by EMA as a planned, progressive approach to bringing a medicine to patients. These pathways make use of existing approval tools, in particular conditional marketing authorisation (in operation in the EU since 2006), and experience gained with strengthened post-marketing monitoring tools. The agency highlights that these are not new routes, whilst pointing out that the novelty is in bringing the different stakeholders precociously into the same table to discuss, demonstrate and reach consensus on ways to optimise requirements (EMA, 2016).

Regulatory authorities have progressively become more open to the possibility of accepting lowest levels of evidence, and even to accept data from experimental animal diseases models (Cavagnaro and Silva Lima, 2015). The PPA means that while pricing and reimbursement negotiations are taking place, the drug is already on the market and available to patients, provided patients fit specific criteria that leads their clinician to submit to the regulatory agency a request for 'special utilisation authorisation' (SUA) (Deliberação n.° 139/CD/2014; Deliberação n.° 76/CA/2015). However, this mechanism granting patients early access, can also lead to higher costs to the PNHS because drugs made available under these conditions are used to collect more evidence on safety and new data on effectiveness, but the price is only set at the end of the evaluation period by pharmaceutical industry. In Portugal, this system has led to an increase in medicines being used under such conditions. During the first eight months of 2016, a total of 1229 authorisations were granted using this mechanism, where more than 60% were medicines for use in oncology (INFARMED, 2016a, 2016b, 2016c, 2016d, 2016e). The following table highlights the top 10 of these authorisations and their respective indication (Table 7.2).

The process instituted works very well, considering that the timeline between the submission of the request and the granting of the authorisation

Table 7.2 Top 10 of medicines granted access via SUA during January–August 2016

Substance	Number of Attributed SUA	Class	Date of EMA Approval*
Aflibercept	131	Ophthalmology	22/11/2012
Nivolumab	96	Oncology	19/06/2015
Pertuzumab	55	Oncology	04/03/2013
Trastuzumab Emtansina	48	Oncology	15/11/2013
Ranibizumab	41	Ophthalmology	22/01/2007
Pemetrexedo	38	Oncology	31/10/2007
Idelalisib	36	Oncology	18/09/2014
Cobimetinib	33	Oncology	20/11/2015
Omalizumab	31	Dermatology	25/10/2005
Bevacizumab	31	Oncology	12/01/2005

* The date of EMA approval indicated refers to the first indication. However, this is not necessarily the same for which the SUA system is being used.

is, on average, 10 days. However, if medicines are timely approved, the SUA would not be needed, and as such INFARMED has recently announced the intention to finish this process in 2017 as it widely recognised that it favours inequity in access to medicines.

7.6 HEPATITIS C MEDICINES

The traditional model of medicines evaluation considers cost-effectiveness of medicines, which is judged by the Health Technology Assessment bodies (HTA). In Portugal, this evaluation is undertaken by INFARMED, who can then nominate individual experts, or consult other nationally reputed bodies in University Centres. In general, citizens are not involved in such decisions, or even consulted. When telaprevir and boceprevir were approved, with a much higher risk-benefit ratio than could today be accepted, citizens were not heavily involved in these processes. Since then, active involvement of patients' organisations has been growing. Ledipasvir was probably the first approved medicine where citizens had an important role in accelerating the process, although still not formally recognised. Now, with sofosbuvir, again patients' organisations had a very active voice.

On January 2014, sofosbuvir was approved by EMA, a medicine considered by INFARMED to be highly effective for the treatment of adult hepatitis C patients, with final cure rates of over 90% (INFARMED, 2015). The medicines containing sofosbuvir have been also described as leading to significant health gains regardless of HIV co-infection status; the estimated ICER was 16,720€/QALY, within the acceptability limit established by European authorities (Silva et al., 2014).

The medicine was launched at a very high price, leading to serious concerns on the health budget implications and therefore leading to an initial strategy of restricting access to a given number of patients per year, those considered to be high priority (*e.g.* those with hepatic cirrhosis) using the so called 'Exceptional Authorisation' mechanism, which at the time lasted, on average 19 days (Deliberação n.° 139/CD/2014). Until the end of 2014, only 70 patients benefited from this medicine. This had obvious ethical implications, strongly fought by patient representatives, who stated that the approach taken could be considered 'white collar genocide'. In 2015, the World Health Organisation (WHO) Model List of Essential Medicines (EML), included for the first time high-cost patented hepatitis C medicines, supporting the patients' claims that access to this medicine is a human right (WHO, 2015b).

In February 2015, INFARMED has decided to reimburse 100% sofosbuvir containing treatments, 13 months after its market approval. The paradigm to be answered was if the PNHS was able to simultaneously provide generalised access to treatment, whilst not risking its sustainability. For this decision INFARMED created an expert consulting group to support the first model of centralised financing, where costs are not imputed to individual hospitals but centrally paid by the Central Administration of the Health System (ACSS, 2017). This decision was based on estimated savings due to avoided hepatic transplants, cirrhosis, cancers and costs of treatment attributable to consequences of the evolution of hepatitis C. However, there was a cap established until the end of 2016 (13,000 patients). In November 2014, a platform has been created to be able to daily monitor the effectiveness of treatment. The most recent data indicate that until the 5th December 2016, a total of 9399 patients had initiated treatment (INFARMED, 2015b). Among those with treatment finalised (n = 4650), 96.3% were cured (INFARMED, 2016a, 2016b, 2016c, 2016d, 2016e). Assuming the prevalence of Hepatitis C to be between 0.5% and 1.5% (Anjo et al., 2014), a minimum of 50,000 individuals would be in need of treatment, implying this cap is insufficient to warrant universal access to treatment. In 2017, the system will be reviewed and eventually the cap may be extended. Furthermore, it should be noticed that the model created to monitor effectiveness may be seen as exemplary.

7.7 ANTIRETROVIRALS

INFARMED's annual report showed that antiretrovirals are amongst the drugs available in Portugal representing higher costs to the PNHS, topped up by emtricitabin + tenofovir, darunavir and abacavir + lamivudine, with respective annual costs registered from January to October 2016 of 47,700,987, 26,559,019 and 23,829,327€ (INFARMED, 2016a, 2016b, 2016c, 2016d, 2016e). The price of a medicine under a contract may be set according to the reference pricing, defined by the average of the three reference countries (in the ambulatory setting) or set at the lowest price of these same reference countries (hospital medicines). However, the contract may foresee a negotiated price, which may define a cap for the maximum number of patients to be treated under that price, or foresee a risk sharing agreement (Directiva 89/105/CEE).

When national regulators are negotiating the price of a medicine with the manufacturer, the latter submits a folder including the official prices in European countries. Hence, the regulator becomes aware of public price but is unaware of prices that include discounts and paybacks, which remain confidential. Portugal has been described as the country in Europe spending more on HIV treatments/1000 inhabitants, although having a high prevalence of disease; one of the reasons being that it is quite a small market, where, therefore, no significant bulk discounts may be applied.

Since the inclusion of antiretrovirals on the Essential Medicines List, for the first time in 2002, where 12 antiretrovirals have been added, ensuring access to these drugs has become a major concern in all member states (WHO, 2002). In Portugal, one of the recognised accessibility problems for HIV is the restriction of being classified as hospital-only and as such, the Government is currently testing out a new distribution model, already available in other countries, where antiretrovirals may be sought via community pharmacies (OPSS, 2016). The implementation implied specific training for pharmacists to become competent in consciously advising and close monitoring effectiveness and safety of these medicines. The pilot currently rolling in Lisbon and to be evaluated by Imperial College will determine the enlargement of this measure to other areas, such as oncology or other infectious diseases (Despacho n° 199/2016).

7.8 IMMUNOMODULATORS

The immunomodulators are the group representing highest costs overall to the PNHS, and with a growing trend. From January to October 2016, the cost was 255 M€, representing 27.6% of total costs with medicines and

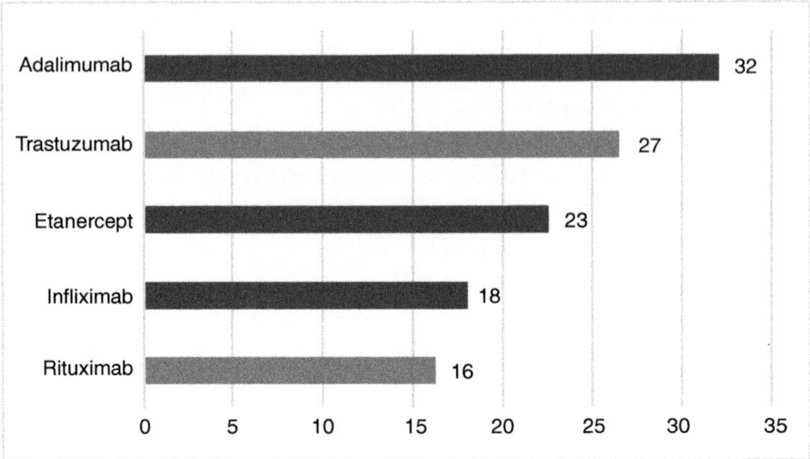

Figure 7.4 ***Top 5 of substances representing higher costs within the PNHS hospitals (January–October 2016), presented in M€.*** *Source: INFARMED, 2016a, 2016b, 2016c, 2016d, 2016e.*

corresponding to a variation of 10.8% in comparison with the homologous period (INFARMED, 2016a, 2016b, 2016c, 2016d, 2016e). Immunomodulators are mostly used for cancer and for rheumatoid arthritis. Therefore, the following figure highlights the substances mostly responsible for the costs, while highlighting their main indication. In green, substances mostly used for arthritis or other immune system disorders, and in blue substances mostly used for different types of cancer (Fig. 7.4).

Immune system disorders are frequently treated with biological medicines. A study comparing the use of TNFα-I across 4 European countries highlighted Portugal as the one with lowest consumption of these agents, where the reported DDD/ inhabitants/day was 0.32 in Portugal, compared to 1.89 in Norway (Hoebert et al., 2012). Other authors, also reporting Portugal to be the country with lowest access among those compared, have found that patients' access to biologics was mostly explained by the country's GDP per capita, the usage of methotrexate and the biologics' distribution channel (Laires et al., 2013).

7.9 ORPHAN DRUGS

Another source of rising costs in the PNHS is orphan drugs. Access has been progressively increasing, with 89 market authorisations registered in 2015 (Sousa, 2016a). The EU legislation, whilst clearly defining the criteria to be considered an orphan drug, also foresees several incentives for marketing an orphan drugs, namely 10 years of market exclusivity and an accelerated process of approval (Regulation EC No. 141/2000l). Another important recent initiative was the creation of the PRIME scheme, which may be considered a development support tool. The PRIME acronym results from Priority Medicines, a scheme launched by EMA to support in various ways the development of medicines that target an unmet clinical need. Applicants need to provide evidence of eligibility to benefit from this scheme, where the advantages may include earlier access to the scheme if the applicants are from the academic sector, having enhanced scientific advice from a multidisciplinary group of experts, fee incentives, to name a few (EMA, 2016).

However, results recently published by EMA evidence that the majority of medicines benefiting from this scheme are cancer drugs. While favouring access to medicines that are needed for a small patient population that without such mechanisms would have an unmet medical need, because the pharmaceutical industry would not have an interest in investing in a market where the profit potential is small (Franco, 2013), it may also create a route for pharmaceutical industry to increase their profits, thus decreasing access on the medium-long run. The best example is imatinib, initially approved as an orphan drug, but then extending its indications, so that it got to hold six orphan drug designations. A recent study has shown that the weight of orphan drugs on the PNHS, excluding the costs of imatinib, which lost its orphan designation in 2011, has varied from 49,945,121.00€ in 2010 to 82,802,658.00€ in 2015. The total costs with orphan drugs represented 6.7% of the PNHS costs in 2015 (Sousa, 2016a). In 2016, INFARMED has already authorised 182 orphan treatments using the SUA mechanism, referring to 21 medicines, corresponding to 15% of the total treatments granted access through SUA. Again, this analysis shows that the majority of medicines are for oncology (INFARMED, 2016a, 2016b, 2016c, 2016d, 2016e).

It has been shown that the price of orphan medicines varies according to regulations in place, where Portugal being a country that regulates prices tends to be classified as those within Europe having a lower price (Simoens, 2011). However, since in Portugal, these drugs are distributed through hospitals, where the regulations in place foresee discounts and clawbacks, this theory may be questioned. The most expensive medicine in the world is the famous Glybera, to treat a rare disease called familial lipoproteinase deficiency, approved by EMA in 2012 (Schwartz, 2015). This medicine is a gene therapy and provides a good example of adaptions that may develop in the regulatory process, as it has been approved following evidence collected from an extremely small sample (Cordeiro, 2014). However, it has been shown that

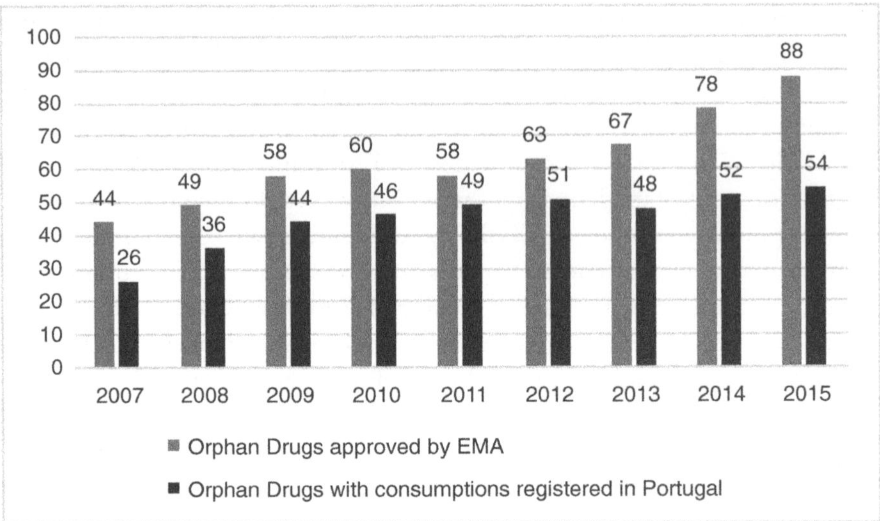

Figure 7.5 ***Distribution of orphan drugs approved by EMA and marketed in Portugal.*** *Source: INFARMED 2016, adapted from Sousa(b), 2016.*

many of these medicines centrally approved do not have any consumption in Portugal, as it is the case for Glybera (Sousa, 2016b). The following figure shows the relation between the number of centrally approved orphan drugs and those with evidence of market use in Portugal (Fig. 7.5).

Although, the ratio between the EMA approved and those marketed in Portugal, has ranged from 59.1% (2007) to 61.4% (2015), with a peak of 84.5% in 2011, this figure shows that the number of orphan drugs available has been steadily increasing both in the European Union and in Portugal.

7.10 ACCESS TO INNOVATION

Access to medicines should be equal in all European countries because approval is made through a centralised process at EMA. This centralised procedure is currently compulsory for most medicines falling into the scope of the Annex to Regulation (EC) No 726/2004, which includes new active substances to treat HIV, cancer, diabetes, advanced-therapy medicines and orphan medicines. This procedure implies that one single market authorisation is issued and is simultaneously valid in all EU Member States and also in the European Economic Area (EEA). However, EMA bases decisions solely on evidence of relative efficacy and safety, whilst leaving reimbursement decisions to be taken by member states.

Member states, including Portugal, will base their decisions on the therapeutic added value (TAV), which will include the notions of comparative efficacy plus commodity and eventually patient reported outcomes (Fontes Ribeiro, 2008). When manufacturers fail to demonstrate TAV, the drug may still be approved but the price is set 10% lower than the previously approved, which may then lead the manufacturer to decide not to market the drug. However, this is only applicable to ambulatory medicines. On the other hand, when a substance is considered to have TAV, it is submitted to the next stage when the economical evaluation takes place. At this stage, several factors are considered, namely the comparator chosen, in terms of therapeutic equivalence, but also in terms of market availability. The way the system is set up has obvious implications as the decision to approve a drug to be made available nationally will also depend on the state budget, leading to some drugs not being available, whilst others may simply see their inclusion delayed. Differences in assessment criteria and requirements for evidence between member states and EMA have been recognised and to impact on patients' access to medicines (Martinalbo et al., 2016).

In Portugal, on average, patients wait more than 18 months to be able to access new medicines reimbursed by the Government (OPSS, 2015). According to the COMPARE study, which analysed access to new medicines in 20 countries between 2009 and 2014, only 16% of analysed medicines had obtained reimbursement in Portugal. This proportion was even worse when restricted to innovative medicines (9%). These findings placed Portugal in the last position of all analysed countries (Fig. 7.6) (Medicines Australia, 2015).

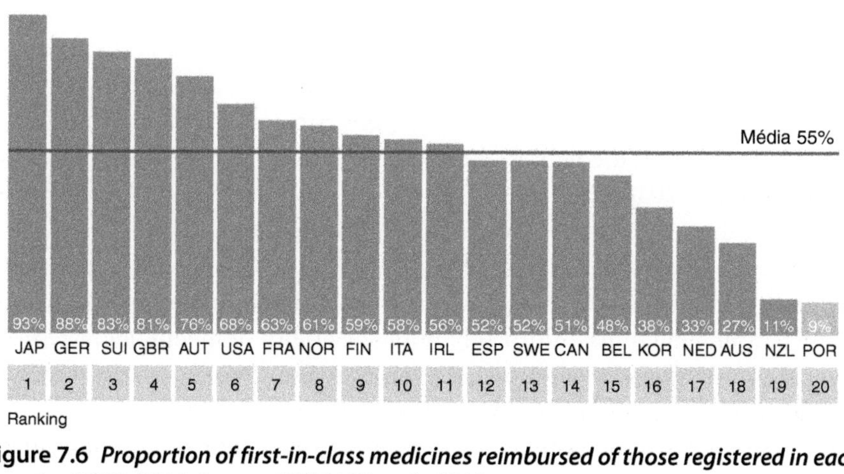

Figure 7.6 ***Proportion of first-in-class medicines reimbursed of those registered in each country, 2009–2014.*** *Source: COMPARE study, 2015.*

Another study looking at the availability of various medicines across EU member states, showed that in Portugal, over 40% of the studied products were not available at all (Hoebert et al., 2013). These data are also supported by national studies, where Portugal has been described as one of the countries in the European context with lowest access to innovation, considering the likeliness of approval and timing for approval (Exigo, 2011).

Recognising this flaw, INFARMED has created a commission to evaluate health-technology (CATs) and recently nominated additional experts so that the process is quicker (Decreto-Lei 97/2015; Deliberação 622/2016). In 2016, 50 medicines considered innovative were approved, over 20% for use in oncology. However, it must be stated that not all are totally innovative but rather present some advantages to the previously existing. A relatively recent category, not considered high-cost medicine, is the NOACs, where the first approved (dabigatran) needed over 3 years to be reimbursed and the more recent (edoxaban) was one of those approved at the end of 2016, with a record time for reimbursement within this class of 1.5 years.

7.11 FUTURE CHALLENGES

In 2015, the National System for Health Technology Assessment (SiNATs) was created, defining the mechanisms through which medicines reimbursement is to be evaluated, whilst also foreseeing their periodic re-evaluation (Decreto-Lei 97/2015; Port. 195-A/2015). The models foreseen for health technology assessment include ex-ante and ex-post cost-effectiveness and comparative effectiveness (Wilsdon and Serota, 2011). This is an initiative potentially leading to cost control and value for money, which could then be better applied to increase patients' access to innovation and specifically to high-cost medicines. However, although announced as a measure focusing on 'the most expensive medicines', the current re-evaluation is focusing on ambulatory medicines, therefore, limiting the potential cost savings (INFARMED, 2016a, 2016b, 2016c, 2016d, 2016e). It would be interesting to extend this evaluation to hospital-only medicines.

On the other hand, it must be seen as a kickback the recent approval of a law that restricts access to health information, including medicines-related information, which may ultimately limit the ability of independent research groups to be able to monitor drug use and the impact of legislative measures in Portugal (Despacho n° 1612-A/2017).

According to the authors of the Report on Access to Essential medicines in Portugal, the pharmaceutical reimbursement system in Portugal is well-defined and sustainable, using clear criteria, and warranting citizens' access to essential medicines (OBIG, 2009). However, the central funding body for medicines in Portugal is the state budget, which is influenced by various factors. The first and perhaps more relevant is the country's GDP, which despite previous estimates, has continued decreasing since 2008, only beginning to surpass the baseline in 2015 (World Bank, Pordata, 2017). Following external intervention, the Memorandum of Understanding set 1% of GDP as a target for public pharmaceutical expenditure to be reached by the end of 2013, covering both ambulatory and hospital. Only in 2014, it was possible to achieve 1.23% of GDP (European Observatory of Health Systems, 2017) and some of the reasons are the aforementioned cost-containment measures but also the fact that the GDP started to finally rise then. The ability to finance access to high-cost medicines in Portugal will depend mostly on the country's GDP, as the health care system's efficiency has been considered quite high. Assuming the GDP to steadily continue rising, the proportion attributed to health should also increase to favour access to high-cost medicines. This decision is also dependent on external factors that Portugal may not control, such as the investment needed, for example, on defence (1.0% in 2015), and the investment also made on other areas that indirectly affect health, such as social security (7.6% in 2015) (Pordata, 2017). Another aspect worth considering for future planning is that costs related to aging have been rising and are expected to continue to rise. In fact, Portugal is the EU country where the projected increase expenditure on health care due to demographic changes from 2013 to 2060 is the highest, accounting for 2.8% of GDP (European Commission, 2015). Portugal has one of the highest proportions of elders in the European Union, but most importantly has also one of the worst living conditions for the elders, as measured by the number of unhealthy years (European Observatory of Health Systems, 2017; Pordata, 2017). Many of these high-cost medicines are used among the elders, and as such the proportion of the state budget needed to finance access to live-saving technologies needs better planning.

REFERENCES

ACSS (Administração Central do Sistema de Saúde). Monitorização Mensal RNCCI – Janeiro de 2017.

Anjo, J., Café, A., Carvalho, A., Doroana, M., Fraga, J., Gíria, J., et al., 2014. O impacto da hepatite C em Portugal. GE. J. Port. Gastrenterol. 21 (2), 44–54.

Caldeira S., Furtado C., Vieira I., Baptista A., PHIS Hospital Pharma Report, http://whocc.goeg.at/Literaturliste/Dokumente/CountryInformationReports/PHIS%20Hospital%20Pharma%20Portugal%202010.pdf accessed 6 July 2017.

Cavagnaro, J., Silva Lima, B., 2015. Regulatory acceptance of animal models of disease to support clinical trials of medicines and advanced therapy medicinal products. Eur. J. Pharmacol. 759, 51–62.

Coelho, R.B., Costa, F.A., 2014. Impact of pharmaceutical counselling in minor health problems in rural Portugal. Pharm. Pract. 12 (4), 451.

Constituição da República Portuguesa.VII Revisão Constitucional. Artigo 64°.(2005).

Cordeiro, J.V., 2014. Ethical and legal challenges of personalized medicine: paradigmatic examples of research, prevention, diagnosis and treatment. Rev. Port. Saude Pública. 32 (2), 164–180.

Costa, F.A., Teixeira, I., Duarte-Ramos, F., Proença, L., Pedro, A.R., Furtado, C., et al., 2016. Effects of economic recession on elderly patients' perceptions of access to health care and medicines in Portugal. Int. J. Clin. Pharm.doi: 10.1007/s11096-016-0405-3.

Deliberação n.° 76/CA/2015, em 18 de Junho de 2015. Diário da República n.° 4/2016 de 7 de Janeiro. Regulation on authorisation for exceptional use.

Deliberação n.° 139/CD/2014. Regulation on early access.

Deliberação 622/2016. Regulation of the Commission for Health Technology Assessment (CATs). Regulation on early access.

Decreto-Lei 282/95. Fee applied to the marketing of medicines.

Decreto-Lei 97/2015, de 1 de Junho. Creation of the Commission for Health Technology Assessment (CATs).

Despacho n.° 1612-A/2017. Determines the prohibition to give away health information.

Direção Geral de Saúde (DGS). Diagnostic and Treatment of Non-Small Cell Lung Cancer. Norma 032/2013.

Eichler, H.G., Abadie, E., Breckenridge, A., Flamion, B., Gustafsson, L.L., Leufkens, H., et al., 2011. Bridging the efficacy-effectiveness gap: a regulator's perspective on addressing variability of drug response. Nat. Rev. Drug Discov. 10, 495–506.

Eichler, H.G., Oye, K., Baird, L.G., Abadie, E., Brown, J., Drum, C.L., et al., 2012. Adaptive licensing: taking the next step in the evolution of drug approval. Nature 91 (3), 426–437.

European Medicines Agency (EMA). Recommendations on eligibility to PRIME scheme. November, 2016.

European Commission—Directorate General Economic and Financial Affairs. The Economic Adjustment Programme for Portugal. Sixth Review—Autumn 2012. European Economy, Occasional Papers 124; 2012. Available at: http://ec.europa.eu/ economy_finance/publications/occasional_paper/2012/pdf/ocp124_ en.pdf] and below the OECD average [OECD. Health at a glance 2015: OECD indicators. OECD Publishing, Paris; 2015. doi:http://dx.doi.org/10.1787/health_glance2015-en.

European Commission. The 2015 Aging Report – Economic and budgetary projections for the 28 EU Member States (2013–2060). ISSN 1725-3217 (online).

European Observatory of Health Systems. Health systems in transition. HIT Portugal. Lisboa, April 2017.

Eurostat, 2016. Eurostat database. Luxembourg, European Commission. Available from: http://ec.europa.eu/eurostat/data/database.

EXIGO CONSULTORES – Financiamento publico dos medicamentos em Portugal (2007–2011): avaliação da acessibilidade e dos critérios de decisão sobre os medicamentos com novas substancias activas ou novas indicações terapêuticas. Lisboa: EXIGO Consultores, Novembro de 2011.

FIP (International Pharmaceutical Federation). Sustainability of Pharmacy Services: advancing Global Health. International overview of remuneration models for community and hospital pharmacy. 2015.

Fontes Ribeiro, C., 2008. Valor terapêutico acrescentado. Rev. Port Clin. Geral. 24, 723–728.

Franco, P., 2013. Orphan drugs: the regulatory environment. Drug Discov. Today 18, 163–172.

Hawlik, K., Devalière, A., 2016. Access to High-Priced Medicines in Hospital Settings in Europe: A Study in Four European Countries. Health Action International, Amsterdam.

Hoebert, J.M., Mantel-Teeuwisse, A.K., van Dijk, L., Bijlsma, J.W., Leufkens, H.G.M., 2012. Do rheumatoid arthritis patients have equal access to treatment with new medicines?: tumour necrosis factor-alpha inhibitors use in four European countries. Health Policy 104 (1), 76–83.

Hoebert, J.M., Irs, A., Mantel-Teeuwisse, A.K., Leufkens, H.G.M., 2013. Future of the European Union regulatory network in the context of the uptake of new medicines. Br. J. Clin. Pharmacol. 76 (1), 1–6.

INFARMED. Comunicado de Imprensa. Acesso à Inovação. Mais de 1200 doentes tratados com AUE. Setembro 2016.

INFARMED. Relatório de Avaliação do Pedido de Comparticipação de Medicamento para Uso Humano. Parecer Harvoni. 18 Fevereiro 2015.

INFARMED. Infarmed reavalia comparticipação de 115 medicamentos mais caros. Comunicado de Imprensa, 17 de Maio de 2016.

INFARMED. Acesso à inovação. Mais de 1200 doentes tratados com AUE. Comunicado de Imprensa, 9 de Setembro de 2016.

INFARMED. Balanço do Programa da Hepatite C. Comunicado de Imprensa, 28-07-2015.

INFARMED. Monitorização Mensal do consumo de medicamentos em Meio hospitalar. Janeiro-Outubro 2016.

INFARMED. Hepatite C - Monitorização dos Tratamentos. 5 de Dezembro 2016. Available at http://www.infarmed.pt/documents/15786/0/Hepatite+C/dd545649-1042-42e9-b2d3-83db2bc34b11?version=1.0 (accessed 21/12/2016).

Laires, P.A., Exposto, F., Mesquita, R., Martins, A.P., Cunha-Miranda, L., Fonseca, J.E., 2013. Patients' access to biologics in rheumatoid arthritis: a comparison between Portugal and other European countries. Eur. J. Health Econ. 14, 875–885.

Leopold, C., Mantel-Teeuwisse, A.K., Vogler, S., Valkova, S., de Joncheere, K., Leufkens, H.G.M., et al., 2014. Effect of the economic recession on pharmaceutical policy and medicine sales in eight European countries. Bull. World Health Organ. 92, 630–640.

Martinalbo, J., Bowen, D., Camarero, J., Chapelin, M., Démolis, P., Foggi, P., et al., 2016. Early market access of oncologic drugs in the EU. Ann. Oncol. 27 (1), 96–105.

Martins, S., van Mil, J.W.F., Costa, F.A., 2015. The organizational framework of community pharmacies in Europe. Int. J. Clin. Pharm. 37, 896.

Medicines Australia. COMPARE Study. March 2015

OBIG. Access to essential medicines in Portugal. Commissioned by Health Action International Europe. July, 2009.

OECD Health Statistics 2016.

Observatório Português dos Sistemas de Saúde (OPSS). Saúde: Síndroma de negação. 2014.

Observatório Português dos Sistemas de Saúde (OPSS). Acesso aos cuidados de saúde: um direito em risco? 2015.

Observatório Português dos Sistemas de Saúde (OPSS). Saúde: procuram-se novos caminhos. 2016.

Panteli, D., Arickx, F., Cleemput, I., Dedet, G., Eckhardt, H., Fogarty, E., et al., 2016. Pharmaceutical regulation in 15 Europenan countries review. Health Syst. Transit. 18 (5), 1–122.

Pordata. Available at http://www.pordata.pt/Portugal Accessed 06 April 2017.

Portaria n.° 195-D/2015. Diário da República, 1.ª série—N.° 125—30 de junho de 2015. Establishes the pharmacotherapeutic groups and subgroups that may be subject to reimbursement.

Portaria n.° 195-A/2015. Diário da República n.° 125/2015, 1° Suplemento, Série I de 2015-06-30. Approves the common procedure for reimbursement and previous evaluation of medicines.

Portaria n.° 359/2017. Diário da República n.° 223/2017, Série I de 2017-11-20. Defines the reference countries to consider in 2018 for the prices of new medicines authorised.
Portaria no 137-A/2012. Diário da República, 1.a série—No. 92 Establishes the rules for prescribing by Common International Denomination.
PWC. (2013). Ensaios Clínicos em Portugal. Junho 2013 http://www.apifarma.pt/publicacoes/siteestudos/Documents/EstudoInvestig.Clinica%20em%20Portugal.%20jun.2013.vf.pdf. Accessed 19/12/2016.
Sakellarides, C., Castelo-Branco, L., Barbosa, P., Azevedo, H., 2014. The impact of the financial crisis on the health system and health in Portugal. European observatory on health systems and policies. WHO Regional Office for Europe, Copenhagen.
Regulation (EC) No 141/2000 of the European Parliament and Council of 16 December 1999 on orphan medicinal products.
RNCCI (Rede Nacional de Cuidados Continuados Integrados). Guia Prático, Instituto da
Schwartz, L. The 9 most expensive medicines in the world – Courtesy of Big Pharma. Alternet, 29 September 2015.
Simoens, S., 2011. Pricing and reimbursement of orphan drugs: the need for more transparency. Orphanet J. Rare Dis. 6, 42.
Silva, M., Félix, J., Ferreira, D., Vandewalle, B., Guerra, I., Cure, S., Aldir, I., Carvalho, A., Macedo, G., Marinho, R.T., Pedroto, I., Ramalho, F., 2014. Sofosbuvir for the treatment of chronic Hepatitis C: A comprehensive cost-effectiveness analysis across Hcv genotypes, pretreatment conditions and Hiv co-infection. Value Health 17, A 3 2 3 – A 6 8 6.
Sousa (a), I., Ramos, R., Costa, M. Analysis of the global spending with orphan drugs on the Portuguese National Health Service. 8th European Conference on Rare Diseases & Orphan Products, 26–28 May 2016, Edinburgh.
Sousa (b), I. Impacto Orçamental de Medicamentos órfãos em Portugal. Trabalho de Projeto do Mestrado em Economia, na especialidade de Economia Financeira, apresentado à Faculdade de Economia da Universidade de Coimbra para obtenção do grau de Mestre.
Teixeira, I, Vieira, I. INFARMED. Pharmaceutical pricing and reimbursement information. Portugal pharma profile. 2008.
Vogler, S., Vitry, A., Babar, Z.-U.-D., 2016. Cancer drugs in 16 European countries, Australia and New Zealand: a cross-country price comparison study. Lancet. Oncol. 17 (1), 39–47.
Weale, A., 1998. Rationing access to health care. BMJ. 316, 410.
WHO, Regional office for Europe (2015), 'Access to new medicines in Europe: technical review of policy initiatives and opportunities for collaboration and research', 2015.
WHO. The selection and use of essential medicines. Report of the WHO Expert Committee, 2002. Technical Report Series 914: 14–17. Geneva: World Health Organization, 2002.
WHO. The 19th WHO model list of essential medicines. Geneva: World Health Organization, 2015. http://www.who.int/medicines/publications/essentialmedicines/EML2015_8-May-15.pdf (accessed 9/10/ 2015).
WorldBank, 2014. World Health Organization Global Health Expenditure database. Available from: https://data.worldbank.org/indicator/SH.XPD.TOTL.ZS.
Wilsdon, T., Serota, A., 2011. Final report: a comparative analysis of the role and impact of Health Technology Assessment. CRA-Charles River Associates.

FURTHER READINGS

Kanavos, P., Vandoros, S., Irwin, R., Nicod, E., Casson, M., 2011. 'Differences in costs of and access to pharmaceutical products in the EU. Brussels: European Parliament'. Policy Dep. Econ. Sci. Policy, 2011.

CHAPTER 8

Improving Access to High-Cost Medicines in Low Income Countries in Africa: Creating a Functioning Pharmaceutical System in Uganda

Brendan Kwesiga*, Anita Katharina Wagner, Morries Seru†, Birna Trap***

*Management Sciences for Health, Kampala, Uganda
**Harvard Medical School and Harvard Pilgrim Health Care Institute, Boston, MA, USA
†Ministry of Health Pharmacy Department, Kampala, Uganda

8.1 INTRODUCTION

In this chapter, we discuss how Uganda is creating a system that is intended to be more efficient, equitable and sustainable. We discuss a holistic approach to addressing supply chain challenges that we think are necessary for low income countries to become efficient and better able to attain cost savings and reduce wastage, a precondition from our perspective, for providing access to highly priced pharmaceuticals.

The reality is that low income countries like Uganda continue to struggle to afford needed medicines on their own; medicines provision still depends mainly on donors. In addition to lack of funds for medicines in general, system inefficiencies and waste squander scarce resources. For this reason, providing access to highly priced medicines cannot be viewed only with respect to pricing and acquisition issues but needs to also consider mechanisms to ensure efficiency and sustainability of resources for medicines. Implementing interventions for strengthening supply chains and procurement processes has been shown as a strategy through which low income countries can save resources (Seidman and Atun, 2017) that could help countries to afford medicines for the growing burden of non-communicable disease (NCDs) and medicines for rare disorders.

NCDs now account for an increasing proportion of morbidity and mortality in Uganda. According to the rapid assessment of morbidity and mortality due to NCDs in Uganda (2011), the common types of NCDs in Uganda are diabetes, cancers, cardiovascular diseases, and respiratory diseases

Equitable Access to High-Cost Pharmaceuticals
http://dx.doi.org/10.1016/B978-0-12-811945-7.00008-7

such as chronic obstructed pulmonary disease, asthma and sick cell anemia. (MOH, 2011). These diseases are chronic and require life-long medication treatments. In the Ugandan context, medicine costs to the health system for treating these conditions are immense and most Ugandans cannot access even established low-cost treatments that are globally available.

At the dawn of the 2000s, Ugandan's could not access new antiretroviral medicines having a cost of more than US$10,000 per person per year. While the country was receiving donor-funded antiretroviral medicines, it also needed to put in place provisions for supplying these products efficiently and sustainably, with donor and, eventually, government funds. We describe challenges faced and the pharmaceutical systems strengthening interventions undertaken in Uganda to provide HIV/AIDS treatments. We describe lessons learned and systems put in place to respond to the challenges posed by HIV treatment that will be critical for enabling access to high cost medicines especially NCDs among people living in low income countries.

8.2 HIGH-COST MEDICINES IN UGANDA

In this chapter, we define high-cost medicines as therapies that account for a large proportion of total pharmaceutical spending, that is, medicines that have high budget impact. In Uganda in 2014/15, treatment for HIV accounted for 70% of total public sector medicines and diagnostics spending, which was US$250 million. When disaggregated by source, treatment for HIV/AIDS accounted for 78% of all medicines and diagnostics funded by donors (US$168 million) and 39% of government medicines spending (US$82 million) (Fig. 8.1).

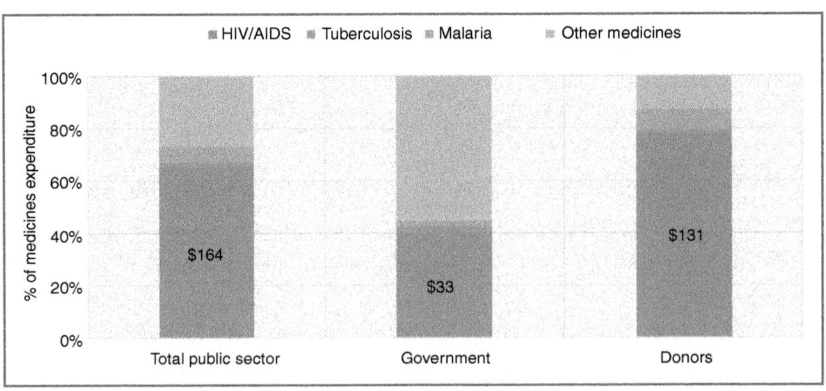

Figure 8.1 ***Funding for medicines and health supplies in Uganda's public sector: 2014/15 (US$ millions).***

In 2015, Uganda provided HIV/AIDS treatment care free of charge for about 900,000 patients enrolled in treatment in government, private not-for-profit and non-governmental facilities—about 60% of the estimated 1,500,000 who need treatment.

Our discussion focusses on interventions implemented in public and not-for-profit pharmaceutical sector systems to improve availability and access to antiretroviral treatment (ART). The system changes were prompted by challenges that the first category of high-cost medicines in Uganda—ART—presented, and they form the basis for enabling access to more expensive chronic treatments for NCDs in the future.

8.3 SYSTEM CHALLENGES HIGHLIGHTED BY PROVIDING ART IN UGANDA

Uganda is a poor East African country with burden of communicable diseases and a growing burden of chronic diseases (MOH, 2015). One in five Ugandans live on less than US$1.25 per day and more than 40% of the population of 36 million is at risk of impoverishment from unexpected expenditures (MOF, 2014). This population depends on a public health care delivery system in which services and medicines are provided free of charge to the patients. A functional system must ensure that medicines are available, accessible to those who need them, appropriately used and sustainable—, that is, affordable—for the system.

The introduction of ART made evident the deficiencies of the public sector medicines system in Uganda. Until recently, the system was an uncoordinated mix of parallel actors funding, procuring, storing, distributing and delivering medicines and related diagnostics. In 2010, more than six donors funded HIV/AIDS medicines, which were procured by more than eight agencies, stored in four national storage sites and distributed to facilities through seven distribution networks (Fig. 8.2) (MOH and SURE, 2010). The uncoordinated system had no standardised process or procedures to ensure that people received the medicines they needed and lacked a mechanism to track the flow of medicines and money, leading to duplicated efforts and wasted medicines and funds.

These system deficiencies are detrimental for patients living with HIV. For example, 31% of HIV-infected children and 48% of adults (UAC, 2015) lacked access to ART in 2014. At the same time, ART valued at about US$100,000 per year expired at each of the central warehouses, depriving

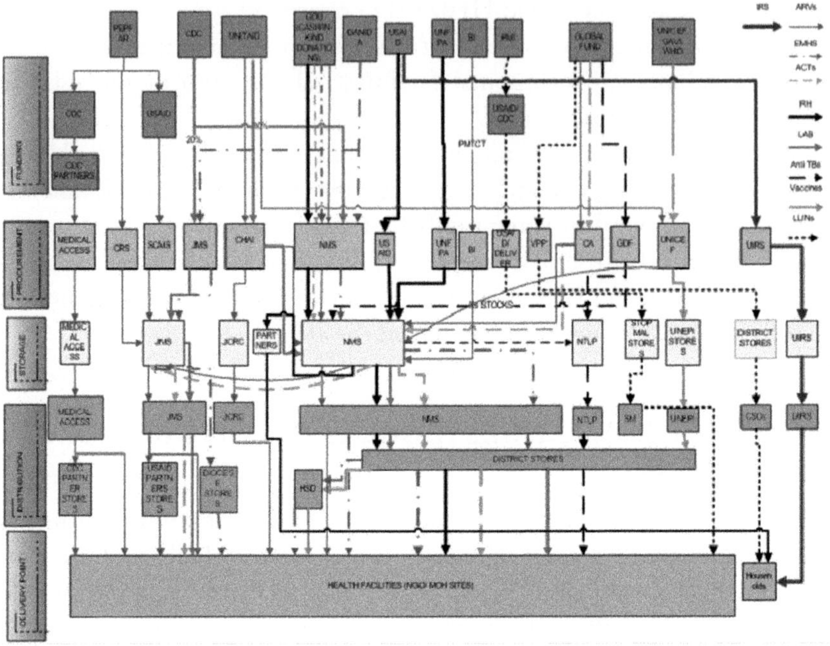

Figure 8.2 ***Public sector medicines provision in Uganda, 2010.***

thousands of patients of effective treatments and wasting enormous amounts of scarce resources.

The Ugandan government and the donors funding ART were thus interested in creating a harmonized and well-coordinated system in which resources allocated to HIV treatment could fully benefit the population. The magnitude of these consequences impelled Uganda to implement a comprehensive long-term strategy to build the foundations of a functional pharmaceutical system. In the remainder of the chapter, we describe the overall system-building strategy and the components that specifically targeted ART.

8.4 SYSTEM APPROACH TO PROVIDING ART IN UGANDA

In 2009, the government of Uganda with support from the US Agency for International Development (USAID) embarked on a comprehensive, multi-pronged strategy to strengthen the public pharmaceutical sector at the central, district and facility levels (SURE, 2014). Four interlinked foci make up the strategy: building the *capacity of health professionals* at all levels to correctly procure, manage and dispenses medicines and manage the funds to do so; *strengthening system structures and processes* to efficiently manage the resources allocated to medicines by donors and government stakeholders;

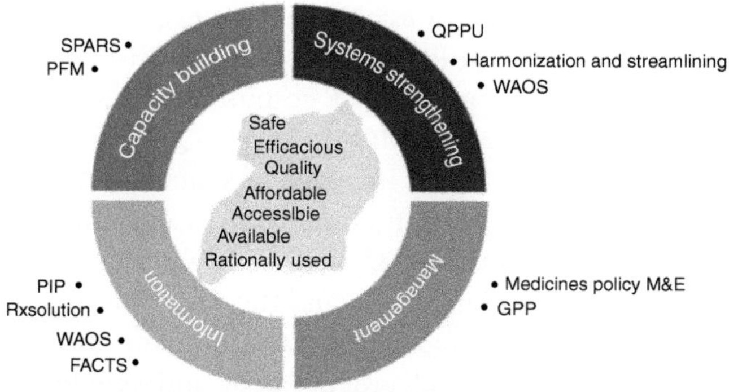

Figure 8.3 ***A comprehensive strategy to strengthen the public pharmaceutical sector.*** SPARS, Supervision, Performance Assessment and Recognition Strategy; PFM, Pharmaceutical Financial Management; QPPU, Quantification, procurement and planning unit; WAOS, Web based ordering and reporting system; GPP, Good Pharmacy Practices; FACTS, Financial and Commodity Tracking System; PIP, Pharmaceutical Information Portal.

increasing the effectiveness of management based on information about system performance; and *providing sound information* for shared decision-making at all levels of the system (Fig. 8.3).

8.4.1 System Strengthening

To address the deficiencies in the system for delivering ART in Uganda, interventions were implemented to strengthen systems, structures and process to make the process more efficient and consequently lead to increased access to ART. The interventions undertaken included establishing a quantification and procurement planning unit, streamlining and rationalisation of the supply chain and ensuring good pharmacy practices (GPP) at ART facilities. These are described in below.

8.5 QUANTIFICATION AND PROCUREMENT PLANNING UNIT

For any supply system to work efficiently, a strong link must exist between forecasting, quantification, procurement, warehousing, inventory management and the logistics information management system. Prior to 2010, Uganda's medicines supply chain lacked coordination and information sharing on stock status, which is needed to avoid stock-outs. Using available funding was challenging because the actual pharmaceutical needs were unclear. Establishing national requirements was difficult because various parallel information sources existed, data to inform quantification was not centralised, and the forecasting methodology was not standardised and procurement was carried out by different donor agencies.

In 2010, Ministry of Health established the Quantification and Procurement Planning Unit (QPPU) within the Pharmacy Department to integrate, coordinate and monitor ART commodities quantification, procurement and supply planning (MOH, 2012). Quantifying ART needs was highly challenging because it involved several central warehouses, 17 treatment regimens and multiple funding sources and other stakeholders. Quantification expertise was needed. Staff from Ministry of Health technical programmes, central warehouses and the QPPU were trained to use ART quantification tools (Quantimed) and pipeline monitoring tools (PipeLine and the Global Fund procurement and supply management system). The unit's function has enabled coordination and centralization of national quantification, stakeholder collaboration, information sharing and decisionmaking and has been fundamental in streamlining the supply chain activities.

The QPPU manages national quantifications, gap analyses and supply planning in coordination with Ministry of Health (MoH) technical staff from the AIDS programme, and on a bimonthly basis develop stock status reports. Initially, these reports included only ART products, but have now been expanded to include tuberculosis and malaria medicines, laboratory supplies, vaccines and reproductive health commodities. Additional expansion will include cancer medicines and 41 essential medicines and health supplies. The bimonthly stock status reports provide the basis for routine risk assessments of the supply chain and for providing critical information on national stock or funding gaps. This allows decision makers to mobilise resources, prioritise purchases and avoid stock-outs by redistributing between central warehouses, placing emergency orders and expediting or delaying shipments. QPPU is also able to track partner ART commitments against what they have delivered. To coordinate commodities-related activities a Commodity Security Group with members from the Pharmacy Department, development partners, implementing partners, Ministry of Health technical programmes and central-level warehouses meets monthly.

Based on Commodity Security Group's agreements between January 2013 and February 2014, the QPPU initiated warehouse transfers of ART worth approximately US$6.8 million, which prevented product shortages and disruption of health services downstream. In August 2014, the Global Fund announced the approval of an additional US$69 million in funding for ART based on QPPU's quantification. In 2016, QPPU estimated the funding gap for ART to be US$94 million. This has informed government efforts for resource mobilization within this period.

8.6 STREAMLINING AND RATIONALIZING OF SUPPLY CHAIN

Before 2010, a facility could receive ART from several warehouses, using different distribution channels and with different order, supply and report schedules, forms and routes (Fig. 8.2). Procurement could not benefit from economies of scale associated with pooled procurement, and storage and distribution. The supply chain was not transparent, resulting in loss of medicines through wastage and theft. There was also duplication of efforts with different distributors making multiple trips to the same facility to deliver different types of medicines.

From 2010 onward, the government took several steps to harmonise and streamline the supply chain:

- **One-facility-one supplier:** Trucks from different warehouses no longer delivered HIV commodities to the same facility, which has optimized distribution. Each health facility is now linked to one central warehouse. To drive the 'one facility–one supplier' approach, ordering had to be structured so that orders could be received and handled only by the facility's designated supplier. It was no longer acceptable for implementing partners and Ministry of Health technical programs to procure, store or manage supplies, something they were not qualified nor legally approved to do in the first place.
- **Coordinated distribution:** Before 2009, the central warehouse delivered to the district store from where the facilities had to organise transport. Because donors funded the distribution cost for ART, it was an opportune time to synchronise bimonthly order and delivery schedules for ART and other essential medicines and health supplies. Harmonising and streamlining order and delivery schedules made it possible to introduce to-the-door delivery from the central warehouse to the facility. This eliminated health facilities' transport burden and reduced the opportunity of theft while in transit. This new harmonised system increased adherence to order cycles from 78% to 89% and delivery cycles from 42% to 63%, and reduced lead time from an average of 59 (20–215) days in 2010 to an average of 41 (8–74) days in 2014/15.
- **One item–one store:** We also introduced harmonisation within the facility. It was common to find multiple programme-specific storage areas within a facility. For example, a health centre level IV had one store for ART, one store for tuberculosis medicines, one pharmacy for other essential medicines and a laboratory that kept its own supplies. It was practically impossible to get an overview of what was in stock and what needed to order to ensure appropriate

and uniform stock management. Under the principle of 'one item–one store' (i.e. one stock card per item), ART and tuberculosis medicines were eventually integrated into the main facility store. Order deadlines for all medicines and related commodities are now uniform, and the maintenance of one stock card for each product has simplified ordering and stock management.

8.7 ENSURING GOOD PHARMACY PRACTICES AT PUBLIC SECTOR FACILITIES

Uganda's medicines regulatory body, the National Drug Authority (NDA) regularly inspected private sector pharmacies. Public sector facility pharmacies were not inspected to ensure they adhered to GPP. NDA decided that public sector facility pharmacies also be GPP- inspected and certified regularly so that both private and public sector facilities had the same requirement for handling medicines including ARVs.

As part of implementation of GPP in public sector facilities, a new electronic inspection tool was developed, inspectors were trained, and the first 455 GPP inspections in public health facilities conducted in 2013/2014. The need was justified when 43% of public facilities failed inspection criteria based on 52 GPP indicators. (Trap, Kikule et al., 2016). GPP certification is now one of the criteria that a health facility needs to become accredited as an ART site, and the MoH tracks facilities' information on the GPP status on its facility master list. The master list, which links to the national health management information system (DHIS2), identifies the health facilities by name, level of care, ownership and physical location (including GIS codes). This master list helps ensure that HIV commodities go to the correct health facilities and are not diverted.

8.8 CAPACITY BUILDING

To assure that medicines are available in the quantities needed and that they are properly stored and appropriately dispensed requires a number of interlinked processes. These processes depend on many factors, including available funds, human resources, information and management capacity. In 2010, an assessment showed weak management: 54% of facilities stored medicines in boxes on the floor; only 4% of facilities performed a monthly physical product count and only 24% based their orders on stock card information; only 19% had knowledge of the current budget allocated to them for medicines; and with less than 8% of 376 pharmacy posts in the public sector filled, other health professionals had to take on the responsibilities of non-existent pharmacists (MOH, 2010; Windisch et al., 2011; MOH, 2014).

In the past, Uganda had invested considerably in building medicines management capacity through training interventions that did not produce significant or sustainable performance improvements (MOH, 2010). To build the needed capacity in medicines and financial management, Uganda's MoH adopted two strategies that combine capacity-building with incentives for both supervisors and health workers called the Supervision, Performance Assessment and Recognition Strategy (SPARS) and Pharmaceutical Financial Management (PFM). Both strategies are based on the tenet that a combination of interventions yields better and more sustainable improvement (Ross-Degnan et al., 1997; Rowe et al., 2005).

8.9 SUPERVISION, PERFORMANCE ASSESSMENT AND RECOGNITION STRATEGY

SPARS uses supportive supervision and on-the-job mentoring provided by district-based public sector medicines management supervisors (MMS) to improve staff medicines management skills in government and private not-for-profit sector facilities (Trap et al., 2016). We developed a national essential medicines and health supplies management manual and job aids and distributed them to all health facilities and MMS. MMS were provided motorcycles, fuel, permits and training in defensive riding. They used standardised indicator-based performance assessment tools during every supervisory visit to measure progress in five domains—dispensing quality, prescribing quality, stock management, storage management, and ordering and reporting—and depicted progress in a spider graph (Fig. 8.4). MMS collect performance data for 25 indicators by reviewing records during supervisory visits, observing staff practices, and talking to patients. The MMS's reports the facility performance data electronically into the central Pharmaceutical Information Portal. In addition, SPARS electronic data collection improves data quality and the web-based portal facilitates data use for decision making and management. The performance recognition strategy motivates MMS and health facility staff through a reward system. These rewards combine personal use items such as tea, sugar, T-shirts, and telephone air time, with items related to supervision and pharmacy services, such as medicine dispensing trays, thermometers, and fuel.

Currently, about 300 trained MMS conduct an average of 2.6 supervisory visits to health facilities per month to work with staff face-to-face. By September 2016, 3100 (85%) public sector facilities in Uganda had had

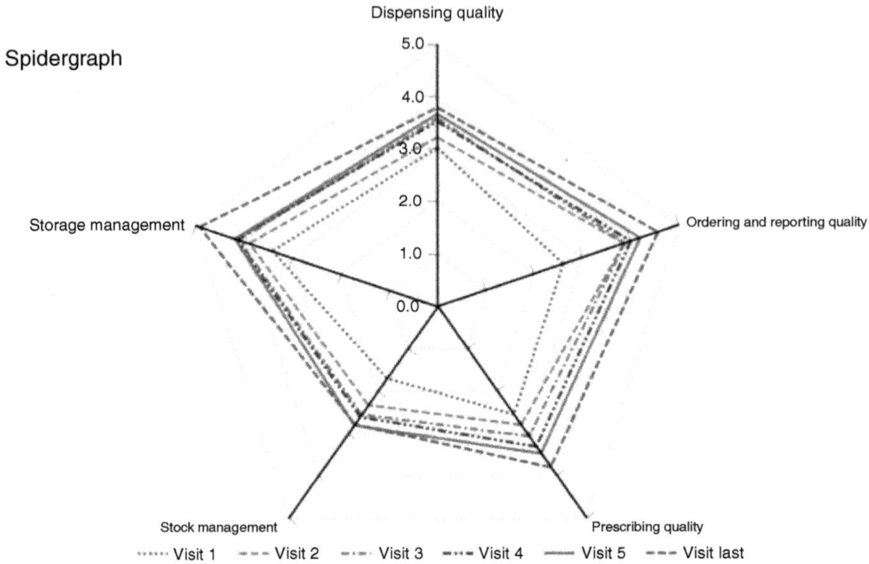

Figure 8.4 ***Illustration of SPARS Indicator based performance assessment.*** *Source: MOH, 2016.*

an average of 5.5 supervision visits. As a multifaceted capacity-building approach, SPARS has produced remarkable achievements in all areas of medicines management as seen in Fig. 8.4. The spider graph illustrates how scores in all five areas of medicines management increased from visit one to the most recent visit. As 5.0 is the highest score possible in each area, 25 would be a perfect SPARS score. During the first 12 months of SPARS, 22% of facilities reached an acceptable SPARS score of 18.75 (75% of 25). Following five SPARS visits the overall performance increased from 44% at the first visit to 73% at the last visit (MOH, 2016).

8.10 PHARMACEUTICAL FINANCIAL MANAGEMENT

In Uganda, all lower level government facilities (i.e. Health Centre II and Health Centre III) receive a predetermined essential medicines and health supplies kit every other month, with types and quantities of medicines dependent on the level of care. This was implemented in 2009 because the staff at the lower levels did not have the capacity to prepare product orders within the available facility budgets. However, an assessment showed that supplying medicines with a 'one size fits all' kit provided only 20% of the facilities with sufficient quantities of medicines; about 40% were undersupplied and 40% were over supplied, which put them at risk of a high rate of expiry (MOH, 2013).

With the introduction of ART, however, the Ministry of Health found that ARVs could not be supplied appropriately through a kit. To facilitate ordering, in particular in facilities with low medicines management capacity, we introduced a web-based ART order system (WAOS, explained below). However, it was clear that health workers' capacity needed to be built not only in medicines management, but also in the development of procurement plans, budget tracking, and generation of orders that fit within the available budget while best meeting clinical needs.

Using SPARS as a foundation, the Ministry of Health developed a PFM capacity-building strategy that is now to being rolled out nationally. Like SPARS, PFM applies a supervision, performance assessment and recognition strategy and the MMS who have been implementing SPARS now implement PFM as well. To assess PFM performance, MMS use an indicator-based tool to measure performance in budgeting, planning procurement, vetting an order, monitoring budgets and commitments, and understanding and developing general financial information. We introduced a PFM manual and appropriate financial tools to support PFM implementation. Facilities need a solid platform in the SPARS area of stock management for PFM to be rolled out successfully. Using the same MMS responsible for SPARS implementation has the advantage of existing facility and staff knowledge, optimising supportive supervision time and leveraging the use of their motorbike, computer and data use (Fig. 8.5).

Results from a pilot study of 51 facilities show that multipronged PFM approaches can increase a facility's capacity to develop procurement plans, prepare appropriate orders and manage and monitor the limited available budgets (Fig. 8.5). Facility scores on the PFM areas improved substantially over four visits. On the basis of the pilot study, the Uganda Ministry of Health is rolling out the PFM strategy nationally, given the sufficient medicines management and procurement planning capacity that is a prerequisite to building financial management capacity (SURE, 2013).

8.11 PHARMACEUTICAL MANAGEMENT INFORMATION

Effective medicines management requires policy makers, program managers, health care workers, and other stakeholders to access information related to medicines management performance, product procurement, and others to determine if limited resources are being used effectively, identify problem areas and make informed decisions.

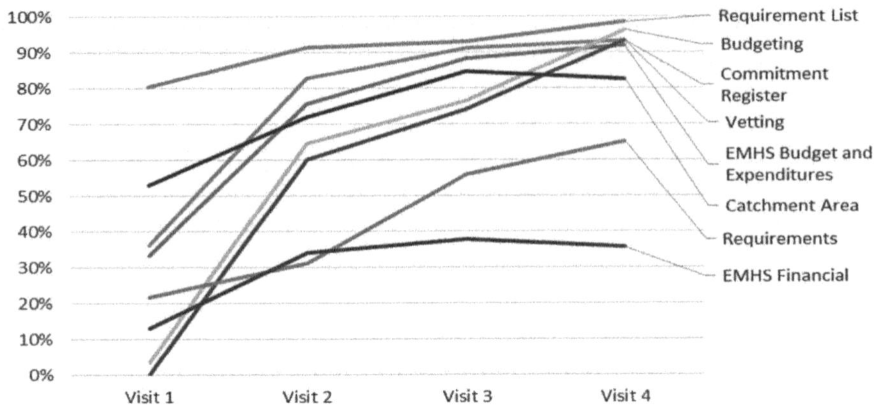

Performance area	Visit	1	2	3	4	Improvement
		%	%	%	%	%
I. EMHS budget		33	76	88	92	179
II. Requirement lists and costing		80	92	93	99	24
III. Vetting		36	83	91	93	158
IV. Budget monitoring sheet		4	65	76	96	2300
V. Commitment Register		0	60	74	93	93
VI. Requirement list/e-tool vetting		22	31	56	65	195
VII. Catchment population data		53	72	85	83	57
VIII. EMHS financial information		13	34	38	36	177

Figure 8.5 ***Facility PFM performance by subarea aross visits over time.***
Source: SURE, 2013.

To coordinate the many different information technology initiatives that implementing partners had initiated—often in isolation—the Ministry of Health developed a national e-health policy that was approved in 2015. Critical elements of the policy ensure that initiatives are integrated into the existing health management information system and that the Ministry of Health takes the lead in coordination and selection of all information technology systems.

New systems that have been introduced to strengthen supply chain functions and ARV management include WAOS, RxSolution, which is a facility-based logistic management system, the Pharmaceutical Information Portal for SPARS data, and a financial and commodity tracking system (FACTS).

8.12 WEB-BASED ARV ORDERING AND REPORTING SYSTEM

To address the challenges of ensuring appropriate supply of ARVs and other HIV commodities by facilities with varying skills in quantification and stock management, and with increasing numbers of ART-certified facilities, the Ministry of Health created Web based ARV ordering and reporting (WAOs), which is a centralised reporting and ordering system that is, part of the existing MoH management information system. WAOS provide facility information on ARV stock status, issues and patient data. Thereby enabling the warehouses to double check and adjust the facility order if needed and correlate consumption to patient data. Having a separate ARV order and report form makes it possible to identify and follow up with poor performing facilities to improve reporting rate and data quality. By 2015, after several years of intensive training, 1700 ART sites now use WAOS, and a similar web-based order and reporting system is being developed for TB commodities.

Linking WAOS to the master list of ART-accredited facilities made it possible to track and follow up on order and reporting rates. Both computerised and non-computerised health facilities can order through WAOS; facilities without computers have the district biostatisticians submit their orders electronically. WAOS has improved reporting rates and data quality and completeness, problems that had made donor requirements for reporting difficult to meet. WAOS has decreased the central level's time-consuming compilation of facility orders and has increased access to accurate order data and patient statistics. The system has proven to provide a substantial advantage over the original paper-based system; for example, among facilities supported by US President's Emergency Plan for AIDS Relief implementing partners, ART reporting rates between 2007 and 2010 averaged from 80% to 90%. Among public sector facilities without support, ART reporting rates for the same period averaged 40% to 50%. The use of WAOS together with other harmonisation efforts also led to reduction in order lead times, which reduced ARV stock-outs at health facilities.

While WAOS improved ARV ordering and patient reporting rates, there was a need to address data quality. An assessment found that over half of all ART facilities overestimated new patient enrolment, which resulted in serious overstocking of ARVs (UHSC, 2015). Unexplained and unexpected changes were seen in patient numbers between order cycles with variations of up to 500 patients in 3% of the health facilities and on average ART facilities overestimated new patient enrolment by 44%.

8.13 RXSOLUTION

Following a feasibility analysis of 16 different logistic management information systems, the Ministry of Health selected RxSolution to be the national system to manage health facility inventory, purchase orders, requisitions and dispensing. Through easily-generated stock alert reports, RxSolution enables a facility to pinpoint common problems with expiries and stock-outs, while providing a consumption data platform to address appropriate use. To facilitate implementation of RxSolution, the Ministry developed the RxBox. It allows the installation of RxSolution without much technical knowledge and includes a self-guided learning course to expand users' comfort with computers through training in basic computer skills, MS Word, MS Excel, MS PowerPoint and email. In total, we have trained more than 600 staff members from health facilities, the Ministry of Health, and other organisations on using computers and different computer systems. We established a mechanism to provide remote installation and technical support, which reduces travel and support time dramatically. By 2016, RxSolution had been rolled out to more than 120 ART- accredited sites. To enable electronic ordering from the national warehouses, standard descriptions and coding for all medicines and supplies has been developed and is being implemented in all central warehouse information systems.

8.14 PHARMACEUTICAL INFORMATION PORTAL

To enable the use of data generated through SPARS, we established a web-based database called the Pharmaceutical Information Portal (PIP). Although initially designed for SPARS data, the PIP platform will be able to host other sources of pharmaceutical sector information, such as PFM, and integrate with Uganda's existing health management information system.

MMS collect data and enter it into the PIP, which allows users to analyse and report on the SPARS intervention areas. PIP users can retrieve information on specific areas of interest, such as availability, stock and storage management, leadtime and rational use of medicines. The information generated through SPARS has been critical in the Ministry of Health's strategic decisionmaking.

8.15 FINANCIAL AND COMMODITY TRACKING SYSTEM

Although different the health commodity flows and processes have been harmonised, a system to track money to fund commodities and how it is being spent has been lacking. The aim of Financial and Commodity

Tracking System (FACTS) is to provide a transparent overview of funding for medicines including ARVs. Having a transparent view of the flow of the medicines funding will not only help ensure the best use of financial resources available for medicines, but will also limit misappropriation and misallocation of both funds and commodities. This system will complement the current information on funding gaps being generated by the QPPU by showing how commodities are being allocated and used, including regular information on the amount of funding per commodity and unmet need.

8.16 PHARMACEUTICAL SECTOR MANAGEMENT

The MoH's long-term vision is to integrate Uganda's pharmaceutical supply chain and financing streams by making information available on one platform and to ensure its use at all levels of the health system. To achieve this vision, the overarching strategy is to assure that the Pharmacy Division is prepared to implement the National Medicine Policy, monitor and manage sector activities and resources and identify and address issues as they arise. To strengthen the Pharmacy Division's capacity, it established a Monitoring and Evaluation (M&E) Unit to assure that data from existing sources such as WAOS, QPPU, RxSolution, central warehouse data systems and SPARS are used to make informed decisions.

In addition to strengthening monitoring and evaluation at the Pharmacy Division, similar skills using data needed to be honed among other health system stakeholders, such as MoH technical programmes, central warehouses, donors, MMS and health managers at all levels. We have trained more than 450 health professionals in using data from PIP, and as a result, PIP use has increased steadily to reach about 343 active users with more than 1300 monthly users.

The Pharmacy Division M&E Unit tracks developments, identifies problems, provides evidence for decision-making and monitors impact on public health. The Unit disseminates regular national and district SPARS reports, QPPU quantification reports, pharmaceutical sector reports that track progress in the 31 medicines policy indicators at central and district meetings to increase visibility of their activities. These reports are also available on the website of Uganda's Ministry of Health (http://www.health.go.ug/) Reports are also being tailored to the specific needs of MoH technical programmes with information from PIP, RxSolution, QPPU, WAOS issue and patient data and health management information system patient, morbidity and mortality data. In addition, Uganda has taken steps to regularly assess and improve data reliability and reproducibility (Blick et al., in press).

The results of the increased efforts to increase availability, understanding and use of pharmaceutical and patient data for management and optimal use of resources for ARVs and other commodities has undoubtedly prepared the Pharmacy Division to oversee Uganda's pharmaceutical sector.

8.17 CONCLUSION

Providing access to ART is considered 'one of the greatest achievements in the history of global health, financing and development' (UNAIDS, 2016). In Uganda, the confluence of global and local responses to the HIV/AIDS epidemic 15 years ago enabled a concerted approach to strengthen the pharmaceutical system, which was needed to support ART scale up (UNAIDS, 2016). Supported by USAID, the Ministry of Health has been collaborating with a lead development partner, Management Sciences for Health, to strengthen and integrate pharmaceutical sector capacity building, management and information systems to comprehensively address the enormous challenges that a high-cost programme such as ART provision posed to the public, not-for-profit and private sectors in this low-resource country. The country has been able to attain efficiency gains from strengthening its pharmaceutical sector. However, ART may no longer be considered as expensively out of reach as it did previously. After all, annual treatment costs of effective generic combination products have decreased from US$10,000 per person in 2000 to less than US$100 in 2011 (MSF, 2011). In a poor country like Uganda, however, the 90-90-90 test and treat target by 2020 will be a challenge.

A functioning pharmaceutical system is a *conditio sine qua non* to effectively treat chronic diseases, including managing highly priced specialty medicines to treat cancers and other NCDs. Decision makers need information, management structures and policies to ensure that appropriate medicines reach those in need, are used appropriately and achieve optimal health outcomes at costs households and the health system can afford. Without such systems, they risk wasting scarce resources on medicines that may do more harm than good when used inappropriately. The pharmaceutical system strengthening efforts implemented in Uganda over the past 10 years has drastically improved the management of ART medicines, and is a starting point for managing much more challenging and more expensive specialty treatments.

However, such a system will require much more extensive tracking of which patients receive these specialty medicines, whether they are appropriately prescribed and dispensed based on indications such as molecular and genetic targets, whether they are appropriately taken, which health outcomes they achieve, and at which cost to patients and the system. Decision makers will need to be able to act on this information with policies and programmes that maximise health outcomes with the resources allocated.

A functioning pharmaceutical system, however, is of course not sufficient for ensuring appropriate, affordable, effective and efficient use of highly priced medicines for NCDs. Tightly interconnected and well-functioning public health, health service delivery and health financing systems are needed for prevention, early diagnosis, initial and advanced treatment, survivorship and palliative care. Referring to these system preconditions, Richard Sullivan said: 'If you think of global health as Mount Everest, cancer control would be a small flag at its peak'(Makri, 2016). In this image, a functioning pharmaceutical system might be part of Mount Everest's base camp.

REFERENCES

Blick B., Nakabugo S., Garabedian L., Seru M., (Forthcoming). "Evaluating inter-rater reliability of indicators to assess performance of medicines management in at health facility in Uganda".

Makri, 2016. "Cancer in poor countries: Too big to tackle?" from http://www.scidev.net/global/systems/scidev-net-at-large/cancer-poor-health-system.html.

MOFPED, 2014. Povety Status Report 2014. Structural Change and Poverty Reduction in Uganda, Economic Development Policy and Research Department, Ministry of Finance, Planning and Economic Development. www.library.health.go.ug/download/file/fid/580728.

MOH, 2010. Annual pharmaceutical sector performance report 2009/10. Ministry of Health, Kampala, Uganda. www.health.go.ug/docs/AHSPR09.pdf.

MOH, 2011. A rapid assessment of morbidity and mortality due to non-communicable diseases in Uganda. Ministry of Health, Kampala, Uganda.

MOH, 2012. Three year strategy and implementation plan 2011/12–2013/14. Quantification and procurement planning unit. Ministry of Health, Kampala, Uganda.

MOH, 2013. Assessment of first region specific essential medicines kit supply system in Uganda. Ministry of Health, Kampala, Uganda. apps.who.int/medicinedocs/documents/s21743en/s21743en.pdf.

MOH, 2014. Annual pharmaceutical performance report 2013/14. Ministry of Health, Kampala, Uganda www.health.go.ug/download/file/fid/1299.

MOH, 2015. Health sector development plan 2015–2020. Ministry of Health, Kampala, Uganda. www. health.go.ug/content/health-sector-development-plan-201516-201920.

MOH, 2016. National performance report on medicines management July–September 2016. Ministry of Health, Kampala, Uganda.

MOH, SURE, 2010. Policy options analysis for Uganda's pharmaceutical supply system. Ministry of Health, Securing Uganda's Right to Essential Medicines, Kampala, Uganda. http://pdf.usaid.gov/pdf_docs/PA00JTFG.pdf.

MSF, 2011. Untangling the web of antiretroviral price reductions. Médecins Sans Frontières, Geneva, Switzerland.

Ross-Degnan, D., Laing, R., Santoso, B., Ofori-Adjei, D., Lamoureux, C., Hogerzeil, H., 1997. Improving pharmaceutical use in primary care in developing countries: a critical review of experience and lack of experience. International Conference on Improving Use of Medicines, Chiang Mai, Thailand.

Rowe, A.K., de Savigny, D., Lanata, C.F., Victora, C.G., 2005. How can we achieve and maintain high-quality performance of health workers in low-resource settings? Lancet 366 (9490), 1026–1035.

Seidman, G., Atun, R., 2017. Do changes to supply chains and procurement processes yield cost savings and improve availability of pharmaceuticals, vaccines or health products? A systematic review of evidence from low-income and middle-income countries. BMJ Glob. Health 2 (2), e000243.

SURE, 2013. Report from PFM implementation pilot. Utilizing limited resources better through Pharmaceutical Financial Management. Management Sciences for Health, Securing Uganda's Rights to Essential Medicines, Kampala, Uganda.

SURE, 2014. Securing Uganda's right to essential medicines program: final report 2009–2014 submitted to USAID. Management Sciences for Health, Arlington, VA. https://www.msh.org/our-work/.../securing-ugandans-right-to-essential-medicines.

Trap, B., Ladwar, D.O., Oteba, M.O., Embrey, M., Khalid, M., Wagner, A.K., 2016. Supervision, performance assessment, and recognition strategy (SPARS)-a multipronged intervention strategy for strengthening medicines management in Uganda: method presentation and facility performance at baseline. J. Pharm. Policy Pract. 9 (1), 1.

UAC, 2015. The HIV and AIDS Uganda Country Progress Report 2014. Uganda AIDS Commission, Kampala, Uganda. www.library.health.go.ug/publications/service-delivery-diseases.../hivaids/hiv-and-aids.

UHSC, 2015. Field study of the quality of data submitted by facilities June–October, 2015. ARV ordering and reporting. Management Sciences for Health, Uganda Health Supply Chain Project, Kampala, Uganda.

UNAIDS (2016). How AIDS changed everything. MDG 6. 15 years, 15 lessons of hope from the AIDS response. www.unaids.org/en/resources/.../MDG6_15years-15lessons-fromtheAIDSresponse.

Windisch, R., Waiswa, P., Neuhann, F., Scheibe, F., de Savigny, D., 2011. Scaling up antiretroviral therapy in Uganda: using supply chain management to appraise health systems strengthening. Globalization and health 7 (1).

CHAPTER 9

Equitable Access to Biosimilars: An Overview

Khurram Rehman*, Nadeem Irfan Bukhari, Zaheer-Ud-Din Babar†,‡**
*Lahore Pharmacy College (A Project of Lahore Medical and Dental College), Lahore, Pakistan
**Punjab University College of Pharmacy, University of the Punjab, Lahore, Pakistan
†University of Huddersfield, Queensgate, Huddersfield, United Kingdom
‡University of Auckland, Auckland, New Zealand

9.1 INTRODUCTION

In the twenty-first century, the outbreak of new diseases (SARS, EBOLA, ZIKA) and research on past diseases (HIV/AIDS, Cancer, etc.) inspire scientists to rapidly discover new cures. Demand for the successful treatments for previous but escalating diseases, like cancer, the prevalence of which alone is expected to increase worldwide from 11.3 million in 2007 to 15.3 million in 2030 (David and Carrie, 2014), also calls for research on the new treatment modalities. As a result, the pharmaceutical scientists are exploring the field of "biologics" by exploiting the processes available in the living organisms. In general, a biologic is biopharmaceutical product made from the natural sources, including humans, animals or microorganisms. Biologics or biopharmaceuticals are proteins or derivatives of proteins that can modulate the immune response, regulate the inflammation and could also support the tumour defence mechanism (Boehncke and Radeke, 2009).

Currently, the biologics comprises a growing portion in the pharmaceutical industry. In US alone biologics are expected to grow to a cost of between $200 and $210 billion by 2016 (Bradford and Gary, 2014; Chow, 2014). The research and production of biologics are costly, since require stringent controlled environment and advance technologies (Bradford and Gary, 2014; Chow, 2014). Nevertheless, several biologics are under research or clinical trials while few biologics has found way to market as successful treatment for several diseases but are at patent stage (Bradford and Gary, 2014; Francois and Pascal, 2015). Albeit biologics are important lifesavings medicinal products but not without a price, healthcare costs for biologics are unsustainable for common consumer. Consequently, biologics either are not available or have limited availability in several countries due to their high price and affordability by common consumers (Bradford and

Equitable Access to High-Cost Pharmaceuticals
http://dx.doi.org/10.1016/B978-0-12-811945-7.00009-9

Gary, 2014; Francois and Pascal, 2015). Fortunately, for many of the biologics patent expiry is approaching which has opened the debate for their new alternatives like "biosimilars" and their easy availability to the patients (Bradford and Gary, 2014; Francois and Pascal, 2015).

Biosimilar is a biotherapeutic product which has similar active substance and is similar in terms of quality, safety, potency and efficacy to, though its name, appearance and packaging may differ to those of already licensed reference biotherapeutic (originator) product (Bradford and Gary, 2014). In real terms, there should be no clinically significant difference between the biosimilar products in terms of safety, potency and thus, such product require analytical studies to demonstrate its "biosimilarity" (Surya and Karen, 2015). World health organization (WHO), United States food and drug administration (FDA) and European medicine agency (EMA) and regulatory authorities of other respective countries are now opening up to the idea of biosimilars with a goal to assure their access to patients and to ensure efficient and secure treatments similar to their originators but at significantly reduced prices (Haustein et al., 2012; Blackstone and Fuhr, 2013; Bradford and Gary, 2014; Francois and Pascal, 2015).

Biosimilars have the potential to provide reduce healthcare economic burden, which may allow ease in access to other biologic therapies and may result into the development of innovative drugs. The leading organizations such as EMA, FDA and WHO have issued the guidelines for the development and approval of biosimilars (WHO, 2009; CHMP, 2014; FDA, 2015b). To receive biosimilar approval, a proposed biologic must demonstrate biosimilarity, that is, it must not demonstrate clinically meaningful difference from the originator product in terms of effectiveness, safety, purity and potency. Establishing biosimilarity between a biologic with its respective originator requires testing by collection of data of the candidate biologic and its originator product through a rigorous step-wise comparison in terms of their analytical, functional, and clinical profiles. The biosimilar products, as lower-cost alternatives of biological product have the potential to provide savings for healthcare systems, especially in countries where affordability of drugs is an issue (Christian et al., 2017). Due to the increasing impact of biosimilars in global healthcare system, biosimilarity is currently an area of discussion among clinical researchers, policy makers and physicians (Dorner and Kay, 2015; Christian et al., 2017). In this context this systematic review of literature was performed. The aim was to review the literature on the access of biosimilars to the patients and the factors involved in controlling its availability.

9.2 METHODOLOGY

The literature search was undertaken between years 2006 and 2017 to identify published peer-reviewed articles and policy papers published by reliable governing bodies such as US Food and Drug Administration (FDA), World Health Organization (WHO), European Medicine Agency (EMA), etc. The databases for search included: Google Scholar, Cochrane Library, Springer links, Science Direct, PubMed, and Medline. The timeline of year 2006–2017 effectively covers all the phases of biosimilars from manufacturing up till market access. Newspaper clippings, general online articles or articles which are not published in English were excluded from the study. The exclusion and inclusion criterion of the study is given in following Table 9.1.

A total of around 2964 articles were identified using database searches for the relevant literature. Articles which were duplicates and titles/abstracts unrelated to health economic evaluations of hospital and pharmacy services (and methodologies utilized) were removed based on our inclusion and exclusion criteria provided in Table 9.1, The number of papers found against

Table 9.1 Exclusion and inclusion criteria of the study

Inclusion/Exclusion	Category	Criteria
Inclusion	Year of publications	2006–2017
	Publication type	Full text articles published in peer reviewed scientific journals
	Language of publication	English
	Region of research	Global
	Medicine type	Biosimilars (generic biologics)
	Methodology	Review of published research and review articles in indexed journals
	Topic of research	Patients' access to biosimilars, cost of biosimilars, its market availability and barrier towards this availability
Exclusion	Publication type	Online articles which are not present in indexed journals and the news reports
	Publication language	Articles published in languages other than English

Table 9.2 Keywords used and the number of publications found from different databases

Keywords	Number of Publications found
Biosimilars (or biosimilar) access	469
Biosimilars (or biosimilar) availability	337
Biosimilars (or biosimilar) cost	740
Biosimilars (or biosimilar) market	787
Biosimilars (or biosimilar) patient access	364
Biosimilars (or biosimilar) patient availability	276

each key word is given in Table 9.2. All the articles from which this review has been extracted are given as references.

9.3 MARKET SCOPE AND ACCESS OF BIOSIMILARS

Currently, only few biological products are registered as biosimilars and are available in global market, therefore the data available for review is also limited. The majority of the biosimilars have been registered and commercialized in Europe (Francois and Pascal, 2015). Apart from Europe and United States, Japan, Australia and some other countries have also introduced biosimlars as alternatives for biological pharmaceuticals in their markets (Rumore et al., 2016). Biosimilars market scope is expected to increase tremendously and the factors influencing this growth are the availability of new innovative technology, market competition, patent expiry, production of efficient, safe medicines at affordable prices, and the worldwide demand (Tsiftsoglou et al., 2013). One of the key factors in the sudden interest in biosimilars research is a huge number of patented biological products are near their patent expiry in upcoming years.

This cluster of patent expiry is termed as "Patent Cliff" (Ghia et al., 2015). This patent cliff would result into an abrupt drop in sales as the biological products reach end of their patent life. The expiration of these patents will encourage manufacturers to develop biosimilars and have access the multi-billion dollars of biologics medicine market (Ghia et al., 2015). Biologics which are near their patent expiry or have been expired in the period of "Patent Cliff" are shown in Table 9.3. The success of biosimilars could influence the sustainability of pharmaceutical business in the next decade. The major competitors will be the big pharmaceutical companies that are interested in increasing their market profit through high prices, therefore discounted price of biosimilars compared to originators is likely to be lesser than desirable (Pasina et al., 2016).

Table 9.3 Estimated expiry year of the patents of biological products

Expiry Year	Patent Products	Drug	Indication
2013	Avonex	Interferon beta-1a	Cytokine used to treat multiple sclerosis
	Byetta	Glucagon-like peptide-1	Hormone used against diabetes mellitus
	Epogen	Epoetin alpha	Artificial protein to produce red blood cells
2014	Remicade	Infliximab	Monoclonal antibody to treat autoimmune diseases
	Novolog	Insulin aspart	Fast acting insulin used against diabetes mellitus
2015	Lantus	Insulin glargine	Artificial hormone used against diabetes mellitus
	Herceptin	Trastuzumab	Monoclonal antibody used against breast cancer
	Neulastra	Pegfilgrastim	Recombinant human granulocyte colony-stimulating factor that simulates white blood cells
	Synagis	Palivizumab	Monoclonal antibody used to prevent respiratory syncytial virus infection
2016	Humira	Adalimumab	Monoclonal antibody used to treat rheumatoid arthritis
	Aranesp	Drabepoetin alfa	Synthetic erythropoietin used to treat anemia
	Enbrel	Etanercept	Protein used to target tumor necrosis factor
	Rituxan	Rituximab	Monoclonal antibody used to treat leukemia and lymphoma
2017	Avastin	Bevacizumab	Monoclonal antibody that is an angiogenesis inhibitor
	Pegasys	Pegylated interferon alfa-2a	Proteins used to treat viral infections including hepatitis C and HIV

9.4 PRICE CONTROL AND PATIENTS ACCESS

The biologics' expenditure is the largest pharmaceutical budgetary spending (Schumack et al., 2014) and due to expensive nature of biologics, patient adherence to treatment is an issue, as they would hesitate in receiving such expensive therapy or refilling' prescriptions. Recently a survey showed that 94% of respondents from low-income and 63% from middle-income countries declared high treatment expenditure as a reason behind hesitation in receiving trastuzumab as adjuvant treatment for patients with breast cancer (Christian et al., 2017). In another survey, conducted in the United States and emerging markets (Brazil, Mexico, Turkey, and Russia), 37%–49% of respondents ascribed infrequent prescribing of trastuzumab as treatment for breast cancer to the lack of insurance coverage, and 37%–44% to scarce drug availability (Cherny et al., 2016). The high cost of biological drugs is considered as a common barrier to prescribing and adherence across all clinical settings. The "high out-of-pocket treatment cost for patient" is a fact that is acknowledged as a barrier to use biologics in the neoadjuvant or adjuvant settings (Cherny et al., 2016). A survey showed that out-of-pocket treatment costs also vary, with patients in some Western and Eastern European countries responsible for the full cost of treatment or >50% after reimbursement, particularly for biologics like pertuzumab, and lapatinib (Christian et al., 2017). Issues related to treatment costs, drug funding, and reimbursement would lead to cancelled or delayed treatment (Cherny et al., 2016).

The demand for cost-effective biological products is growing. Steps are needed to ensure affordable access to biosimilars (alternatives of biologics) for patients suffering from diseases like arthritis, diabetes and cancer. The market access of biosimilars for these diseases would also be economically beneficial as it is believed that biosimilars would be around 10%–40% less expensive than their counter biological products (Rumore et al., 2016), which would be sufficient for adoption of biosimilars in hospital settings as a replacement therapy for biological reference product (Rumore et al., 2016). Biosimilars have also reported to influence the reduction of market price of couple of biological reference products (as shown in Table 9.4). Therefore, the competition among biosimilars and innovator biologics would be interesting once the biosimilars gain full access to the market that could result into massive price reduction of innovator biologics, thus leading to improved patient access.

From year 2009 to 2019, around $50 billion of the market value of biologics in the United States alone will lose patent protection. For

Table 9.4 Biological reference products which market price reduced as a result of biosimilar products

Biologics innovators	Price reduction (%)	Country
Erythropoietin	33	Germany
Infliximab	70	Norway

example, Genentech would end up losing $10.7 billion in sales with patent expiration for Avastin, Herceptin, and Rituxan (Blackstone and Fuhr, 2013; Ghia et al., 2015). This would result into a gap and opportunity for biosimilars for their access in market resulting into more reduction in biological patents and reference products. The Biologic Price Competition and Innovation Act (BPCIA) is responsible for providing affordable access to biological products including biosimilars (Rumore et al., 2016). Price control over biosimilars may increase their affordability and improve patient access. An independent analysis in 2014 predicted that the availability of biosimilars would result in a $44.2 billion reduction in biologic spending between 2014 and 2024, or approximately 4% of total biologic spending over the period (Surya and Karen, 2015). Promise of reduction in biologics prices have been source of encouragement for the biosimilars, especially in case of expensive oncology treatments. A study showed that patients suffering from lymphoma or plasma disorder receiving treatment of Tbo-filgrastim, a biosimilar with granulocyte colony stimulating factor activity, resulted into a significant cost savings of $260,000 based on the whole sale price of granulocyte colony-stimulating factor in USA (Avalos, 2015). Across European countries, availability of biosimilar granulocyte colony-stimulating factor have resulted in an increase in market access especially in Croatia, Hungary, Romania, Czech Republic and Belgium (Khraishi et al., 2016). Biosimilars have been widely encouraged across the Europe and are being approved to ease their market access which would lead to cost savings in pharmacotherapy related to biologics. Some of the biosimilars approved in European countries are given in Table 9.5.

Table 9.5 Approved biosimilars by European countries

Product name	Active ingredient	Approval year
Binocrit	Epoetin alfa	2007
Silapo	Epoetin alfa	2007
Retacrit	Epoetin alfa	2007
Benepali	Etanercept	2016
Accofil	Filgrastim	2014
Biogastim	Filgrastim	2008
Grastofil	Filgrastim	2013
Flixabi	Infliximab	2016
Infledra	Infliximab	2013
Insulin glargine	Abasglar	2014

The WHO Prequalification of Medicines Program ensures that medicines purchased by international procurement agencies (e.g., UNICEF) for the purpose of distribution of medicine in low-income countries meet acceptable standards of quality, safety, and efficacy. The Lancet Commission on Essential Medicines recommended that the prequalification program should expand the range of essential medicines, including biosimilars. The incentive for governments to embrace biosimilars is to reduce healthcare economic burden, which in turn should increase access and improve population health-care outcomes (Lancet, 2017). However, the introduction of biosimilars has not resulted into significant reduction of health care economic burden as it happened in case of generic drugs. This might be because the development of biosimilars is more costly and time consuming as compared to generics. Still there are many examples such as in Norway, there has been significant reduction in healthcare economic burden by switching to biosimilar versions. WHO prequalification will hopefully increase competition in the biosimilar market to further reduce the price and increase access to these medicines in low-income countries (Lancet, 2017).

9.5 BARRIERS TOWARDS ACCESS TO BIOSIMILARS

Despite the evolution and growth, the development of biosimilars continues to be expensive and time consuming, as they need to meet technical, manufacturing, and analytical challenges. In addition to this, the biosimilars also face regulatory, clinical and commercialization challenges (Rathore, 2009; Bui et al., 2015). Biosimilars developers will need to adapt to the regulatory criteria that will continue to evolve as the biosimilars increase their market share. Thus, there are concerns and doubts regarding the ability of biosimilars to be commercially successful, especially in developed countries where biosimilars must go through stringent and evolving regulatory processes (Konara et al., 2016). Following are some of the key elements which serve as barriers for the access to biosimilars.

9.5.1 High Expenditure for Development of Biosimilars

The development and manufacturing of biologics, as well as biosimilars, is a highly complex, time-consuming and costly procedure that is sensitive to a number of determinants, and specific to a particular product. Even minor changes in manufacturing procedure may lead to significant variations of the cellular systems used for biologic production, and may affect stability, and biology of the end product. Additional expenditures are incurred to meet the strict environmental control, complex quality assessment procedures during development of the biologics (Bui et al., 2015; Surya and Karen, 2015) and the stringent requirements of the regulatory authorities (WHO, 2009; CHMP, 2014; FDA, 2015b). This is because any variation in a biologic from its reference product can potentially affect the tolerability and efficacy of the marketed product, as well as can increase the risk of adverse immune responses. Additionally, the proposed biosimilar has the same sequence of primary amino acids as that of the originator and the both must be similar in terms of structure, safety, mechanism of action and biological activity. Hence biosimilars require implementation of dedicated analytical and functional assessments.

Furthermore, drug regulatory authorities require that there should be no clinically significant difference between the biosimilar and the reference drug in terms of safety, and potency which again warrant development of validated analytical studies to demonstrate their biosimilarity. The development of biosimilars also involves expensive clinical studies that are conducted by using appropriate and sensitive study populations and endpoints to demonstrate similarity between the proposed biosimilar and originator products in terms of their safety, immunogenicity and efficacy profiles (WHO, 2009; CHMP, 2014; FDA, 2015b). All of the above serve as the major barriers for biologics and their biosimilar to access and availability to the patients in need.

9.5.2 Stringent Regulatory Regulations, Legislations and Requirements for Biosimilars

The stringent regulatory regulations, legislations and requirements concerned with biologics and biosimilars are the other factors acting as barriers for access to biosimilars. Although the regulatory guidelines for biosimilars is well defined but are continuously evolving and there is still disagreement on which studies must be implemented to approve a biosimilar. Overall, uncertainties remain the key issue surrounding biosimilars. Policy makers, physicians, and other stakeholders, that have interest in economic burden of health care system, must address the issues raised by health authorities in this field. The EMA first established a regulatory pathway for the approval of biosimilars in 2005, taking a conservative approach. Since then, guidelines have been updated and revised several times, and a specific guideline for biosimilars was issued in 2013 (EMA, 2012; Dorner and Kay, 2015; FDA, 2015a). Due to these repeated revisions of regulations, uncertainty among policy makers, and difference of opinion in regulatory bodies of Europe and USA, there are no uniform guidelines to follow.

9.5.3 Requirement of Distinguishing Nomenclature for Generic and Originator Brands

Unlike the drug other than the biologics where nonproprietary names may be used in market, a common nonproprietary name cannot be used for biologics to ascribe the adverse events to specific products. Thus a specific nomenclature is required to distinguish biosimilars from their originators and from each other to ensure accurate prescribing and avoid confusion among biosimilars and originators (Dorner and Kay, 2015). To achieve this goal, it would be more appropriate to use the brand name, the international nonproprietary names (INNs) plus the brand name, or some other unique identifier (Corrado et al., 2017). Alternatively, WHO has proposed a 4-digit code for a biologic qualifier that could be used to distinguish originators from biosimilars (WHO, 2012).

The European Commission issued the Directive 2012/52/EU, which requires the use of brand names "to ensure clear identification of biological medicinal products (EC, 2012)," a requirement that also applies to biosimilars. In addition, the batch number is required to be notified to the regulatory authority to ensure proper traceability because there is a risk of a product drift (unintentional changes during manufacturing of biosimilars from the original product or previous batch of biosimilar). The United Stated food and drug administration (FDA) regulations have created confusion regarding nomenclature for biosimilars (Rumore et al., 2016). According to these regulations nonproprietary (generic) names of biosimilars should contain a unique suffix identifier (e.g., filgrastim-sndz). This may cause confusion among prescriber, pharmacist, patients and is also resulted into patent litigation that is influencing the delay in biosimilars entering into the US market (e.g., filgrastim-sndz vs filgrastim) (Rumore et al., 2016).

9.5.4 Biobetters and Next Generation Biologics

The performance of biosimilars have also been impacted by the fact that competition is limited to the first-generation reference products. The market entry of biobetters and next generation biologics is an important consideration in evaluating the market impact of biosimilars and their potential savings to the health-care system (Beck, 2011; Ghia et al., 2015; Surya and Karen, 2015; Kuyucak and Kayser, 2017). As biosimilars are exactly similar to the originator product, the biobetters are intentionally modified as compared to the original molecule to produce better quality, safety and efficacy (Beck, 2011; Ghia et al., 2015). This difference between the biosimilars and biobetters has a significant regulatory perspective because unlike biosimilars, biobetters will be registered as new innovative medicines. Similarly next generation biologics have alterations in their molecules to improve their immune function, half life and are capable of triggering other mechanism of actions (Beck, 2011). Thus the next generation of biologics biobetters has better safety quality and efficacy from the previous generation product (Ghia et al., 2015; Surya and Karen, 2015; Kuyucak and Kayser, 2017). If biosimilars gain a substantial share of sales from their referenced products (of previous generation), their share of overall patient treatments may be limited if physicians and patients preferred biobetters or next generation of biological products (Grabowski et al., 2014).

9.5.5 Patients' Concerns

Patients are known to show reservations about whether biosimilars are as effective as their originators and about their adverse effects. Considering the patients' concerns the UK National Rheumatoid Arthritis Society has welcomed the entry biosimilars into the market but has also highlights the importance of prescribing biosimilars based on clinical reasons and not merely as cost saving alternative (Corrado et al., 2017).

9.6 KNOWLEDGE OF HEALTHCARE PROFESSIONALS ABOUT BIOSIMILARS

The use of biosimilars presents challenges for healthcare professionals in terms of biosimilarity, interchangeability, risk management and switchability. Limited literature is available on healthcare professionals' knowledge and views of biosimilars. Pharmacists should be knowledgeable about the particularities and key issues of biosimilars because they will play a key role for the introduction of biosimilars in clinical practice. Given that the current legal framework under which substituting biologic products is evolving and that there are economic concerns, pharmacists have to remain vigilant and ensure their regular continuing education in order to provide the safe and optimal use of biologic products and biosimilars in their clinical practice (Ade et al., 2017).

As biosimilars are more complex than generic small molecules, the need to provide education to patient is also very vital. For this purpose, a clear specific nomenclature and full transparency of labelling may be helpful in increasing the confidence of both physicians and patients. As more studies are being conducted on biosimilars and the recommendations are also evolving with time based on evidence-based data, this will help build confidence of both healthcare professionals and patients, and widen their understanding of biosimilar use (Rumore et al., 2016; Ade et al., 2017).

9.7 CONCLUSION

The global demand for health services has increased dramatically in recent years due to emergence of new illnesses and medical technologies and changes in health care system. Biologics have revolutionized the treatment of many life threatening diseases such as cancer, rheumatoid arthiritis, multiple sclerosis, etc. Over the past, biologics have played a significant role in healthcare around the world and are considered as lifesavings drug products.

With the use of biologics rapidly increasing, patent expiries, and the low numbers of competitors, companies are presented with a new attractive market with production of biosimilars. The current healthcare scenario requires more therapeutic choices for patients and physicians. The biosimilars are now viewed as a potential source of cost savings in the healthcare system. Therefore, the reduced costs of biosimilars together with clinical reassurance will enable broader acceptance and usage of biosimilars in most markets. But still there are many challenges that biosimilars face to access the market. There is a need to increase the confidence of health care professionals and patients on biosimilar usage. Many new firms entering the biological space appear to be focused on next generation biologicals or 'biobetters' rather than biosimilars in the recognition of these dynamic developments. It remains to be seen how competition will evolve for the more complex biological products with patent expirations as well as biosimilars and biobetters on the horizon in the case of the European and US markets. In conclusion, the shared opinion is that, although cost savings are highly desirable but the prescribing of biosimilars should be based on clinical evidence; the approval process for biosimilars needs to place tolerability and efficacy, supported by scientifically sound evidence, as the highest priorities.

REFERENCES

Ade, A., Bourdon, O., Bussieres, J.F., 2017. A survey of pharmacists' knowledge and views of biosimilars in Quebec and France. Ann. Pharm. Fr. 75, 267–275.

Avalos, R.B., 2015. Bring on the biosimilars! Biol. Blood Marrow Transplant. 21, 18589–21862.

Beck, A., 2011. Biosimilar, biobetter and next generation therapeutic antibodies. mAbs 3, 107–110.

Blackstone, A.E., Fuhr, Jr., P.J., 2013. The economics of biosimilars. Am. Health Drug Benefits 6, 469–478.
Boehncke, W.H., Radeke, H.H., 2009. Biologics in general medicine. Springer, New York.
Bradford, R.H., Gary, H.L., 2014. Biosimilars: a cure to the U.S. health care cost conundrum? Blood Rev. 28, 263–268.
Bui, L.A., Hurst, S., Finch, G.L., Ingram, B., Jacoba, I.A., Kirchoff, C.F., et al., 2015. Key considerations in the preclinical development of biosimilars. Drug Discov. Today 20, 3–15.
Cherny, N., Sullivan, R., Torode, J., Saar, M., Eniu, A., 2016. ESMO European Consortium Study on the availability, out-of-pocket costs and accessibility of antineo-plastic medicines in Europe. Ann. Oncol. 27, 1423–1443.
CHMP, 2014. Committee for medicinal products for human use: guideline on similar biological medicinal products. European Medicinies Agency, London, England.
Chow, S.C., 2014. Biosimilars design and analysis of follow on biologics. CRC Press, Boca Raton, Florida.
Christian, J., Philip, L., Ira, J., 2017. Evolving landscape of human epidermal growth factor receptor 2-positive breast cancer treatment and the future of biosimilars. The Breast. 32, 199–216.
Corrado, B., Pier, L.M., Giovanni, L., 2017. Comparing originator biologics and biosimilars: a review of the relevant issues. Clin. Ther. 39, 1026–1039.
David, H., Carrie, T., 2014. Pharmacoeconomics of cancer therapies: considerations with the introduction of biosimilars. Semin Oncol. 41, 13–20.
Dorner, T., Kay, J., 2015. Biosimilars in rheumatology: current perspectives and lessons learnt. Nat. Rev. Rheumatol. 11, 713–724.
EC, 2012.Commission implementing directive 2012/52/EU of 20 December 2012 laying down measures to facilitate the recognition of medical prescriptions issued in another Member State European Commission.
EMA, 2012. EMA/CHMP/BMWP/86289/ 2010: Guideline on immunogenicity assessment of monoclonal antibod-ies intended for in vivo use. European Medicine Agency, London.
FDA, 2015a. Biosimilars: questions and answers regarding implementation of the biologics price competition and innovation act of 2009: guid-ance for industry. Food and Drug Administration, Silver Spring, Maryland.
FDA, 2015b. US Food and drug administration: scientific considerations in demonstrating biosimilarity to a reference product: guidance for industry. US Department of Health and Human Services, Food and Drug Administration, Center for Drug Evaluation and Research (CDER), Center for Biologics Evaluation and Research (CBER), Silver Spring, Maryland.
Francois, B., Pascal, P., 2015. A long war begins: biosimilars versus patented biologics. J. Med. Econ. 18, 1071–1073.
Ghia, C., Shah, D., Rambhad, G., Mubashir, A., Upadhyaya, S., 2015. Biologics, biosimilars, intended copies and the era of competitive medicine. Apollo Med. 12, 103–111.
Grabowski, H., Guha, R., Salgado, M., 2014. Biosimilar competition: lessons from europe. Drug Discov. 13, 99–100.
Haustein, R., De Millas, C., Hoer, A., 2012. Saving money in the european healthcare systems with biosimilar. Generics Biosimilars Initiat J. 1, 120–126.
Khraishi, M., Stead, D., Lukas, M., Scotte, F., Schmid, H., 2016. Biosimilars: a multidisciplinary perspective. Clin. Ther. 38, 1238–1249.
Konara, S.C., Barnard, T.R., Damian, H., Siegel, E., Ferro, V., 2016. The tortoise and the hare: evolving regulatory landscapes for biosimilars. Trends Biotechnol. 34, 70–83.
Kuyucak, S., Kayser, V., 2017. Biobetters from an integrated computational/experimental approach. Comput. Struct. Biotechnol. J. 15, 138–145.
Lancet, 2017. Improving access to biosimilars in low-income countries. The Lancet 389, 1860.

Pasina, L., Casadei, G., Nobili, A., 2016. Biological agents and biosimilars: essential information for the internist. Eur. J. Intern. Med. 33, 28–35.
Rathore, A.S., 2009. Follow-on protiend products: scientific issues, developments and challenges. Trends Biotechnol. 27, 698–705.
Rumore, M.M., Cobb, E., Sullivan, M., Wittman, D., 2016. Biosimilars: opportunities and challenges for nurse practitioners. J. Nurse Pract.V 12, 181–191.
Schumack, G.T., Li, E.C., Suda, K.J., Matusaik, L.M., Hunkler, R.J., Vermeulen, L.C., et al., 2014. National trends in prescription drug expenditures and projections for 2014. Am. J. Health Syst. Pharm. 71, 482–499.
Surya, C.S., Karen, M.B., 2015. The enconomic implications of biosimilars. Am. J. Manag. Care 21, 331–340.
Tsiftsoglou, A.S., Ruiz, S., Schneider, C.K., 2013. Development and regulation of biosimilars: current status and future challenges. Bio. Drugs 27, 203–211.
WHO, 2009. Expert Committee on biological standardization: guidelines on evaluation of similar biotherapeutic products (SBPs). World Health Organization, Geneva, Switzerland.
WHO, 2012. 55th Consultation on inter-national nonproprietary names for pharmaceutical substances. World Health Organization, Geneva.

CHAPTER 10

Access to High-Cost Medicines in Europe

Sabine Vogler
Gesundheit Österreich GmbH (GÖG/Austrian Public Health Institute), Vienna, Austria

10.1 INTRODUCTION

Access to high-cost medicines has become a major issue in the political debate in European countries, including high-income countries. With a rising number of new premium priced medicines offered to, at least, some of the European markets, even high-income countries have been struggling to develop approaches to ensure access to such high-priced medicines to their population. This is jeopardising the financial sustainability of the pharmaceutical systems. Also, lower-income countries in Europe have increasingly been confronted with the non-availability of high-priced medicines since they are not able to pay for them.

This chapter will provide an overview of the current situation related to affordable access to high-cost medicines in European countries. It will discuss different strategies that European countries have chosen and are discussing individually as well as in cooperation with other countries to ensure access to high-priced medicines.

Information provided in this chapter is based on the literature published in peer-reviewed journals as well as grey literature known to the author. In some cases, the author has drawn information from unpublished data provided by members of Pharmaceutical Pricing and Reimbursement Information (PPRI) network of competent authorities (Vogler et al., 2014).

10.2 DEFINITIONS

10.2.1 High-Cost Medicines

The concept of high-cost medicines has not yet been clearly defined internationally (WHO Collaborating Centre for Pharmaceutical Pricing and Reimbursement Policies, 2013). In some cases, it refers to, or includes, speciality medicines and highly complex medicines (Pan American Health Organization, 2010), including orphan medicines.

Equitable Access to High-Cost Pharmaceuticals
http://dx.doi.org/10.1016/B978-0-12-811945-7.00010-5

Frequently, high-cost medicines appear to be used as a synonym for high-priced medicines. This is a reasonable approach since the high expenditure (i.e. high cost) of these medicines is often attributable to their high prices. However, since expenditure is the result of both price and volume, high cost (high expenditure) can also be caused by high dispensing volumes of low-priced medicines (Vogler et al., 2016d). For the purpose of this book, high-cost medicines refer only to products whose high prices cause high expenditure for public payers; the term 'high cost' will thus be used as a synonym to 'high-priced' or 'premium-priced' medicines.

Quantitative figures to define high-cost medicines are not common in the European countries though some countries (the Netherlands—till 2012, Slovakia) have had specific lists of high-cost medicines (WHO Regional Office for Europe, 2015). In a report, the Regional Office for Europe of the World Health Organization (WHO) applied a broad definition of a new, premium-priced medicine as one whose acquisition cost is greater than 10,000€ per patient per year for the public payer, and which replaces an existing medicine (also covered by the public payer) (Permanand and Bak Pedersen, 2015).

In this chapter, the term 'innovative medicines' will not be used, since, as to be shown below, the added value of some of these medicines is not as high as expected. These medicines will be referred to as 'new medicines'.

10.2.2 European Countries

Europe has approximately 50 countries. The number differs somewhat depending on the classification used (United Nations, for instance, also includes Central Asian countries). This chapter will focus on the Member States of the European Union (EU) and of the European Free Trade Association (EFTA) such as Norway and Switzerland. According to the latest World Bank classification (as of July 2016), 26 of the 28 EU Member States and all EFTA countries are high-income economies; the EU Member States Bulgaria and Romania are considered as upper-middle-income economies (The World Bank, 2016).

10.3 CHALLENGES OF AFFORDABLE ACCESS TO HIGH-COST MEDICINES

Despite the relative wealth of many European countries compared to other economies, the world over, these countries have also been observing major and increasing limitations related to affordable and sustainable access to high-cost medicines during the last few years.

10.3.1 Limitations in Availability

The availability of medicines on the market varies among European countries (Vogler et al., 2008; Kanavos et al., 2011; Carone et al., 2012; Bouvy and Vogler, 2013; van Harten et al., 2016). In particular, lower-income economies and small countries (so-called small markets) appear to face major difficulties in getting (timely) access to high-cost medicines.

Limited or delayed availability of medicines on the market can result from a company's decision to bring a product on the market at a later stage, or to not market it at all. Marketing authorisation holders apply strategic launch sequences in response to the practice of external price referencing—EPR (i.e. price setting based on the prices in other countries) that authorities commonly use in European countries (Vogler et al., 2016a).

Delays might also result from pricing and reimbursement procedures. According to the latest available WAIT (Patients Waiting to Access Innovative Therapies) report produced by the European pharmaceutical industry association, EFPIA, the time period between the marketing authorisation and the pricing/reimbursement decision ranged from 116 to 515 days for a sample of 66 outpatient medicines, centrally authorised by EMA during 2008–2010, in 20 European countries (EFPIA, 2011). It was argued that these differences are attributable to delays in the pricing and reimbursement decisions. At the same time, marketing authorisation holders were also accountable for delays in regulatory processes because their dossiers were not complete or did not contain the required information (Bouvy and Vogler, 2013).

Even if authorities had taken a pricing and reimbursement decision, medicines might not have been launched immediately. Based on the IMS data, the indicator 'time to market' (time between marketing authorisation and actual sales of more than 1% of the maximum sales in the first 24 months after market entry) was, on average, approximately 8 months but varied among European countries. It ranged from Germany (2 months) and Austria, Denmark, Finland and Sweden (4–5 months) to Belgium (11 months) and Italy and Portugal (12 months) (Panteli et al., 2016).

Furthermore, companies may decide not to market their products at all in lower-resourced countries because the public payer cannot afford them at the price the marketing authorisation holder asks for or because the market is not attractive due to its small size (Heads of Medicines Agencies, 2007; Kanavos et al., 2011).

In addition, limited availability can be attributed to shortages of medicines that were initially marketed but cannot be supplied. Shortages, again, have different reasons: besides global manufacturing capacity problems, one cause is parallel trade that is allowed and encouraged within the European Union and that incentivises traders to make use of the arbitrage between lower- and higher-priced countries (Kanavos et al., 2011; Gray and Manasse, 2012; Pauwels et al., 2014b; De Weerdt et al., 2015).

10.3.2 High Prices and Unsustainable Funding

The Hepatitis C medicine sofosbuvir has been frequently mentioned as an example for a high-priced and unaffordable medicine. In fact, research revealed that its prices were variable and unaffordable globally: if a patient had to pay for the treatment out of pocket, the total cost of a full course of sofosbuvir alone would be equivalent to 1 year or more of average earnings for individuals in 12 of the 30 investigated countries, thereof several European countries. Across the 22 European countries of that study, the purchasing power parity (PPP)-adjusted ex-factory price of a 12-week course of sofosbuvir ranged from USD 28,092 in Norway to USD 101,063 in Poland. Overall, Central and Eastern European countries had higher PPP adjusted prices than other European countries. Based on PPP-adjusted total pharmaceutical expenditure and without the cost of ribavirin and other treatment costs, treating the entire Hepatitis C viraemic population with these regimens at the PPP-adjusted prices with a 23% price reduction would amount to at least one-tenth of the current total pharmaceutical expenditure across the countries included in this study, ranging from 10.5% in the Netherlands to 190.5% in Poland (Iyengar et al., 2016).

Besides medicines for the treatment of Hepatitis C, cancer medicines and TNF alpha inhibitors have frequently been referred to in scientific and public debate about premium-priced medicines. In addition, orphan medicines have also raised public attention.

In Europe, one-half of healthcare costs of cancer (on average equivalent to 102€ per citizen in 2009, with large variations ranging from 16€ in Bulgaria to 184€ in Luxembourg) were spent on medication (Luengo-Fernandez et al., 2013). Annual price estimates for three medicines for the treatment of chronic myeloid leukaemia amounted to several thousands of US dollars in the United States as well as European countries (e.g. Germany: USD 54,000 for imatinib, USD 60,000 for nilotinib and USD 90,000 for dasatinib; France: USD 40,000, USD 51,500, USD 71,000, respectively; Norway: USD 50,500, USD 61,000 and USD 82,500, respectively; USD 33,500, USD 33,500 and USD 48,500, respectively) (Abboud et al., 2013). A study that compared the prices of 31 originator cancer medicines of

16 European countries, Australia and New Zealand found large variations, up to 388%, between countries, with Greece and UK prices ranking at the low levels and prices in Sweden, Switzerland and Germany in comparably high ranges (Vogler et al., 2016c). Another study on the actual prices paid for cancer medicines in European countries confirmed high variations between countries (both for list prices and discounted prices) and showed a large difference in the reductions on the list prices, with Spain and Italy being granted higher discounts than some Eastern European countries (van Harten et al., 2016).

The high prices have also been criticised because there is limited evidence about the added value in terms of clinical benefit of these medicines (Fojo and Grady, 2009; Kelly and Smith, 2014). Data from the United States showed, for instance, that eleven of the twelve medicines approved by the Foods and Drugs Administration (FDA) for various cancer indications in 2012 were priced above USD 100,000 per year, and only three of them prolonged survival—two by less than 2 months (Kantarjian et al., 2013).

Orphan medicinal products (OMPs) have particularly high prices. In the EU, these medicines are defined as medicines intended for the diagnosis, prevention or treatment of life-threatening or very serious conditions that affect no more than five in 10,000 people (European Commission, 2016a). As of 2017, the European Commission has authorised 128 orphan medicines for the benefit of patients suffering from rare diseases and has designated 1418 products as orphan medicinal products (EMA, 2017). Cancer medicines account for a relatively high share of orphan medicines (approximately 40% of those 67 orphan medicines that received marketing authorisation between 2002 and 2012; Pauwels et al., 2014b). The fact that meanwhile more than 1000 medicines have been given an OMP designation reflects that despite the low number of patients in each rare disease indication, the collective number of patients living with a rare disease is considerable (27–36 million across the EU) (von der Schulenburg and Frank, 2014).

As of 2009, the average annual cost of 19 orphan medicines per patient was generally around 150,000€ in France, Spain and UK, around 200,000€ in Germany and nearly 250,000€ (Aballea et al., 2010; Michel and Toumi, 2012). A survey of 60 orphan medicines done by EURODIS in 2010 displayed again price variations between 10 responding EU Member States, with price differences up to 160%. Countries with lower prices were Romania, followed by France, Belgium and the Netherlands, and countries with higher prices were Italy, Greece and Denmark. The same survey also showed limited availability of and access of patients to several orphan medicines, particularly those recently authorised in the European countries (especially in Greece, Romania and Spain) (Le Cam, 2010). A study about reimbursed orphan medicines in Belgium found that 13 orphan medicines for which a therapeutic alternative was available had a lower annual cost per patient than nine orphan medicines without such alternatives (Picavet et al., 2011).

10.4 POLICIES OF EUROPEAN COUNTRIES

In the EU, new medicines have to be granted a marketing authorisation by the European Medicines Agency EMA (through a centralised procedure, valid for most new medicines with added value, or a decentralised procedure), or by the national medicines agencies (less relevant for high-cost medicines). Having received the centralised or decentralised marketing authorisation, pharmaceutical companies can launch their product in any EU Member State. Since they have an interest to have their medicine costs covered, at least partially, by public payers, they will apply for a price of their product and public funding. Pricing and reimbursement decisions are the national responsibility of the EU Member States.

In their efforts to grant access to high-cost medicines while aiming to keep the healthcare systems sustainable, it is observed that European countries tend to particularly apply the following strategies or consider an increased future use of them: (1) managed entry agreements (MEAs) and similar discount arrangements, (2) generation of evidence to better assess the benefit of medicines (e.g. through a Health Technology Assessment—HTA), (3) specific funding models for high-cost medicines, (4) horizon scanning and (5) searching for cost optimisation through biosimilar medicines. According to a 2014 survey of policy makers in European countries, MEA and HTA were reported to be key approaches in order to deal with high-cost though several countries also reported that they did not yet have specific policies for the pricing and reimbursement for these medicines (WHO Regional Office for Europe, 2015; Zimmermann et al., 2015).

10.4.1 Managed Entry Agreements

The umbrella term MEAs covers different types of arrangements between a manufacturer and a payer/provider that enables access to (coverage/reimbursement of) a health technology subject to specified conditions (WHO

Collaborating Centre for Pharmaceutical Pricing and Reimbursement Policies, 2013). MEAs can take different forms and also vary in complexity. The major distinction is between financial MEAs that are not outcome-based, such as simple discount arrangements, price volume agreements, utilisation caps and performance-based (or outcome-based) MEAs that tie the level of reimbursement to a defined outcome. Examples of the latter are coverage with evidence development (CED), patient access schemes (PAS), risk sharing schemes (RSS), conditional reimbursement and outcome guarantee arrangements (Klemp et al., 2011).

MEAs are particularly used for orphan medicines (Morel et al., 2013a, b; Gammie et al., 2015) and additional high-cost medicines such as those for cancer treatment (Cheema et al., 2012; Pauwels et al., 2014a). The EMINet survey of 2011/2012 showed that antineoplastic and immune-modulating agents represented 37% of all MEAs in the 14 European countries that responded (Ferrario and Kanavos, 2013). There are variations in the number of MEAs between the European countries, with Italy and UK appearing to have the highest number of MEAs. These countries also started to conclude MEAs earlier than other countries. As of today, there appears to be no country in Europe that has not arranged some kind of MEA for high-cost medicines (Adamski et al., 2010; Ferrario and Kanavos, 2013, 2015; Garrison et al., 2013; Iskrov and Stefanov, 2015; Vogler et al., 2017) There are indications that most of the countries opted for financial MEAs: these arrangements are easier to handle than performance-based MEAs (Neumann et al., 2011; Ferrario and Kanavos, 2013).

Stakeholder views on MEAs are mixed (Ferrario and Kanavos, 2013, 2015; Pauwels et al., 2015): For payers and patients, MEAs help ensure (earlier) access to high-cost medicines that are considered not to be affordable otherwise or could only be introduced at a later stage. MEAs allow payers to manage uncertainty since the added therapeutic value has not yet been fully proven for several of the new medicines. Industry uses MEA as a tool for price discrimination since, in a first step, an authority sets prices in its country based on the prices in other countries (policy of EPR). EPR is commonly used, at least for parts of the medicines in Europe and also worldwide (Espin et al., 2011). All 28 EU Member States except Sweden and UK have EPR as a pricing policy defined in their legislation; further European countries (e.g. Iceland, Norway, Switzerland, Turkey) apply EPR as well (Vogler et al., 2016a). With regard to high-cost medicines, EPR is, however, only applied as a starting point in most countries, and a lower price is agreed in negotiations.

These discounted prices agreed in MEAs are always confidential even in the countries (e.g. Scotland, England, Belgium) where the existence and the content of the agreements are public (Vogler et al., 2017). Given the confidentiality of MEAs and discount agreements, authorities have to refer to officially published list prices in other countries, and they thus risk overpaying. Price studies that calculated alternative scenarios taking assumptions on discounts highlighted the potential of discounts. For instance, a price study did a comparison of list prices in European countries and an alternative comparison with discounted prices based on the published mandatory manufacturer discounts in Germany (and list prices in other countries). It showed that Germany was the country that most frequently had the highest prices (in 40% of the 30 medicines), followed by Sweden (23%) and Denmark (13%) in the list price comparison. However, if discounted medicines instead of list prices were considered for Germany, Sweden was most frequently the highest priced country (37% of the medicines), followed by Denmark (17%). Germany ranked third, together with Austria and the UK (10%) (Schneider and Vogler, 2015). Another study that simulated the consideration of discounted prices in Germany, Greece and Ireland (again only based on published mandatory manufacturer discounts that exist in these three countries) showed that the average price in all other countries using EPR according to its current design would drop by 27% after 10 years (Vogler et al., 2016a).

The design of an MEA, even in the case of a financial MEA, can be more complex than a flat discount and could, for instance, consider volume figures and performance data. In such a case, even if the content of the MEA were disclosed, the calculation of the actual discounted price to be considered in the EPR policy might be difficult.

10.4.2 HTA and Pharmacoeconomics

In the light of the emergence of new high-cost medicines, with little knowledge about their added clinical benefit, competent authorities are increasingly using (economic) evaluations to base their funding decisions on evidence (Carone et al., 2012; Paris and Belloni, 2013). More than a decade ago, some funding institutions used different economic evaluations, such as cost-effectiveness and cost-minimisation analyses as part of their reimbursement processes (Vogler et al., 2008). In 2002, the three Baltic countries Estonia, Latvia and Lithuania approved the Baltic Guideline for Economic Evaluation of Pharmaceuticals that specified the main principles for performing pharmacoeconomic analyses (Behmane and Innus, 2011).

A major feature of health economic and pharmacoeconomic evaluations concerns the perspective they take: A more limited approach is the health system perspective that only considers direct costs of the healthcare system. This approach is, for instance, applied in Belgium, England and Scotland. A broader approach is taken in Norway, Sweden or the Netherlands with the societal perspective which also takes into account indirect costs of diseases and treatments (Paris and Belloni, 2013).

The National Institute for Health Care and Excellence (NICE) in England, the Haute Autorité de Santé (HAS) in France and the Institut für Qualität und Wirtschaftlichkeit im Gesundheitswesen (IQWIG) in Germany are among the leading and most well-known HTA institutions in Europe. However, several other European countries have HTA institutions. Some small countries have been discussing whether or not they also want to establish an HTA institution in their country, or whether to use evidence generated by HTA institutions in other countries and translate it into their national context (e.g. Cyprus; Wouters and Kanavos, 2015).

For several years, activities have been undertaken to strengthen HTA in the European context. Joint efforts have been made through the EU-netHTA project that has been organised as a so-called Joint Action since 2010. A Joint Action is a multi-stakeholder project co-funded by the European Commission. The strategic objectives of EUnetHTA are to reduce overlap and duplication of efforts and hence promote more effective use of resources. This is also to increase HTA input into decision-making in EU Member States, to strengthen the link between HTA and healthcare policy making in the EU and its Member States, and to support countries with limited experience of HTA. Under EUnetHTA, methodological models for doing a HTA (and thus providing a basis for comparative assessments) were developed such as the 'core model' that defines the elements of a full-fledged HTA report and a 'rapid assessment' model (Kristensen et al., 2009). Criticism has been raised that the work done under EUnetHTA was not sufficiently practical for policy-makers, and that the process of joint assessments that were made were considered as too slow. Currently, there is a debate about the future model for the cooperation of HTA (European Commission DS, 2016; see also Section 14.5).

While the value of HTA and pharmacoeconomics is seen in its contribution to generate evidence, concerns have been raised for those cases where reimbursement decisions were completely based on single criteria, such as the cost per QALY. An explicit threshold per QALY tends to incentivise marketing authorisation holders to push the price up to the threshold

(Hughes, 2011). In the case of such a value-based approach, medicines with perceived high value are likely to be granted higher prices, which might present opportunities to the industry for 'gaming', in particular, related to the choice of the comparator and the threshold (Kanavos et al., 2010).

In order to address the methodological limitations of HTA, the use of a multi-criteria decision analysis (MCDA) was proposed. MCDA is a tool that allows for a systematic and explicit consideration of multiple factors that influence the decision, through identified criteria that each are assigned a weight in order to make their values and objectives explicit. When criteria and weights are identified based on the decision problem, policy makers score the performance of the healthcare intervention under appraisal with regard to each criterion (Goetghebeur et al., 2012).

There have been high expectations on HTA as being the solution to manage high-cost medicines but it has been increasingly understood that HTA is simply a tool to support pricing and reimbursement decisions. Refinements of pharmacoeconomic evaluations will continue in Europe, both in terms of addressing methodological challenges and translating results into practice. At the same time, these tools will increasingly be used given the emergence of new medicines.

10.4.3 Specific Funding Models

Some European countries introduced specific funds with the aim to finance defined (high-cost) medicines instead of covering them out of the general budget.

In 2005, Italy introduced a fund for orphan medicinal products and high-cost medicines. This so-called 'Fondo AIFA 5%' (financed by pharmaceutical companies' contributions equivalent to 5% of their annual spending on promotional activities) aimed to provide access to medicines for rare diseases before marketing authorisation (Garau and Mestre-Ferrandiz, 2009; Tordrup et al., 2014). However, with the frequent use of managed entry agreements in Italy this fund might today play a minor role (half of the fund is used to promote independent research and related activities).

In response to public debate about the refusal of cancer medicines by NICE, the Cancer Drug Fund (CDF) was established in England in 2010. The CDF was originally created as a temporary measure and initially consisted of GBP 50 million. Later it received GBP 200 million per year to cover new cancer treatments. CDF money was spent on relatively few medicines, and growth in utilisation was reported. A reform of the CDF was called for with the aim of focusing on cost-effective medicines

(Stephens and Thomson, 2012; Pauwels et al., 2014a; Buxton et al., 2014). In 2016 the previous CDF system was closed and replaced by a new system that included NICE appraisals for medicines to be covered (NHS England, 2016).

The example of the Cancer Drug Fund highlights the fact that the establishment of specific funds for high-cost medicines tends to create incentives that an increasing number of medicines be prescribed.

A few European countries introduced funding models that aimed to bridge the outpatient and hospital sectors. The rationale for these funding solutions was to respond to the incentive for payers in fragmented healthcare systems (with different payers for the outpatient and hospital sectors) to shift patients, treatments and thus costs between sectors (Vogler et al., 2017). In France and the Netherlands, health insurers fund certain high-cost medicines used in hospitals whereas other medicines are funded out of the hospital budget (Vogler et al., 2010). Since 2006, Norway has been transferring the funding responsibility for a selected number of medicines (TNF alpha inhibitors, medicines for the treatment of Multiple Sclerosis, anti-cancer medicines) to hospitals even if these medicines were used in the outpatient sector (WHO Regional Office for Europe, 2015).

10.4.4 Horizon Scanning

Policy makers stated that they were not prepared to the launch of the high-priced Hepatitis C medication sofosbuvir (Vogler et al., 2016e). As a lesson learned, horizon scanning is considered to be a strategic tool in European countries. Despite the perceived importance of this tool, there are a few examples of horizon scanning programmes in European countries, such as in Italy and England (Vogler et al., 2017).

In Italy, the horizon scanning project was introduced in the region of Veneto, with the aim to inform payers at regional and national levels. In this project, three reports were produced: the reports which were produced 36 months before possible market authorisation contained information on the mechanisms of action of emerging medicines, phase II trial data and the indications of ongoing phase III trials; the reports 18 months before possible market authorisation assessed available results of the first phase III completed trials, and the reports 12 months before possible market authorisation critically assessed available data on efficacy and safety of the new medicines versus current standards. These reports also include the possible advantages over existing treatments (level of innovation), the possible place in therapy, estimated direct costs and information on other potentially relevant indications in development or on competitors in development for the same indication (Joppi et al., 2009).

In England, the National Horizon Scanning Centre (NHSC) provides an advance notice of new and emerging health technologies and interventions that are likely to have a significant impact on the English NHS and/or patients within the next two to three years. Established as an independent research team at the University of Birmingham in 1998, it was incorporated as a research program within the United Kingdom's National Institute for Health Research (NIHR) in 2006 (Packer et al., 2012). The Scottish Medicines Consortium (SMC) appraises potential new medicines around six to eighteen months before their likely launch, and produces a confidential annual report for health board financial officers to help with their planning (Wettermark et al., 2010). Austria has a horizon scanning programme for cancer medicines (Nachtnebel et al., 2012).

However, it has been critically discussed that some of the results produced under horizon scanning are not systematically used in decision making and that some horizon scanning programmes might be discontinued due to lack of funding. As a way forward, it is advised that horizon scanning should not be set up as an academic exercise disconnected to the policy practice but done in a way that can inform policy makers, as the Veneto, English and Scottish models were intended. Since horizon scanning is very resource-intensive, it is an issue to be addressed in cooperation projects such as in the Beneluxa collaboration (Bundesministerium für Gesundheit [Federal Ministry of Health], 2016; Henrarda and Arickxb, 2016; Ministre des Affaires Sociales et de la Santé Publique, 2016).

10.4.5 Biosimilar Medicines

In the last few decades, there has been increasing evidence about the cost-containment potential of generic medicines (Simoens and De Coster, 2006; Cameron et al., 2012; Godman et al., 2012; Heinze et al., 2014). It has not only been an issue of bringing prices down but also of using these savings to treat more patients: generics have contributed to increased utilisation of medicines (Ubeda et al., 2007; Godman et al., 2012).

Not surprisingly, payers have high expectations about biosimilar medicines and their possible contribution to a more affordable solution in access to medicines. Norway, for instance, has been able to reduce the prices of biosimilar medicines and, at the same time, ensure sufficient uptake of these medicines which compensates biosimilar suppliers for low prices and eventually allows the treatment of more patients (Vogler et al., 2017). In

Norway, biosimilar medicines have been tendered, and large discounts (of up to 80%) have been achieved (GaBI Online, 2015). A tendering policy for biosimilar medicines is rather unique; most other European countries set the price of the biosimilar medicine at a certain percentage below the price of the originator. They apply this pricing policy to generic medicines (so-called 'generic price link' (WHO Collaborating Centre for Pharmaceutical Pricing and Reimbursement Policies, 2013)) as well; however, the required difference between biosimilar and originator is smaller compared to the difference between originator and generic (e.g. 30% for generics and 15% for biosimilars in Croatia and 50% for generics and 30% for biosimilars in Lithuania) (Vogler et al., 2016b). The relatively higher prices appear to be based on the perception that biosimilar medicines should not be treated as 'generics' (Mestre-Ferrandiz et al., 2016).

Prices are only one part of the equation. Norway has been successful in benefiting from the low prices of biosimilar medicines because they were utilised. The Norwegian procurement agency for public hospitals closely works with clinicians to educate and encourage them to prescribe the tendered biosimilar medicine. One issue that still needs to be addressed in such discussions is the concern that a switch to a biosimilar medicine might not be safe. A few studies on this topic are on-going in European countries (European Commission, 2016b). The most well-known among them is the NOR-SWITCH study, again done in Norway; this has recently been finalised. It showed that a switch from originator infliximab to biosimilar infliximab is safe (Goll et al., 2016).

10.5 STRATEGIES AT EUROPEAN LEVEL

As said earlier, pricing and reimbursement policies fall into the national responsibility of the EU Member States. Although marketing authorisation is harmonised, there are no harmonised pricing and reimbursement policies in the EU. As a result, pharmaceutical companies deal with 28 different jurisdictions (and in some countries, there are further payers at regional levels). The negotiation power of the purchasers is split among 28 Member States, and their relevance varies, depending on the economic situation, the market size and epidemiology of the respective countries.

Concern of how to ensure access to high-cost medicines has been put on the agenda of recent EU Presidencies (the Presidency of the Council of the European Union rotates among EU Member States every six months; the Presidency is responsible for the functioning of the Council of the

European Union that represents the executive governments of the EU's Member States and is part of the EU bicameral legislature with the other legislative body being the European Parliament). Improved cooperation (both vertical and horizontal) has been proposed as a way forward (European Commission, 2014a; Council of the European Union, 2015, 2016).

There has been in the past rather informal cooperation between policy makers, such as the Pharmaceutical Pricing and Reimbursement Information (PPRI) network of competent authorities of pharmaceutical pricing and reimbursement (not limited to the EU) (Vogler et al., 2014) or the Competent Authorities Responsible for Pharmaceutical Pricing and Reimbursement (CAPR) network (Pani et al., 2016) of EU Member States created in 2008. Recent documents call for strengthened and improved cooperation and networks in the context of the EU. For instance, the Council Conclusions in June 2016 asked for a continuation of investment in the work of the CAPR network (Council of the European Union, 2016).

Another example concerns the current and future European cooperation related to HTA: the multi-stakeholder initiative European Network for Health Technology Assessment (EUnetHTA) that started from a cooperation of HTA bodies is currently in its third round. Discussions are on-going about how to better use the expertise generated in EUnetHTA for policy making. There are reflections about the future of the HTA cooperation at European level for the period beyond 2020, when the current cooperation model will come to an end. Possible scenarios range from a continuation of the status quo (non-legislative, voluntary collaboration) to a model of cooperation through the collection, sharing and use of common tools and data based on a legal framework and the setting up of an organisational structure at EU level. This is to coordinate the participation of all EU Member States in the joint full assessments, followed by their mandatory uptake (European Commission DS, 2016).

Developments have also been observed in vertical cooperation, that is, among decision making on marketing authorisation (by EMA), HTA agencies, competent authorities for pharmaceutical pricing and public payers. Since 2010, EMA has been offering in its 'early dialogue' parallel scientific advice together with HTA bodies (European Medicines Agency (EMA), 2013); thanks to this process, pharmaceutical companies receive simultaneous feedback from both regulators (EMA) and HTA bodies on their development plans for new medicines.

These improvements, however, do not appear far reaching enough, and there has been a debate as to whether or not EU Member States could jointly procure medicines. For the time being this does not seem possible. A legal framework to support joint procurement, the 'Joint Procurement Agreement (JPA) on medical countermeasures' (European Commission, 2014b), was established in 2014 and subsequently signed by EU Member States. But this JPA is targeted at medical countermeasures against communicable diseases considered as serious cross-border threats to health (for procurement of vaccines, for instance, to be prepared for an outbreak of a pandemic). It was discussed whether or not this instrument could be extended to a joint procurement of high-priced medicines against cancer, multiple sclerosis, and of orphan medicines. But the European Commission clarified that this would be beyond of the scope of this agreement (Vogler et al., 2016a).

Reflections have been made about the policy option of differential pricing within the European Union. Such a policy would involve the setting of a European price by EU Member States, possibly in cooperation with the European Commission, and the definition of different national prices based on mark ups or mark downs that consider the economic situation of the countries. The European Commission commissioned a study to explore the feasibility of such a differential pricing policy for EU Member States. This study identified major obstacles to be addressed before a full-fledged differential pricing policy could be introduced in the EU, including action to prevent leakage due to parallel trade and strong political commitment to agree to differential pricing and its principles and mechanisms (Vogler et al., 2016a).

Cooperation in pricing might be able to achieve price transparency between countries. As explained in Section 14.4.1, confidential arrangements (MEAs and similar) have been frequently applied for high-priced medicines. It would be extremely helpful for pricing authorities and payers (even those who do not apply EPR) to know the real (discounted) prices in the other countries. Despite high awareness of policy makers about the distortion of prices due to discounts and increasing calls for price transparency by policy making, administration and research (ESIP AIM, 2011; Espin et al., 2011; WHO Regional Office for Europe, 2015; Vogler et al., 2016b; Vogler and Paterson, 2017), no European country has pioneered in disclosing discounted prices. This is due to the fear that the manufacturers would stop offering price discounts or would even no longer supply these medicines. As a first step, Austria has been labelling those medicines in its reimbursement list for which a discount agreement has been negotiated (Vogler et al., 2017).

As EU wide cooperation on joint pricing and purchasing seems not yet to be feasible for implementation, some countries, typically those that are similar in size and economic situation, have started voluntary cooperation. For instance, the so-called Beneluxa cooperation (Austria, Belgium, Luxembourg and the Netherlands) aims to collaborate in horizon scanning and HTA as well as in joint negotiations with pharmaceutical companies (Bundesministerium für Gesundheit [Federal Ministry of Health], 2016; Henrarda and Arickxb, 2016; Ministre des Affaires Sociales et de la Santé Publique, 2016).

10.6 OUTLOOK

High-cost medicines will remain an issue for European policy makers. Traditional pricing and reimbursement policies have proved insufficient to ensure patient access to these medicines. As a result, new approaches are needed. The European model for the future to deal with high-cost medicines might be a mixture of different approaches: first, existing policies could be optimised, for example, through an increased generation of evidence to better inform decisions. In this respect, transparency (on prices and discounts in other European countries) could help. Second, new policies beyond pricing and reimbursement are likely to be increasingly used, such as horizon scanning and further pre-launch and post-launch policies. Third, we will likely see increased cross-country cooperation of purchasers and public payers that bundle efforts to improve purchasing power.

ABBREVIATIONS

CAPR	Competent Authorities Responsible for Pharmaceutical Pricing and Reimbursement
CDF	Cancer Drug Fund
CED	Coverage with evidence development
EFPIA	European Pharmaceutical Industry Association
EFTA	European Free Trade Association
EMA	European Medicines Agency
EPR	External price referencing
EU	European Union
EUnetHTA	European Network for Health Technology Assessment
FDA	Foods and Drugs Administration
GBP	Great Britain Pound
HAS	Haute Autorité de Santé
HTA	Health technology assessment
IMS	Intercontinental Marketing Statistics

IQWIG	Institut für Qualität und Wirtschaftlichkeit im Gesundheitswesen
JPA	Joint Procurement Agreement
MCDA	Multi-Criteria Decision Analysis
MEA	Managed entry agreement(s)
NHSC	National Horizon Scanning Centre
NICE	National Institute for Health and Care Excellence
NIHR	National Institute for Health Research
OMP	Orphan medicinal products
PAS	Patient access scheme(s)
PPP	Purchasing power parity
PPRI	Pharmaceutical Pricing and Reimbursement Information
QALY	Quality-adjusted life year
RSS	Risk sharing scheme(s)
SMC	Scottish Medicines Consortium
TNF	Tumour necrosis factor
USD	United States Dollar
WAIT	Patients Waiting to Access Innovative Therapies
WHO	World Health Organization

REFERENCES

Aballea, S., Toumi, M., Vataire, A., Millier, A., Lamure, M., 15–19 May 2010. Quantitative analysis of the influence of disease and product characteristics on orphan drug prices in Europe. Poster. ISPOR 15th Annual International Meeting. Atlanta.

Abboud, C., Berman, E., Cohen, A., Cortes, J., DeAngelo, D., Deininger, M., et al., 2013. The price of drugs for chronic myeloid leukemia (CML) is a reflection of the unsustainable prices of cancer drugs: from the perspective of a large group of CML experts. Blood 121 (22), 4439–4442.

Adamski, J., Godman, B., Ofierska-Sujkowska, G., Osinska, B., Herholz, H., Wendykowska, K., et al., 2010. Risk sharing arrangements for pharmaceuticals: potential considerations and recommendations for European payers. BMC Health Services Research 10, 153.

Behmane, D., Innus, J., 2011. Pharmaceutical policy and the effects of the economic crisis: Latvia. Eurohealth 17 (1), 8–10.

Bouvy, J., Vogler, S., 2013. Background Paper 8.3 pricing and reimbursement policies: impacts on innovation. In: World Health Organization (Ed.), Priority Medicines for Europe and the World 'A Public Health Approach to Innovation' Update on 2004 Background Paper, Geneva.

Bundesministerium für Gesundheit [Federal Ministry of Health], 17 June 2016. Oberhauser: Österreich tritt Benelux-Kooperation für Arzneimittelpolitik bei [Oberhauser: Austria joins the Benelux cooperation on pharmaceutical policy]. Available from: http://www.bmgf.gv.at/home/Presse/Pressemeldungen/Oberhauser_Oesterreich_tritt_Benelux_Kooperation_fuer_Arzneimittelpolitik_bei (accessed 13.02.17).

Buxton, M., Longworth, L., Raftery, J., Sculpher, M., Towse, A., 2014. Reforming the cancer drug fund. British Medical Journal 349 (2), g7276.

Cameron, A., Mantel-Teeuwisse, A.K., Leufkens, H.G.M., Laing, R.O., 2012. Switching from originator brand medicines to generic equivalents in selected developing countries: how much could be saved? Value in Health 15 (5), 664–673.

Carone, G., Schwierz, C., Xavier, A., 2012. Cost-Containment Policies in Public Pharmaceutical Spending in the EU. European Commission, Directorate-General for Economics and Financial Affairs, Brussels.

Cheema, P., Gavura, S., Migus, M., Godman, B., Yeung, L., Trudeau, M., 2012. International variability in the reimbursement of cancer drugs by publically funded drug programs. Current Oncology 19 (3), e165–e176.

Council of the European Union, 2015. Council conclusions on personalised medicine for patients. Available from: http://data.consilium.europa.eu/doc/document/ST-15054-2015-INIT/en/pdf (accessed 08.02.17).

Council of the European Union, 2016. Council conclusions on strengthening the balance in the pharmaceutical systems in the EU and its Member States. Available from: http://www.consilium.europa.eu/press-releases-pdf/2016/6/47244642812_en.pdf (accessed 03.07.16).

De Weerdt, E., Simoens, S., Hombroeckx, L., Casteels, M., Huys, I., 2015. Causes of drug shortages in the legal pharmaceutical framework. Regulatory Toxicology and Pharmacology 71 (2), 251–258.

EFPIA, 2011. Patients' WAIT Indicator-report 2011. Available from: http://www.efpia.eu/uploads/Patients_WAIT_Report_2011_FINAL_070811_1.doc (accessed 13.02.17).

EMA, 2017. Orphan Medicinal Products. European Medicines Agency, London, Available from: http://ec.europa.eu/health/human-use/orphan-medicines_en.

ESIP, AIM, 2011. Review of Council Directive 89/105/EEC of 21 December 1988 relating to the transparency of measures regulating the pricing of medicinal products for human use and their inclusion in the scope of national health insurance systems (Transparency Directive) Joint Position Paper. Submitted by European Social Insurance Platform (ESIP)/Association Internationale de la Mutualité (AIM) on 10 February 2011. Available from: https://www.yumpu.com/en/document/view/30373504/esip-aim-position-on-a-review-of-the-transparency-directivepdf (accessed 13.02.17).

Espin, J., Rovira, J., de Labry, A.O., 2011. Working paper 1: External price referencing — review series on pharmaceutical pricing policies and interventions. World Health Organization and Health Action International, Geneva.

European Commission, 2014a. Council conclusions on innovation for the benefit of patients (2014/C 438/06). European Commission, Brussels.

European Commission, 2014b. Medical counter measures that could be procured in common under the joint procurement agreement. European Commission, Luxembourg. Available from: http://ec.europa.eu/health/preparedness_response/docs/jpa_note_scope_en.pdf (accessed 13.02.17).

European Commission, 2016a. Orphan medicinal products 2016. Available from: http://ec.europa.eu/health/human-use/orphan-medicines_en (accessed 27.12.16).

European Commission, 2016b. Multi-stakeholder workshop on biosimilar medicinal products summary. Available from: http://ec.europa.eu/DocsRoom/documents/19302/attachments/1/translations/en/renditions/native (accessed 03.11.16).

European Commission DS, 2016. Inception impact assessment—strengthening of the EU cooperation on health technology assessment (HTA).

European Medicines Agency (EMA), 2013. Early dialogue between regulators and health technology assessment bodies key to medicines development. EMA and multiple stakeholders to develop tools for industry. Available from: http://www.ema.europa.eu/ema/index.jsp?curl(pages/news_and_events/news/2013/11/news_detail_001979.jsp&mid(WC0b01ac058004d5c1 (accessed 13.02.17) [press release].

Ferrario, A., Kanavos, P., 2013. Managed entry agreements for pharmaceuticals: the European experience, EMINet. Availabe from: http://whocc.goeg.at/Literaturliste/Dokumente/FurtherReading/ferrario_2013_mea_report_en.pdf.

Ferrario, A., Kanavos, P., 2015. Dealing with uncertainty and high prices of new medicines: a comparative analysis of the use of managed entry agreements in Belgium, England, the Netherlands and Sweden. Social Science & Medicine 124 (1), 39–47.

Fojo, T., Grady, C., 2009. How much is life worth: cetuximab, non-small cell lung cancer, and the $440 billion question. Journal of the National Cancer Institute 101 (15), 1044–1048.
GaBI Online, 2015. Huge discount on biosimilar infliximab in Norway. GaBI (Generics and Biosimilars Initiative Journal). http://www.gabionline.net/Biosimilars/General/Huge-discount-on-biosimilar-infliximab-in-Norway (accessed 03.11.16).
Gammie, T., Lu, C.Y., Babar, Z.U.-D., 2015. Access to orphan drugs: a comprehensive review of legislations, regulations and policies in 35 countries. PLoS ONE 10 (10), e0140002.
Garau, M., Mestre-Ferrandiz, J., 2009. Access mechanisms for orphan drugs: a comparative study of selected European countries. Office of Health Economics Briefing. No. 52 October 2009.
Garrison, L.P., Towse, A., Briggs, A., de Pouvourville, G., Grueger, J., Mohr, P.E., et al., 2013. Performance-based risk-sharing arrangements—good practices for design, implementation, and evaluation: report of the ISPOR good practices for performance-based risk-sharing arrangements task force. Value in Health 16 (5), 703–719.
Godman, B., Bennie, M., Baumgärtel, C., Sović-Brkičić, L., Burkhardt, T., Fürst, J., et al., 2012. Essential to increase the use of generics in Europe to maintain comprehensive health care? Farmeconomia Health Economics and Therapeutic Pathways 13 (3S), 5–20.
Goetghebeur, M.M., Wagner, M., Khoury, H., Levitt, R.J., Erickson, L.J., Rindress, D., 2012. Bridging health technology assessment (HTA) and efficient health care decision making with multicriteria decision analysis (MCDA) applying the EVIDEM framework to medicines appraisal. Medical Decision Making 32 (2), 376–388.
Goll, G.L., Olsen, I.C., Jorgensen, K.K., Lorentzen, M., Bolstad, N., Haavardsholm, E.A., et al., 2016. Biosimilar infliximab (CT-P13) is not inferior to originator infliximab: results from a 52-week randomized switch trial in Norway. Arthritis Rheumatology 968 (Suppl. 10), Available from: http://acrabstracts.org/abstract/biosimilar-infliximab-ct-p13-is-not-inferior-to-originator-infliximab-results-from-a-52-week-randomized-switch-trial-in-norway/ (accessed 03.11.16).
Gray, A., Manasse, Jr, H.R., 2012. Shortages of medicines: a complex global challenge. Bulletin of the World Health Organization 90 (3), 158.
Heads of Medicines Agencies, 2007. Report of task force of HMA. Availability of Human Medicinal Products. Heads of Medicines Agencies, Madeira.
Heinze, G., Hronsky, M., Reichardt, B., Baumgärtel, C., Müllner, M., Bucsics, A., et al., 2014. Potential savings in prescription drug costs for hypertension, hyperlipidemia, and diabetes mellitus by equivalent drug substitution in Austria: a nationwide cohort study. Applied Health Economics and Health Policy 13 (2), 1–13.
Henrarda, S., Arickxb, F., 2016. Negotiating prices of drugs for rare diseases. Bulletin of the World Health Organization 94 (10), 779.
Hughes, D.A., 2011. Value-based pricing. incentive for innovation or zero net benefit? Pharmacoeconomics 29 (9), 731–735.
Iskrov, G., Stefanov, R., 2015. Prospects of risk-sharing agreements for innovative therapies in a context of deficit spending in Bulgaria. Frontiers in Public Health 3, 1–4.
Iyengar, S., Tay-Teo, K., Vogler, S., Beyer, P., Wiktor, S., de Joncheere, K., et al., 2016. Prices, costs, and affordability of new medicines for hepatitis C in 30 countries: an economic analysis. PLoS Medicine 13 (5), e1002032.
Joppi, R., Demattè, L., Menti, A.M., Pase, D., Poggiani, C., Mezzalira, L., 2009. The Italian horizon scanning project. European Journal of Clinical Pharmacology 65 (8), 775–781.
Kanavos, P., Nicod, E., Espin, J., 2010. Short- and long-term effects of value-based pricing vs. External price referencing. Available from: http://whocc.goeg.at/Literaturliste/Dokumente/FurtherReading/Short-%20and%20long-term%20effect%20of%20value-based%20pricing.pdf.
Kanavos, P., Vandoros, S., Irwin, R., Nicod, E., Casson, M., 2011. Differences in Costs of and Access to Pharmaceutical Products in the EU. European Parliament, Brussels.

Kantarjian, H.M., Fojo, T., Mathisen, M., Zwelling, L.A., 2013. Cancer drugs in the United States: Justum Pretium—the just price. Journal of Clinical Oncology 31 (28), 3600–3604.
Kelly, R.J., Smith, T.J., 2014. Delivering maximum clinical benefit at an affordable price: engaging stakeholders in cancer care. The Lancet Oncology 15 (3), e112–e118.
Klemp, M., Frønsdal, K.B., Facey, K., 2011. What principles should govern the use of managed entry agreements? International Journal of Technology Assessment in Health Care 27 (1), 77–83.
Kristensen, F.B., Lampe, K., Chase, D.L., Lee-Robin, S.H., Wild, C., Moharra, M., et al., 2009. Practical tools and methods for health technology assessment in Europe: structures, methodologies, and tools developed by the European Network for Health Technology Assessment, EUnetHTA. International Journal of Technology Assessment in Health Care 25 (Suppl. 2), 1–8.
Le Cam, Y., 2010. Inventory of access and prices of orphan drugs across Europe: a collaborative work between national alliances on rare diseases & Eurordis. Presentation, Paris.
Luengo-Fernandez, R., Leal, J., Gray, A., Sullivan, R., 2013. Economic burden of cancer across the European Union: a population-based cost analysis. The Lancet Oncology 14 (12), 1165–1174.
Mestre-Ferrandiz, J., Towse, A., Berdud, M., Biosimilars:, 2016. How can payers get long-term savings? PharmacoEconomics 34 (6), 609–616.
Michel, M., Toumi, M., 2012. Access to orphan drugs in Europe: current and future issues. Expert Rev. Pharmacoecon. Outcomes Res. 12(1), 23–29.
Ministre des Affaires Sociales et de la Santé Publique, 2016. The Grand Duchy of Luxemburg Joins Belgium-Netherlands Initiative on Orphan Drugs, Communiqué de presse 24 September 2015. Available from: http://www.deblock.belgium.be/fr/grand-duchy-luxemburg-joins-belgium-netherlands-initiative-orphan-drugs.
Morel, T., Arickx, F., Befrits, G., Siviero, P., van der Meijden, C., Xoxi, E., et al., 2013a. Managed entry agreements and orphan drugs: a European Comparative Study (2006–2012). Value in Health 16 (7), A391.
Morel, T., Arickx, F., Befrits, G., Siviero, P., van der Meijden, C., Xoxi, E., et al., 2013b. Reconciling uncertainty of costs and outcomes with the need for access to orphan medicinal products: a comparative study of managed entry agreements across seven European countries. Orphanet Journal of Rare Diseases 8, 198.
Nachtnebel, A., Geiger-Gritsch, S., Hintringer, K., Wild, C., 2012. Scanning the horizon: development and implementation of an early awareness system for anticancer drugs in Austria. Health Policy 104 (1), 1–11.
Neumann, P.J., Chambers, J.D., Simon, F., Meckley, L.M., 2011. Risk-sharing arrangements that link payment for drugs to health outcomes are proving hard to implement. Health Affairs 30 (12), 2329–2337.
NHS England, 2016. Appraisal and Funding of Cancer Drugs from July 2016 (including the new Cancer Drugs Fund). NHS England, London.
Packer, C., Fung, M., Stevens, A., 2012. Analyzing 10 years of early awareness and alert activity in the United Kingdom. International Journal of Technology Assessment in Health Care 28 (03), 308–314.
Pan American Health Organization, 2010. Access to High-Cost medicines in the Americas: Situation Challenges and Perspective. Technical Series No. 1. Essential Medicines, Access and Innovation. Pan American Health Organization, Washington, DC.
Pani, L., Montilla, S., Németh, G., Russo, P., Viceconte, G., Vogler, S., 2016. Balancing access to medicines and sustainability in Europe: an analysis from the network of competent authorities on pricing and reimbursement (CAPR). Pharmacological Research 111, 247–250.
Panteli, D., Arickx, F., Cleemput, I., Dedet, G., Eckhardt, H., Fogarty, E., et al., 2016. Pharmaceutical regulation in 15 European countries. Contract No. 5.

Paris, V., Belloni A., 2013. Value in Pharmaceutical Pricing. OECD Health Working Papers, No. 63. OECD Publishing, Paris.

Pauwels, K., Huys, I., Casteels, M., De Nys, K., Simoens, S., 2014a. Market access of cancer drugs in European countries: improving resource allocation. Targeted Oncology 9 (2), 95–110.

Pauwels, K., Huys, I., Casteels, M., Simoens, S., 2014b. Drug shortages in European countries: a trade-off between market attractiveness and cost containment? BMC Health Services Research 14 (1), 1–9.

Pauwels, K., Huys, I., Bielen, E., Bormans, S., Vincken, R., Zheng, H., et al., 2015. Financial based agreements and performance based agreements: the Belgian experience. Journal of Pharmaceutical Policy and Practice 8 (Suppl. 1), O1.

Permanand, G., Bak Pedersen, H., 2015. Managing new premium-priced medicines in Europe. Journal of Pharmaceutical Policy and Practice 8 (1), K2.

Picavet, E., Dooms, M., Cassiman, D., Simoens, S., 2011. Drugs for rare diseases: influence of orphan designation status on price. Applied Health Economics and Health Policy 9 (4), 275–279.

Schneider, P., Vogler, S., 2015. Impact of discounts on medicine prices. Journal of Pharmaceutical Policy and Practice 8 (Suppl. 1), O4.

Simoens, S., De Coster, S., 2006. Sustaining generic medicines markets in Europe. Journal of Generic Medicines 3 (4), 268.

Stephens, P., Thomson, D., 2012. The cancer drug fund 1 year on—success or failure? The Lancet Oncology 13 (8), 754–757.

The World Bank, 2016. World Bank Country and Lending Groups 2016. Available from: https://datahelpdesk.worldbank.org/knowledgebase/articles/906519 (accessed 27.12.16).

Tordrup, D., Tzouma, V., Kanavos, P., 2014. Orphan drug considerations in health technology assessment in eight European countries. Rare Diseases and Orphan Drugs: An International Journal of Public Health 1 (3), 86–97.

Ubeda, A., Cardo, E., Sellés, N., Broseta, R., Trillo, J.L., Fernández-Llimós, F., 2007. Antidepressant utilization in primary care in a Spanish region. Social Psychiatry and Psychiatric Epidemiology 42 (3), 181–188.

van Harten, W.H., Wind, A., de Paoli, P., Saghatchian, M., Oberst, S., 2016. Actual costs of cancer drugs in 15 European countries. The Lancet Oncology 17 (1), 18–20.

Vogler, S., Paterson, K.R., 2017. Can price transparency contribute to more affordable patient access to medicines? PharmacoEconomics - Open, Published online: 3 May 2017.

Vogler, S., Habl, C., Leopold, C., Rosian-Schikuta, I., de Joncheere, K., Lyager Thomsen, T., 2008. PPRI Report. Pharmaceutical Pricing and Reimbursement Information, Vienna.

Vogler, S., Habl, C., Leopold, C., Mazag, J., Morak, S., Zimmermann, N., 2010. PHIS hospital pharma report. Pharmaceutical Health Information System (PHIS), Vienna; commissioned by the European Commission and the Austrian Federal Ministry of Health. http://whocc.goeg.at/Literaturliste/Dokumente/BooksReports/PHIS_HospitalPharma_Report.pdf (accessed 02.04.17).

Vogler, S., Leopold, C., Zimmermann, N., Habl, C., de Joncheere, K., 2014. The pharmaceutical pricing and reimbursement information (PPRI) initiative—experiences from engaging with pharmaceutical policy makers. Health Policy and Technology 3 (2), 139–148.

Vogler, S., Lepuschütz, L., Schneider, P., Stühlinger, V., 2016a. Study on Enhanced Cross-Country Coordination in the Area of Pharmaceutical Product Pricing. Gesundheit Österreich Forschungs- und Planungs GmbH, Vienna.

Vogler, S., Peter, S., Gombocz, M., Zimmermann, N., 2016b. Differences in pricing policies for generic and biosimilar medicines. Value in Health 19 (7), A350.

Vogler, S., Vitry, A., Babar, Z.-U.-D., 2016c. Cancer drugs in 16 European countries, Australia, and New Zealand: a cross-country price comparison study. The Lancet Oncology 17 (1), 39–47.

Vogler, S., Zimmermann, N., Babar, Z.-U.-D., 2016d. Price comparison of high-cost originator medicines in European countries. Expert Review of Pharmacoeconomics & Outcomes Research 17 (2), 221–230.

Vogler, S., Zimmermann, N., Ferrario, A., Wirtz, V.J., de Joncheere, K., Pedersen, H.B., et al., 2016e. Pharmaceutical policies in a crisis? Challenges and solutions identified at the PPRI Conference. Journal of Pharmaceutical Policy and Practice 9 (1), 1.

Vogler, S., Paris, V., Ferrario, A., Wirtz, V.J., de Joncheere, K., Schneider, P., 2017. How can pricing and reimbursement policies improve affordable access to medicines? Lessons learned from European countries. Applied Health Economics and Health Policy 1 (3), 145–147.

von der Schulenburg, J.-M.G., Frank, M., 2014. Rare is frequent and frequent is costly: rare diseases as a challenge for health care systems. The European Journal of Health Economics 16 (2), 113–118.

Wettermark, B., Godman, B., Eriksson, C., van Ganse, E., Garattini, S., Joppi, R., et al., 2010. Einführung neuer Arzneimittel in europäische Gesundheitssysteme. GGW (G + G Wissenschaft) 10 (3), 24–34.

WHO Collaborating Centre for Pharmaceutical Pricing and Reimbursement Policies, 2013. Glossary of pharmaceutical terms. Update 2013. WHO Collaborating Centre for Pharmaceutical Pricing and Reimbursement Policies, Vienna. Available from: http://whocc.goeg.at/Literaturliste/Dokumente/MethodologyTemplate/PHISGlossary_Update2013_final_gesamt.pdf (accessed 15.11.14).

WHO Regional Office for Europe, 2015. Access to new medicines in Europe: technical review of policy initiatives and opportunities for collaboration and research. WHO Regional Office for Europe, Copenhagen.

Wouters, O.J., Kanavos, P.G., 2015. Transitioning to a national health system in Cyprus: a stakeholder analysis of pharmaceutical policy reform. Bulletin of the World Health Organization 93 (9), 606–613.

Zimmermann, N., Vogler, S., Bak Pedersen, H., 2015. Policy options to deal with high-cost medicines—survey with European policy-makers. Journal of Pharmaceutical Policy and Practice 8 (Suppl. 1), 8.

CHAPTER 11

Access to High-Cost Medicines in Australia

Agnes Isabelle Vitry, Russell Shute
Sansom Institute, University of South Australia, SA, Australia

11.1 INTRODUCTION

The first objective of the Australian National Medicines Policy is to provide 'timely access to the medicines that Australians need, at a cost individuals and the community can afford' (The Australian Government, 1999). Access to medicines in Australia is funded mostly through the PBS which is the national public pharmaceutical insurance system. It covers outpatients and patients in private hospitals. Medicines dispensed in public hospitals are covered by the state budgets except for Section 100 medicines (see below). In 2015–16, PBS expenditure was $10,838 million. In 2014, pharmaceutical spending in Australia represented 1.32% of Gross Domestic Product, which was higher than Sweden (1.08) or United Kingdom (1.21), but lower than that in other similar countries including France (1.60), Germany (1.67) or the United States (2.04) (Organisation for Economic Co-operation and Development, 2014).

Of the total PBS expenditure, 85.1% was subsidised by the government, the remainder were patient contributions (PBS Information Pharmaceutical Policy Branch, 2016). In 2016, general patients and concessional patients had to pay a co-payment of $38.30 and $6.20, respectively, for each medicine dispensed with a price above the co-payment level until they reach an annual safety net threshold ($1475.7 and $372.0, respectively). In 2014–15, 25.9% of total PBS prescriptions were dispensed at a price below the co-payment level and patients had to pay the full price of their medicines. Concerns have been raised about the level of co-payment which may affect accessibility of medicines (Vitry et al., 2015a, b). However, the co-payment remains the same even for high-cost medicines, therefore patients are protected from the true cost of these medicines when they are funded.

In 2015–16, the average price per prescription was $45 but with a wide range across therapeutic classes: the immunosuppressants, antivirals and antineoplastic agents had the highest average price per prescription, $965, $938 and $859, respectively. In 2015–16, the new medicines with the highest cost

Equitable Access to High-Cost Pharmaceuticals
http://dx.doi.org/10.1016/B978-0-12-811945-7.00011-7

Table 11.1 PBS Expenditure (in dollars) on Section 100 Programmes in 2015–16 (PBS Information Pharmaceutical Policy Branch, 2016)

Highly specialised drugs	1,583,754,673
Efficient funding of chemotherapy	702,421,712
Botulinum toxin programme	36,473,730
Human growth hormones	29,098,993
In vitro fertilisation programme	143,529,836
Opiate dependence treatment programme	49,404,634
Other programmes	180,249,749
Total	2,724,933,327

to the government were medicines for hepatitis C, for example, the combination ledipasvir with sofosbuvir ($357.9 million), immunomodulating drugs such as adalimumab for rheumatoid arthritis ($334.7 million) and ranibizumab for macular degeneration ($217.8 million). The therapeutic class of antineoplastic and immunomodulating agents represented the highest cost to the government ($1671 million, 21% of community expenditure).

A number of medicines are available as pharmaceutical benefits but are distributed under alternative arrangements, the Section 100 programmes. These include the Highly Specialised Drugs, the Efficient Funding of Chemotherapy (both for medicines prescribed in public and private hospitals), the Botulinum Toxin Program, the Growth Hormone Program, the In Vitro Fertilisation programme and the Opiate Dependence Treatment Program (Table 11.1) (The Australian Government, 2016a, b). In 2015–16, all Section 100 programmes represented 25% ($2725 million) of PBS expenditure.

Since 2007, the Australian government has implemented a number of pricing policy reforms in order to decrease the price of generic medicines which had been found to be higher than those in similar countries (Vitry et al., 2015a, b). For this reason, pharmaceutical expenditures overall have remained stable over the last few years despite the listing of high-cost medicines on the PBS (Harvey and de Boer, 2015; PBS Information Pharmaceutical Policy Branch, 2016). However, PBS programmes which provide access to high-cost medicines have shown rapid rates of growth. Between 2009–10 and 2013–14, expenditures on the Efficient Funding of Chemotherapy and the Highly Specialised Drugs Program were the fastest growing Section 100 programmes with an average annual growth rate of 62.61% and 6.38% (Harvey and de Boer, 2015). In 2015–16, the Highly Specialised Drugs programme represented 13.3% ($1584 million) of PBS expenditure, a 31% increase compared to the previous financial year (PBS Information

Pharmaceutical Policy Branch, 2016). In 2016, a significant contributor to the increase in government expenditure was the high usage of the new hepatitis medicines following their PBS listing in March 2016 (The Australian Government, 2016a, b). Given predictions about the increasing prevalence of diseases such as cancer in the growing Australian ageing population and the high number of new, expensive medicines in development, it is likely that pharmaceutical expenditures will continue to rise and the Australian government will face difficult decisions for balancing PBS sustainability and access to new expensive medicines.

Although not part of the PBS, the Life Saving Drugs Programme (LSDP) provides access to a limited number of high-cost medicines for rare and life-threatening medical conditions (The Australian Government, 2016a, b). Currently 12 medicines are funded for eight conditions:

- imigulcerase (Cerezyme), velaglucerase (VPRIV), taliglucerase (Elelyso) and miglustat (Zavesca) to treat Gaucher disease
- agalsidase alfa (Replagal) and agalsidase beta (Fabrazyme) for Fabry's disease
- laronidase (Aldurazyme) for Mucopolysaccharidosis (MPS) Type I
- idursulfase (Elaprase) for MPS Type II
- galsulfase (Naglazyme) for MPS Type VI
- alglucosidase alfa (Myozyme) for Infantile-onset, Juvenile Late-onset or Adult Late-onset Pompe disease
- eculizumab (Soliris) for Paroxysmal Noctural Haemoglobinuria
- nitisinone (Orfadin) for Hereditary Tyrosinaemia

In 2015–16, 335 patients were provided access to the LSDP (The Australian Government, 2016a, b). This programme, which is currently under review (Australian Government and Department of Health, 2015), grew at a rate of 12.7% from 2009–10 to 2013–14 (Harvey and de Boer, 2015).

11.2 VALUE-BASED FUNDING

Historically, Australia has been at the forefront of establishing value-based funding for medicines (Whitty and Littlejohns, 2015). The funding and pricing of new medicines which have been approved by the Therapeutic Goods Administration (TGA) are examined by the Pharmaceutical Benefits Advisory Committee (PBAC), an independent expert body, which is required by law to consider the cost-effectiveness of any new medicine. Medicines which have similar efficacy and safety as another listed treatment are given the same price. An incremental cost effectiveness ratio (ICER) compared to existing therapy is calculated for medicines for which there is evidence for superior efficacy or safety compared to the standard treatment. Overall, it is not clear whether value-based funding has led to lower prices of new high-cost medicines in Australia compared to that in similar countries (Harris et al., 2016; Vitry et al., 2016). Furthermore, Australian law precludes price reviews once a medicine is listed on the PBS. This means that the price of a new medicine cannot be decreased when the comparator loses its patent and its price drops as a result of the generic pricing policy (Karnon et al., 2016). Given such limitations, value for money is no longer ensured.

In addition to cost-effectiveness, the PBAC also considers a number of other factors such as the clinical need, the lack of alternative treatment and the budget impact. There is no fixed ICER threshold above which a medicine is not funded although a medicine is less likely to be funded when the ICER is above $70 to 75,000 per Quality-Adjusted Life Year (Chim et al., 2010; Whitty and Littlejohns, 2015; Harris et al., 2016). The same criteria are applied to all medicines including cancer medicines (Chim et al., 2010) or orphan medicines (Wonder and Chin, 2015). In practice, medicines for which manufacturers seek high prices such as cancer medicines might be less likely to be funded because of the high ICER or high budget impact (Chim et al., 2010). One factor included in the PBAC's decision criteria is the "Rule of Rescue", a term created "to describe the imperative people feel to rescue individuals facing avoidable death" (McKie and Richardson, 2003), with disregard for the opportunity costs of doing so (Whitty and Littlejohns, 2015). Although there is no explicit increased ICER threshold for end-of-life treatments, a study found that the odds for being funded were increased by 4.41 (95% CI 1.28–15.24) times, equivalent to an increase in value of $46,000 if the condition was life-threatening and the medicine had no active comparator (Harris et al., 2016).

11.3 PRICING POLICIES

The main objective for governments when listing high-cost medicines is to minimise the impact on global pharmaceutical expenditures. The first way of doing so is by minimising off-label use or use inconsistent with evidence. The PBS includes prescribing restriction rules for some medicines either at initiation or continuation of the medicine. Medicines with 'restricted benefits' can only be prescribed for specific therapeutic uses, and medicines with 'authority required benefits' can only be prescribed after the Department of Health's approval. Continuation of some medicines is subject to the provision of documentation of adequate benefit (Vitry and Roughead, 2014). For example, imatinib, a cancer medicine, can be continued by a patient only if a complete haematological response is observed. At the population level, the Drug Utilisation Sub Committee of the PBAC analyses data on actual and projected usage of medicines to inform PBAC decisions and post-market reviews of listings.

The second way is by negotiating the price of new high-cost medicines with the manufacturer through risk-share arrangements that involve price reductions for sales exceeding a pre-agreed volume or rebate arrangements that involve repayment of costs beyond an agreed annual subsidisation cap. There is limited information on these pricing arrangements which remain confidential. A 2013 survey established that there were at least 71 special pricing arrangements in place (Vitry and Roughead, 2014). The Australian Department of Health's annual reports mentioned that the Department had recovered $99.3 million and $588 million in 2014–15 and 2015–16, respectively, 'with cost-sharing agreements between the Commonwealth and pharmaceutical companies' but no further detail was provided.

11.4 COVERAGE WITH EVIDENCE DEVELOPMENT

For many high-cost medicines, difficulties in funding decisions may arise from uncertainties about clinical benefits, in particular, for new cancer medicines (Vitry et al., 2016). An analysis of submissions to the PBAC for cancer medicines between 2005 and 2012 established that half of major submissions had significant problems with supporting clinical evidence (Wonder and Dunlop, 2015). Furthermore, the therapeutic benefits may be very limited (Niraula et al., 2012; Ellis et al., 2014; Fojo and Mailankody, 2014; Kim and Prasad, 2015).

Since May 2010, a new funding scheme, the Managed Entry Scheme (MES), has been implemented to enable the funding of medicines when there is a high clinical need and that new clinical data would resolve the issues of uncertainty (Australian Government and Department of Health, 2011a, b). Funding is given pending provision of further evidence (i.e. coverage with evidence development). The MES is formalised in a Deed of Agreement with explicit specification of how emerging data should be collected and modelled for PBAC reconsideration. If later evidence does not support expected results, the price may be lowered and the sponsor expected to rebate the cost of difference in performance between observed versus predicted benefits of the medicine.

Four MES have been agreed on so far and one is under discussion (Table 11.2) (Australian Government and Department of Health, 2016a–e). All were for medicines for advanced cancer. Two MES have been completed,

Table 11.2 Managed Entry Agreements (Australian Government and Department of Health 2016)

Name	Indication	Date PBAC Meeting	Comments
Ipilimumab Yervoy	Stage III or stage IV malignant melanoma	Nov. 2012	The PBAC wanted to verify the anticipated overall survival benefits of Ipilimumab in real world clinical practice. The "Australian Outcomes Program" is planned to collect data on the outcomes of patients using Ipilimumab as monotherapy. These results were required to be submitted in September 2016 for PBAC consideration
Trametinib Mekinist	Advanced melanoma	Nov. 2014	The PBAC proposed to review the trial evidence within two years. In July 2016, after reviewing the finalised results of the COMBI-D and COMBI-V trials, the PBAC considered that the clinical benefit of Trametinib in terms of prolongation of progression-free survival and overall survival had been over-estimated when approved in November 2014. As a result, the PBAC recommended that the effective price of Trametinib be reduced to maintain acceptable cost-effectiveness
Crizotinib Xalkori	Non-small-cell lung cancer	Nov. 2014	The PBAC requested information on the proportion of the first 50 consecutive patients who are alive 365 days after starting therapy with crizotinib after any PBS listing begins because on the uncertainty about incremental overall survival gain (to be provided within 14 months after the 50th study eligible patient is initiated on crizotinib)

Pembrolizumab Keytruda	Stage III or Stage IV malignant melanoma	March 2015	The PBAC recommended a managed entry framework with an initial risk share arrangement to achieve the same cost per patient as Ipilimumab Adjustment to the Pembrolizumab price would occur upon provision of outcomes from trial KN-006.The sponsor would also provide compassionate access to Pembrolizumab for any patient refractory to Ipilimumab. In November 2016, the PBAC examined these results but rejected a price increase compared to Ipilimumab
Nivolumab Opdivo	Locally advanced or metastatic squamous or non-squamous non-small-cell lung cancer	Nov. 2016	The PBAC recommended discussions with the sponsor in order to develop a proposal for a MES because of concerns regarding the variation in the extent of effectiveness in patients over 75 years and high ICER
Opdivo	Advanced or metastatic squamous or non-squamous non-small-cell lung cancer	2016	To develop a proposal for a MES because of concerns regarding the variation in the extent of effectiveness in patients over 75 years and high ICER

one for trametinib where it was found that the price should be reduced as the results were less favourable than expected; the second one for pembrolizumab, where the price was maintained despite the company's request for an increase.

If results were less than expected and if the lowered price was still above an acceptable ICER, this may require mitigating options such as partial or full disinvestment (Mitchell and Viney, 2016). However, early subsidised access may not be reversed easily (Vitry et al., 2015a, b).

11.5 ACCESS TO NON-PBS FUNDED HIGH-COST MEDICINES

Additional avenues are available for patients to access non-PBS funded high-cost medicines. They include clinical trials, access through the Special Access Scheme (SAS), public hospitals, Medicines Access Programs (MAPs), social media crowdfunding, charities or buyers' clubs. However, access processes may be complex and medicines can be unaffordable to patients. In 2015, the Leukaemia Foundation released a brochure to help patients to get access to non-PBS-funded cancer medicines (Leukaemia Foundation, 2015).

Participating in clinical trials for accessing medicines in early development or for new indications may be one avenue for early access to potentially life-saving and life-extending drugs. However, it may not be a possibility for a significant number of Australian patients because of the location of the trials and the trial eligibility criteria.

At the national level, the SAS refers to regulatory arrangements which allow for the supply of an unapproved medicine, in particular, for patients who are seriously ill or at risk of premature death (The Australian Government, 2016a, b). High-cost medicines accessed through SAS may have to be paid in full by the patient or provided by a public hospital or through a MAP.

Hospital patients may get access to unapproved or unfunded medicines in special circumstances. For example, in South Australia, individual patient use medicine requests may be submitted by the prescribers to the Drug and Therapeutics Committee of the treating hospital with appropriate justification (Government of South Australia, 2016). There is limited information on the types and quantities of non-PBS funded high-cost medicines which are dispensed in Australian hospitals. The level of access may vary considerably between hospitals and between states, and access to expensive medicines is likely to be limited by capped hospital budgets. In some cases, patients may be able to claim some or all the cost of treatment with a new medicine not listed on the PBS if they have a private health insurance (Leukaemia Foundation, 2015).

MAPs in Australia is an umbrella term that refers to programmes created by pharmaceutical companies to supply new and unfunded medicines to patients either at no cost or at a reduced cost. In contrast with compassionate use programmes in Europe or Expanded Access programmes in the United States which may give access exclusively to new medicines not approved by regulatory agencies yet, the Australian MAPs mainly give access to medicines which may be approved by or in the process of being approved by the TGA but are not listed on the PBS yet. In 2014–15, a study identified 51 MAPs for cancer medicines operational in Australia (Grover et al., in press). Interviews of stakeholders identified several important issues with MAPs including the lack of clinical monitoring, inequity to access, operational issues and lack of transparency (Grover et al., in press). Concerns were raised that some of these programmes may be accessed by desperate cancer patients at a great personal financial cost but without gaining any tangible benefit and sometimes at the risk of severe toxicity (Grover et al., in press). The existence of cost-sharing arrangements in some of these programmes also raise equity issues when only some patients may have the capacity to self-fund access to these medicines (Azad and Franco, 2013). The Council of Australian Therapeutic Advisory Groups (CATAG) has recently published guiding principles for appropriate governance and implementation of MAPs (Council of Australian Therapeutic Advisory Groups, 2015) but these guidelines are neither mandated nor regulated. The existence of these MAPs is somewhat acknowledged by the PBAC. For example, when the PBAC approved pembrolizumab for the treatment of stage III or stage IV melanoma who have not been exposed to ipilimumab, it noted that 'the sponsor would subsidise ongoing access to pembrolizumab for patients who are refractory to ipilimumab' (Pharmaceutical Benefits Advisory Committee, 2015).

More and more patients try to get access to new unfunded medicines or experimental treatments through crowdfunding platforms like Mycause (2016). Rare Cancers Australia, (2016) has also set up a patient treatment fund to help Australians faced with high-cost treatment options.

Before the new hepatitis C treatments became available on the PBS, a hepatitis C buyers' club, FixHepC, was set up by a Tasmanian GP to help patients import generic versions of hepatitis C medications through parallel importations of generic medicines (FixHepC, 2016; Freeman and Hill, 2016). The SocialMedwork (2016) located in Netherlands is also offering Australian medicines for breast cancer, leukaemia and multiple sclerosis, which are not available in Australia.

11.6 CHALLENGES FOR THE FUTURE

The burden of high-cost medicines on pharmaceutical expenditures is a serious concern for policy makers. Earlier subsidised access to high-cost medicines may provide hope for patients with urgent high unmet clinical need. However, it has potentially important opportunity costs. It has been shown that the PBAC was quite consistent in its assessments and its decisions are usually well accepted by the Australian community (Harris et al., 2008, 2016). A recent study could not detect any effect of external pressures on PBAC decisions (Harris et al., 2016). However, in this study, such pressures were only gauged by the number of articles published in Australian newspapers in the year before, and this could be a crude and insensitive measure (Harris et al., 2016). The PBAC has refused to bow to strong public campaigns including a recent campaign requiring the listing of a new expensive treatment for cystic fibrosis, Orkambi (combination of lumacaftor and ivacaftor) (Brodie, 2016). However, on a number of occasions, the PBAC advice to the Australian Health Minister not to list a new medicine has led to community backlash. An example was the rejection for listing of Herceptin (trastuzumab), a medicine indicated for the treatment of advanced breast cancer by the PBAC in 2005 because of the high price requested by the manufacturer and the uncertainty of scientific evidence (MacKenzie et al., 2008). In response to a campaign by patient advocacy groups, the Australian Government chose to provide access to this medicine by creating a special fund separate from the PBS, the Herceptin programme. There was public outcry when the PBAC refused to recommend, Gardasil, the first anticancer vaccine for the prevention of cervical cancer (Roughead et al., 2008). The PBAC had to reconvene an urgent meeting and finally recommended the listing of Gardasil on the PBS at a reduced price.

Over the last few years, concerns have been growing on the lack of access to new medicines in Australia, in particular, cancer medicines. A study investigating variability into the reimbursement of cancer medicines amongst 13 nations by publicly funded pharmaceutical programmes found New Zealand and Australia to be in the bottom five in regard to funding to the chosen cancer medicines. Australia funded 46% and New Zealand 25% of the 44 listed indications (Cheema et al., 2012). When the PBAC rejects or defers a funding application, the government may be accused in the media of neglecting dying patients' needs, while the benefits of the new medicines may be exaggerated, and exorbitant prices are rarely mentioned (MacKenzie et al., 2008). In 2015, Roche, the manufacturer of Gazyva (obinutuzumab), a new medicine for leukaemia, was fined $100,000 for having run a wide media campaign that was 'overly optimistic about the likely outcomes from treatment with Gazyva and may have the effect of encouraging people with leukaemia to seek treatment with the product' (Medicines Australia, 2016). Roche did have agreements with both the healthcare professional and the patient quoted in the media. In 2016, Janssen-Cilag's promotion for Zytiga (abiraterone), a new medicine for advanced prostate cancer, used claims such as 'MORE energy', 'MORE to live for'. These claims were found to be misleading and Janssen-Cilag was fined $100,000 (Medicines Australia, 2016).

In this highly sensitive context, a number of options have been discussed to optimise the funding of medicines including streamlining the TGA and PBAC processes, modifying the evidence criteria for some medicines, improving access to clinical trials, or setting up an 'exceptional circumstances funding programme' (Samson et al., 2015; The Senate Community Affairs References Committee, 2015).

Since January 2011, parallel TGA and PBAC processes have been introduced, thus reducing the time lag between regulatory approval and funding decision (The Australian Government, 2011). A single entry point has also been established for fast-moving applications of medicines with a 'co-dependent' diagnostic technology (such as a genetic test for a 'targeted therapy') (Australian Government and Department of Health, 2011a, b). In response to the Review of Medicines and Medical Devices Regulation (Samson et al., 2015), the TGA has undertaken public consultations on new processes including consideration of assessments conducted by comparable overseas regulators (Australian Government, Department of Health , 2016a–e), expedited pathways (Australian Government, Department of Health, 2016a–e). Medicines eligible for the Priority Review pathway (within 150 working days) would require 'substantial evidence demonstrating that the medicine provides a major therapeutic advantage in efficacy and/or safety over existing treatments'. Medicines eligible for the Provisional Approval pathway would require 'promising evidence from early data indicating that the medicine is likely to provide major therapeutic advantages in efficacy and/or safety over existing treatments'. Concerns have been raised internationally about expedited approval pathways because of the increased risk of exposing patients to medicines with uncertain efficacy but potentially severe adverse effects (Moore and Furberg, 2012; Frank et al., 2014).

PBAC guidelines on how to prepare a submission to list a new medicine on the PBS have just been reviewed and have not fundamentally changed (The Australian Government and Department of Health, 2016a–e ; Pharmaceutical Benefits Advisory Committee, 2016). New medicines are compared to standard medical management. Outcomes presented in submissions should be relevant and meaningful for patients. The sponsor should nominate and justify a minimal clinically important difference. However, there is currently no collectively shared definition for relevant clinical benefit.

11.7 BETTER INFORMATION FOR THE PUBLIC AND ENGAGEMENT IN DECISION-MAKING

The creation of public indignation and organised access campaigns when funding of a new medicine is rejected or deferred by the PBAC indicates the need for better information provision to the public and the importance of participation in decision-making by public and patient groups. Patients (and their families) with conditions that may be helped by new high-cost medicines have a particular interest in, and not surprisingly prefer to have access to, medicines that afford them the best chance of survival and/or quality of life. Most people indicate that they want as much information as is available about their treatment options (Kaser et al., 2010). However, they may overestimate the benefits of available medicines. At a consumer hearing on the listing of pembroluzimab, the PBAC noted with concern the mismatch between the sponsor's data and public expectations of the medicine: patient groups indicated that they believed the response rate with pembrolizumab was 90% rather than 33%–37% as reflected in the sponsor's data (Pharmaceutical Benefits Advisory Committee, 2015). Currently, neither the TGA's Australian Public Assessment Reports nor the PBAC's Public Summary Documents which detail decisions on registration and funding of medicines and are posted online include plain English summaries (The Australian Government and Department of Health, 2016a–e). Provision of consumer-friendly information on PBAC decisions would facilitate knowledge-sharing and acceptance of funding choices. Transparency could also be improved by releasing data supporting funding of new medicines which currently remain commercial-in-confidence.

Whitty and Littlejohns have described the role of social values in priority setting related to health technology assessment processes in Australia using Clark and Weale's conceptual framework (Clark and Weale, 2012). Although transparency and accountability of the PBAC current processes are apparent (Whitty and Littlejohns, 2015), there is limited public information available on how social values are considered in PBAC decisions. It is also not known to which extent current pharmaceutical funding decisions reflect preferences of the Australian public.

There is general acceptance that increasing consumer involvement in decision-making about regulating access to high-cost medicines is important as it may lead to more transparent decisions and possibly to better health outcomes (Wortley et al., 2016). Currently, there are two consumer representatives on the PBAC. Consumers may also send comments on submissions prior to PBAC meetings. More recently, the PBAC has started consultations with consumer groups prior to its meetings. Only the most proactive members of the general public or those interested in a specific topic are likely to provide input to the PBAC processes. The Australian Senate inquiry into the availability of new, innovative and specialist cancer drugs in 2015 has advised increasing consumer involvement in decision-making (The Senate Community Affairs References Committee, 2015).

Participation in decision-making could be improved if a better defined patient and public engagement policy was formulated (Whitty and Littlejohns, 2015). However, there continue to be questions as to how consumer preferences are elicited and policy implemented in a way that accurately represents the broader community and that can have some influence in a country with finite health resources (Guindo et al., 2012; Whitty et al., 2014; Hunter 2016; Wortley et al., 2016). The LSDP review sees the value of broader community consultation, for example, establishing a UK NICE-style community panel to consider the broader issues of criteria that could be considered in decision-making, such as access, equity and affordability for all Australians with rare conditions although the implementation of a community panel could be complex and resource-intensive and delay funding approval further.

11.8 CONCLUSION

Balancing public expectations for access to high-cost medicines and maintaining the sustainability and the equity of the pharmaceutical insurance scheme will continue to pose complex challenges for policy makers in Australia. Improving information of the public and engagement in decision-making would definitely increase understanding and acceptance of funding decisions. Other innovative access pathways developed in other countries, such as the trial programme implemented by the French National Cancer

Institute, the AcSé programme, which provides access to targeted cancer medicines to genetically selected patients across France might also be considered (Buzyn et al., 2016). Ultimately, the astronomical prices for new medicines requested by pharmaceutical companies need to be addressed at the international level. Greater transparency about pricing and new business models for medication innovations are required to ensure access to truly innovative medicines in both developed and developing countries.

REFERENCES

Australian Government, 2016a. Department of Health and Therapeutic Goods Administration 2016. Consultation: Criteria for comparable overseas regulators, Retrieved 23 December from https://www.tga.gov.au/consultation/consultation-criteria-comparable-overseas-regulators.

Australian Government, 2016b. Department of Health and Therapeutic Goods Administration 2016. Consultation: Expedited pathways for prescription medicines, Retrieved 23 December, from https://www.tga.gov.au/consultation/consultation-expedited-pathways-prescription-medicines.

Australian Government and Department of Health, 2011. "Co-dependent and hybrid technologies." Retrieved 13 December, 2015, from http://www.health.gov.au/internet/hta/publishing.nsf/Content/co-1.

Australian Government and Department of Health, 2011. "Framework for the introduction of a Managed Entry Scheme for submissions to the Pharmaceutical Benefits Advisory Committee." Retrieved 14 June 2013, from http://www.pbs.gov.au/info/publication/factsheets/shared/framework-for-introduction-of-managed-entry-scheme-for-PBAC-submissions.

Australian Government and Department of Health, 2015. Post-market review of the Life Saving Drugs Programme (LSDP)., Retrieved 31 December, 2016 from http://www.pbs.gov.au/info/reviews/life-saving-drugs.

Australian Government and Department of Health, 2016. Annual Report 2015–16. Available from: http://www.health.gov.au/internet/main/publishing.nsf/Content/annual-report2015-16-cnt1/$File/department-of-health-annual-report-2015-16.pdf.

Australian Government Department of Health, 2016b. AusPAR user survey results, Retrieved 23 December, 2016 from https://www.tga.gov.au/book/export/html/732969.

Australian Government Department of Health, 2016c. Life Savings Drugs Programs (LSDP), Retrieved 31 December 2016 from http://www.health.gov.au/LSDP.

Australian Government and Department of Health, 2016. Pharmaceutical Benefits Advisory Committee Guidelines Review. Available from: http://www.pbs.gov.au/info/reviews/pbac-guidelines-review.

Australian Government and Department of Health, 2016. Public Summary Documents. Available from: http://www.pbs.gov.au/info/industry/listing/elements/pbac-meetings/psd.

Azad, A., Franco, M., 2013. Co-funded expanded access programmes for new oncology drugs: creating a two-tier system for Australian cancer patients? Internal Medicine Journal 43 (7), 843–844.

Brodie, M., 2016. PBAC unmoved by community appeal. Pharma in focus.

Buzyn, A., Blay, J.-Y., Hoog-Labouret, N., Jimenez, M., Nowak, F., Deley, M.-C.L., Pérol, D., Cailliot, C., Raynaud, J., Vassal, G., 2016. Equal access to innovative therapies and precision cancer care. Nature Reviews. Clinical Oncology 13 (6), 385.

Cheema, P.K., Gavura, S., Migus, M., Godman, B., Yeung, L., Trudeau, M.E., 2012. International variability in the reimbursement of cancer drugs by publically funded drug programs. Current Oncology 19 (3), e165–176.
Chim, L., Kelly, P.J., Salkeld, G., Stockler, M.R., 2010. Are cancer drugs less likely to be recommended for listing by the pharmaceutical benefits advisory committee in Australia? Pharmacoeconomics 28 (6), 463–475.
Clark, S., Weale, A., 2012. Social values in health priority setting: a conceptual framework. Journal of Health Organization and Management 26 (3), 293–316.
Council of Australian Therapeutic Advisory Groups, 2015. Managing Medicines Access Programs. Guiding principles for the governance of Medicines Access Programs in Australian hospitals. Available from: http://www.catag.org.au/wp-content/uploads/2012/08/OKA10428-CATAG-Guiding-Principles-for-Australian-Hospitals-FINAL-pdf.pdf.
Ellis, L.M., Bernstein, D.S., Voest, E.E., Berlin, J.D., Sargent, D., Cortazar, P., Garrett-Mayer, E., Herbst, R.S., Lilenbaum, R.C., Sima, C., Venook, A.P., Gonen, M., Schilsky, R.L., Meropol, N.J., Schnipper, L.E., 2014. American Society of Clinical Oncology Perspective: Raising the Bar for Clinical Trials by Defining Clinically Meaningful Outcomes. Journal of Clinical Oncology 32 (12), 1277.
FixHepC, 2016. FixHepC. Available from: http://fixhepc.com/.
Fojo, T., Mailankody, S., LO, A., 2014. Unintended consequences of expensive cancer therapeutics-the pursuit of marginal indications and a me-too mentality that stifles innovation and creativity: the John Conley lecture. JAMA Otolaryngology Head and Neck Surgery 140 (12), 1225–1236.
Frank, C., Himmelstein, D.U., Woolhandler, S., Bor, D.H., Wolfe, S.M., Heymann, O., Zallman, L., Lasser, K.E., 2014. Era of faster FDA drug approval has also seen increased black-box warnings and market withdrawals. Health Affairs 33 (8), 1453–1459.
Freeman, J.A.D., Hill, A., 2016. The use of generic medications for hepatitis C. Liver International 36 (7), 929–932.
Government of South Australia, S. H., 2016. South Australian Medicines Formulary. Available from: http://www.sahealth.sa.gov.au/wps/wcm/connect/public+content/sa+health+internet/clinical+resources/clinical+topics/medicines+and+drugs/south+australian+medicines+formulary.
Grover P., Babar Z., Oehmen R. and Vitry A., Medicines access programs to cancer medicines in Australia and New Zealand: an exploratory study, *Health Policy, in press*.
Guindo, L.A., Wagner, M., Baltussen, R., Rindress, D., van Til, J., Kind, P., Goetghebeur, M.M., 2012. From efficacy to equity: literature review of decision criteria for resource allocation and healthcare decisionmaking. Cost Effectiveness and Resource Allocation 10 (1), 1–13.
Harris, A.H., Hill, S.R., Chin, G., Li, J.J., Walkom, E., 2008. The role of value for money in public insurance coverage decisions for drugs in Australia: a retrospective analysis 1994–2004. Medical Decision Making 28 (5), 713–722.
Harris, A., Li, J.J., Yong, K., 2016. What can we expect from value-based funding of medicines? A retrospective study. Pharmacoeconomics 34 (4), 393–402.
Harvey, R., de Boer, R., 2015. Growth in expenditure on high cost drugs in Australia. Research paper series, 2014-15. D. o. p. s, Parliament of Australia. Canberra.
Hunter, D.J., et al., 2016. Public involvement in health priority setting: future challenges for policy, research and society. Journal of Health Organization and Management Information 30 (5), 796–808.
Karnon, J., Shafie, A.S., Orji, N., Usman, S.K., 2016. What are we paying for? A cost-effectiveness analysis of patented denosumab and generic alendronate for postmenopausal osteoporotic women in Australia. Cost Effectiveness and Resource Allocation 14 (1), 11.
Kaser, E., Shaw, J., Marven, M., Swinburne, L., Boyle, F., 2010. Communication about high-cost drugs in oncology—the patient view. Annals of Oncology 21 (9), 1910–1914.

Kim, C., Prasad, V., 2015. Cancer drugs approved on the basis of a surrogate end point and subsequent overall survival. An analysis of 5 Years of US Food and Drug Administration approvals. JAMA Internal Medicine 175 (12).

Leukaemia Foundation, 2015. Accessing non-PBS funded blood cancer drugs in Australia, Retrieved 12 September 2016 from http://www.leukaemia.org.au/news/new-guide-to-accessing-blood-cancer-drugs.

MacKenzie, R., Chapman, S., Salkeld, G., Holding, S., 2008. Media influence on Herceptin subsidization in Australia: application of the rule of rescue? Journal of the Royal Society of Medicine 101 (6), 305–312.

McKie, J., Richardson, J., 2003. The rule of rescue. Social Science & Medicine 56 (12), 2407–2419.

Medicines Australia, 2016. Code of Conduct Annual Report 2015–2016. Available from: https://medicinesaustralia.com.au/wp-content/uploads/sites/52/2014/02/20161020-FINAL-CoC-AnnualReport-2015_2016-REVISED.pdf.

Mitchell, A., Viney, R., 2016. Predicting future evidence in drug reimbursement: a government policy and decision-making perspective. ISPOR ISPOR 7th Asia-Pacific Conference, Singapore.

Moore, T.J., Furberg, C.D., 2012. The safety risks of innovation the FDA's expedited drug development pathway. Journal of the American Medical Association 308 (9), 869–870.

Mycause, 2016. Mycause. Available from: https://www.mycause.com.au/personal-cause-crowdfunding/cancer.

Niraula, S., Seruga, B., Ocana, A., Shao, T., Goldstein, R., Tannock, I.F., Amir, E., 2012. The price we pay for progress: a meta-analysis of harms of newly approved anticancer drugs. Journal of Clinical Oncology 30 (24), 3012–3019.

Organisation for Economic Co-operation Development, 2014. Pharmaceutical Spending, Retrieved 2017, 3 January, from https://data.oecd.org/healthres/pharmaceutical-spending.htm.

PBS Information, M. S., Pharmaceutical Policy Branch, 2016. Expenditure and Prescriptions Twelve Months to 30 June 2016. Available from: https://www.pbs.gov.au/statistics/expenditure-prescriptions/2015-2016/expenditure-prescriptions-report-2015-16.pdf.

Pharmaceutical Benefits Advisory Committee, 2015. Public Summary Document – March 2015 PBAC Meeting. Pembrolizumab 50 mg vial, 100 mg vial; Keytruda®. Available from: http://www.pbs.gov.au/info/industry/listing/elements/pbac-meetings/psd/2015-03/pembrolizumab-keytruda-psd-03-2015.

Pharmaceutical Benefits Advisory Committee, 2016. Guidelines for Preparing a Submission to the Pharmaceutical Benefits Advisory Committee. Version 5.0. September 2016. Available from: https://pbac.pbs.gov.au/content/information/files/pbac-guidelines-version-5.pdf.

Rare Cancers Australia, 2016. Patient Treatment Fund. Available from: https://www.rarecancers.org.au/page/1138/patient-treatment-fund.

Roughead, E.E., Gilbert, A.L., Vitry, A.I., 2008. The Australian funding debate on quadrivalent HPV vaccine: a case study for the national pharmaceutical policy. Health Policy 88 (2–3), 250–257.

Samson, L., Delaat, W., Horvath, J., 2015. Review of Medicines and Medical Devices Regulation. Stage One Report. Available from: https://www.tga.gov.au/media-release/expert-review-medicines-and-medical-devices-regulation.

The Australian Government, D. o. H., 1999. National Medicines Policy. Available from: http://www.health.gov.au/nationalmedicinespolicy.

The Australian Government, D. o. H., 2011. Framework for the Introduction of Parallel TGA and PBAC Processes. Available from: http://www.pbs.gov.au/info/publication/factsheets/shared/framework-for-introduction-of-parallel-TGA-and-PBAC-processes.

The Australian Government, D. o. H., 2016. Section 100 Item List. Available from: https://www.pbs.gov.au/browse/section100.

The Australian Government, D. o. H., Therapeutic Goods Administration, 2016. Special Access Scheme. Available from: https://www.tga.gov.au/form/special-access-scheme.
The Senate Community Affairs References Committee, 2015. Availability of New, Innovative and Specialist Cancer Drugs in Australia. Available from: http://www.aph.gov.au/Parliamentary_Business/Committees/Senate/Community_Affairs/Cancer_Drugs.
The SocialMedwork, 2016. The SocialMedwork. Available from: https://thesocialmedwork.com/crowdfunding/.
Vitry, A., Roughead, E., 2014. Managed entry agreements for pharmaceuticals in Australia. Health Policy 117 (3), 345–352.
Vitry, A., Nguyen, T., Entwistle, V., Roughead, E., 2015a. Regulatory withdrawal of medicines marketed with uncertain benefits: the bevacizumab case study. Journal of Pharmaceutical Policy And Practice 8, 25.
Vitry, A., Thai, L., Roughead, E., 2015b. Pharmaceutical pricing policies in Australia. Pharmaceutical Prices in the 21st Century. Springer, Z. Babar.
Vitry, A., Mintzes, B., Lipworth, W., 2016. Access to new cancer medicines in Australia: dispelling the myths and informing a public debate. Journal of Pharmaceutical Policy and Practice 9, 13.
Whitty, J.A., Littlejohns, P., 2015. Social values and health priority setting in Australia: an analysis applied to the context of health technology assessment. Health Policy 119 (2), 127–136.
Whitty, J.A., Ratcliffe, J., Chen, G., Scuffham, P.A., 2014. Australian public preferences for the funding of new health technologies: a comparison of discrete choice and profile case best-worst scaling methods. Medical Decision Making 34 (5), 638–654.
Wonder, M., Chin, G., 2015. What impact does 'conventional' economic evaluation have on patient access to new orphan medicines? A comparative study of their reimbursement in Australia (2005–2012). Expert Review of Pharmacoeconomics & Outcomes Research 15 (5), 843–850.
Wonder, M., Dunlop, S., 2015. Assessment of the quality of the clinical evidence in submissions to the Australian pharmaceutical benefits advisory committee: fit for purpose. Value in Health 18 (4), 467–476.
Wortley, S., Tong, A., Howard, K., 2016. Preferences for engagement in health technology assessment decision-making: a nominal group technique with members of the public. BMJ Open 6 (2), e010265.

FURTHER READINGS

Australian Government, 2013. Department of Health and Pharmaceutical Benefits Pricing Authority (PBPA) "PBPA Policies, Procedures and Methods 2009. Pricing of new products proposed for listing on the Pharmaceutical Benefits Scheme (PBS)., Retrieved 14 June from http://www.health.gov.au/internet/publications/publishing.nsf/Content/pbs-pbpa-policies-contents~pbs-pbpa-policies-ch3.
Vogler, S., Vitry, A., Babar, Z.U.D., 2016. Cancer drugs in 16 European countries, Australia, and New Zealand: a cross-country price comparison study. Lancet Oncology 17 (1), 39–47.

CHAPTER 12

Access to High-Cost Medicines in New Zealand

Louise E. Curley*, Maree Jensen*, Zaheer-Ud-Din Babar,*, Sanya Ram***

*University of Auckland, Auckland, New Zealand

**University of Huddersfield, Queensgate, Huddersfield, United Kingdom

12.1 INTRODUCTION

The World Health Organisation's (WHO) essential medicine list (EML) provides a list of the minimum medicine needs that should be available in a country for a basic healthcare system (World Health Organization, n.d.). The list includes the most efficacious, safe and cost-effective medicines for priority conditions and is updated every 2 years, to reflect the current and estimated public health relevance (World Health Organisation, 2015). In the 2015 review of the EML, five new direct-acting oral antiretroviral drugs were added for the treatment of chronic hepatitis C. Furthermore, 16 new oncology medicines were also added to the EML (Mayor, 2015). These medicines are expensive and consequently place strain on the budget of many healthcare systems (McCormack et al., 2010). In addition to more expensive medicines, worldwide the population is ageing, which subsequently increases the demand and use of medications. Combined with consumer expectation, both the aforementioned factors contribute to the challenge of medicine expenditure and the policies that allow access to high-cost medicines. In New Zealand, there are additional concerns regarding equitable access to medicines for Maori and Pacific Island people (Babar and Francis, 2014).

New Zealand is well-known internationally for having implemented national medicines policies that aim for equitable access for medicines (Babar and Vitry, 2014). When compared to other OECD countries, New Zealand achieves an equivalent spend of 40% to that of other countries in the OECD (Babar and Vitry, 2014; Organisation for Economic Co-operation and Development, 2013) and is able to achieve these cost savings through the use of a combination of programme budgeting, tough price negotiations and different procurement mechanisms, such as encouraging

Equitable Access to High-Cost Pharmaceuticals
http://dx.doi.org/10.1016/B978-0-12-811945-7.00012-9

the development of generics by competition for sole supply or by running competitive tenders (Babar and Vitry, 2014; Cumming et al., 2010). Medicines are largely funded from taxation, which provides drugs free of charge in public hospitals and a pre-specified list of drugs at a subsidised cost to people outside the hospital setting (Cumming et al., 2010).

However, New Zealand medicines access is not without its controversy (Babar and Vitry, 2014; Cumming et al., 2010); submissions to a public consultation by the Pharmaceutical Management Agency (PHARMAC) reported negative experiences in access to some medications. For example, there have been complaints that the access to new medicines is less than that of other similar countries (Grainger and Harrison, 2005) or when certain brands have become unfunded (Gillies et al., 2005). When compared to its neighbour Australia, New Zealand had 43% of Australia's available medicines (Pharmaceutical Management Agency, 2013). In a review for the Minister of Health (2010), McCormack et al. (2010) report that "New Zealand has less access to new, high-cost medicines than other countries, in particular Australia".

There has been considerable discussion over access to high-cost medicines in New Zealand. In a report to the Minister of Health (2010), high-cost medicines are defined as 'medicines that, compared to others, are expensive relative to the health benefits patients receive from them .... Although there are no precise definitions for New Zealand, their cost is likely to be in excess of $20,000 per patient per year, and sometimes considerably more' (McCormack et al., 2010).

The debate around whether and which high-cost medicines should be funded has been ongoing for a number of years. In 2006, PHARMAC released a report that indicated that there was no reason that funding high-cost medicines should be treated differently from other medicines (Pharmaceutical Management Agency, 2006). Since then, there have been further reports released by PHARMAC and the pharmaceutical industry arguing different views on this topic.

Access to high-cost medicines has also become a political agenda. The National Party pledged to improve access to high-cost medicines during their campaign and after being elected in 2009 the funding for Herceptin was extended (Fenton, 2010). This move was criticised, as this did not resolve the ongoing issue with access to high-cost medicines (Funding of Cancer Drug, 2008). However, in May 2009, an independent panel was established to provide advice on access to high-cost medicines (New Zealand Government, 2010). This panel released a report in 2010 which stated that New Zealanders have less access to new high-cost medicines than comparable countries and this could result in poor health and death (Access to High-cost Medicines, 2010). The potential solutions presented in the recommendations were increased government spending, increased patient co-payments on prescriptions and reducing wastage in the health system (Access to High-cost Medicines, 2010). A recent published study by (Vogler et al., 2016) compared the funding of cancer drugs across 13 countries; New Zealand was the country that funded the fewest indications (Vogler et al., 2016). Furthermore, the time to market has also been criticized; a study conducted by Wonder and Milne (2011) reported that the average time that a medicine was registered in New Zealand 9 months after Australia and time from registration to listing was 2 years longer than that of Australia. However, PHARMAC released a report to dispute these claims, stating that 'most of the additional medicines funded in Australia but not in New Zealand do not offer health gains that would be considered clinically meaningful by international cancer specialists in recent research' (Pharmaceutical Management Agency, 2015).

This chapter will give a description of approval of medicines in New Zealand and PHARMAC, the funding agency for pharmaceuticals, and describes the avenues to access high-cost medicines in New Zealand.

12.2 APPROVAL OF MEDICINES IN NEW ZEALAND

Medicines in New Zealand are approved by the Minister of Health, under advice by Medsafe, the Medicines and Medical Devices Safety Authority (BPAC, 2013; Medsafe, 2013). The Medicines Adverse Reaction Committee (MARC) and Medsafe advise the Minister of Health on the safety of the medicine, specifically the risk–benefit of each medicine (BPAC, 2013; Medsafe, 2013).

Prior to this approval being granted, each medicine and medical device has to go through a regulatory process; this process ensures medicines and medical devices meet appropriate standards of safety and quality (BPAC, 2013; Medsafe, 2013). In accordance with the Medicines Act 1981, for a medication to be approved, the company that markets the medication must apply for consent. Furthermore, the medication is only approved for the specific indication that it has applied for (Medsafe, 2013).

The Centre for Adverse Reactions Monitoring (CARM) collects reports of suspected adverse reactions to medicines and informs Medsafe of potential safety issues with approved medicines (BPAC, 2013). If a significant safety or quality issue is identified, a warning or recall is requested by Medsafe, and in extreme cases, the Minister of Health can withdraw consent for the approval of the medicine (BPAC, 2013).

12.3 PHARMAC

PHARMAC was established in 1993 in response to the growing spending on pharmaceuticals (Cumming et al., 2010; Pharmaceutical Management Agency, 2017a–h). In the 1980s, expenditure on medications was rising by approximately 15%–20% per year (Cumming et al., 2010; Pharmaceutical Management Agency, 2017a–h), which was faster than any other component of healthcare, and this growth was unsustainable. When established, PHARMAC's objective was to actively manage government spending on medicines (Pharmaceutical Management Agency, 2017a–h).

PHARMAC acts on behalf of the 20 District Health Boards throughout New Zealand (Cumming et al., 2010) and is an independent government appointed board that reports to the Minister of Health in New Zealand (Babar and Francis, 2014).

Today PHARMAC works within a capped budget to manage the budget for medications including negotiating the prices of medicines and the supply of some hospital medicines and promoting the optimal use of medicines (Ragupathy et al., 2014). In addition, PHARMAC also manages selected cancer drugs and exceptional circumstances schemes that supply drug funding for people with rare conditions (Pharmaceutical Management Agency, 2017a–h).

PHARMAC's objective is to 'secure for eligible people in need of pharmaceuticals the best health outcomes that are reasonably achievable from pharmaceutical treatment and from within the funding provided' (Pharmaceutical Management Agency, 2017a–h).

12.4 SUBSIDISED AND PARTLY SUBSIDISED MEDICATIONS

Once the approval process has taken place and a medicine has been approved for sale in New Zealand, pharmaceutical companies can apply for government funding to PHARMAC. PHARMAC need to decide whether the medication will be funded, how much the government will pay and also what if any are the conditions to access this medicine (Cumming et al., 2010).

The application that the company submits details information on the cost and the benefits of the medication. This information historically was assessed based on nine criteria by the pharmacology and therapeutics advisory committee at PHARMAC and makes a recommendation; recently, a new model has been developed and has been made publicly available on PHARMAC's web site (Pharmaceutical Management Agency, 2017a–h). The factors for consideration are represented in a circular diagram, representing four dimensions of the funding decisions: needs, health benefits, costs and savings, and suitability. Within these four dimensions, there are also three levels: the impact to the person, the person's family, whanau and wider society and also to the broader health system. The extent to which any one particular factor is relevant, if at all, and the influence of each factor is for PHARMAC to determine on each occasion within the context of its legal obligations (Pharmaceutical Management Agency, 2017a–h).

All medicines that are subsidised or partly subsidised by the government are listed in the pharmaceutical schedule, in addition to all the medicines that may be given in District Health Board (DHB) hospitals (Pharmaceutical Management Agency, 2017a–h). A hospital pharmaceutical is only funded if it is administered at DHB hospitals. All other registered medicines need to be paid for by the patient.

Patients who are prescribed a drug that is subsidised by the government pay a co-payment of $5 per item, if they are eligible for publicly-funded health and disability services and they are prescribed a medicine from an eligible prescriber. As of 1 July 2015, children who are under the age of 13 are exempt from paying a prescription co-payment (Ministry of Health, 2017). In addition to this subsidy, for patients and/or their families who have collected 20 prescription items in one year, they are also exempt from paying the co-payment for future prescriptions until February of the following year (Ministry of Health, 2017). If the patient is prescribed a subsidised medicine by a prescriber that is not eligible, as determined by the PHARMAC, on behalf of the District Health Boards, the patient pays a co-payment of $15 (Ministry of Health, 2017).

Medications that are partly subsidised pay an additional charge; this is due to the fact that PHARMAC have arranged the subsidy level for that particular medication at a lower price than the drug company charge (Ministry of Health, 2017).

New Zealand has made the decision to keep the co-payment charges for subsidised medicines relatively low. In comparison, Australian co-payment charges for general patients are A$36.90 or A$6 for people with concession cards. A higher co-payment has been reported to lead to equity issues, a study that evaluated the effects of an increase in co-payments showed that an increase in the co-payments that occurred in 2005 in Australia adversely affected prescription medicine use (Hynd et al., 2008).

12.5 SPECIAL AUTHORITY PHARMACEUTICALS

Special authority criteria may apply to some patients with specific medical conditions who meet pre-specified criteria (Pharmaceutical Management Agency, 2016a, b, 2017a–h). The pre-specified criteria are stipulated in the PHARMAC schedule below each special authority community pharmaceutical (Pharmaceutical Management Agency, 2016a, b). The process in which this funding is sought is via an application made on behalf of a particular patient by the prescriber (Pharmaceutical Management Agency, 2016a, b). Most Special Authority applications are processed by the Ministry of Health (Pharmaceutical Management Agency, 2017a–h). If the person meets the criteria, and a special authority is granted, the patient will be issued a special authority number, which must appear on the prescription when the drug in question is prescribed (Pharmaceutical Management Agency, 2016a, b).

Examples of recently added special authority pharmaceuticals are the anti-retrovirals for Hepatitis C; Harvoni ((ledipasvir with sofosbuvir) and Viekira Pak (paritaprevir with ritonavir and ombitasvir copackaged with dasabuvir)/Viekira Pak-RBV (paritaprevir with ritonavir and ombitasvir copackaged with dasabuvir and ribavirin) (Pharmaceutical Management Agency, 2017a–h)).

12.6 EXCEPTIONS

PHARMAC's role is also to consider whether medications that are not currently subsidised should be funded under exceptional circumstances. The consideration of these exceptional circumstances is outlined in the Exceptional Circumstances Framework which outlines the way in which PHARMAC considers these applications before determining whether or not to fund that supply of that medicine for that patient. The Exceptions Framework includes the Named Patient Pharmaceutical Assessment (NPPA) policy and other means by which a patient's exceptional circumstances may be considered (Pharmaceutical Management Agency, 2017a–h).

The NPPA policy has three core principles: "(1) to provide a pathway to consider those whose clinical circumstances cannot be met through the current schedule; (2) to complement the PHARMAC schedule and its decision-making process and (3) it is designed for individual assessment" (Pharmaceutical Management Agency, 2017a–h). If the application, made by the patient's prescriber, is consistent with these three core principles then PHARMAC will assess the application against the decision criteria, which are outlined in PHARMAC's Operating Policies and Procedures (Pharmaceutical Management Agency, 2017a–h). Once a decision is made, this decision applies to the patient for which the application has been made only (Pharmaceutical Management Agency, 2017a–h).

In a hospital setting, if a medication was needed and the need is urgent, that is, then it is not feasible within the clinical timeframe to undergo the process of applying via the standard NPPA scheme, then a Rapid Hospital Assessment can be made to the District Health Board. In the Exceptional Circumstances Framework, it states that it is expected that "DHBs will follow the same process as PHARMAC in considering the NPPA Rapid Hospital Assessment" (Pharmaceutical Management Agency, 2017a–h).

There have been reports by specialists that the NPPA process is inefficient, and in some cases can impact on the patient's care whilst waiting for the approval and can impact on a clinician's time (Babar and Francis, 2014). In the study by (Babar and Francis, 2014), the authors discuss the process of NPPA and suggest that due to the high proportion of approval rates under the NPPA scheme (only 15 applications being declined compared with 555 approvals), whether an alternative could be an evidence-based facilitator to ease the burden of the clinicians regarding the application (Babar and Francis, 2014).

Other means in which a patient may be considered is if a particular medicine is funded under special authority conditions, and the patient does not meet those exact conditions. There are some cases whereby the person's clinical circumstances meet the intent of the Schedule, but not the Special Authority criteria, at the discretion of the Ministry of Health, a Special Authority waiver may be granted (Pharmaceutical Management Agency, 2017a–h).

12.7 UNAPPROVED MEDICINES

When a company applies for, and is granted approval for a medicine, the Ministry of Health provides consent that stipulates the marketing of that medicine, including the indication (BPAC, 2013; Medsafe, 2009, 2014). Section 25 of the Medicines Act 1981 allows an authorised prescriber to "procure the sale or supply of any medicine" (BPAC, 2013; Medsafe, 2009, 2014). Thus, this includes both medicines that are approved, and those that are unapproved in New Zealand (BPAC, 2013). This also includes approved medicines for unapproved uses or routes of administration. This unapproved medicine has to be for a named person, that is, "enabling the medicine to be administered to a particular patient who is known and identifiable at the time when the medicine is sold or supplied to the authorised prescriber". Pursuant to this, Section 29 of the Medicines Act states that the supplier of the unapproved medicine must notify in writing the Director General of Health (BPAC, 2013). However, no notification is required of an approved medication with an unapproved use or route of administration (BPAC, 2013).

The consumer should also be fully informed that the medication is unapproved, including its use and any safety concerns. If the medicine is experimental, written consent is also required (BPAC, 2013).

Although the PHARMAC Schedule has mainly approved medicines, being an approved medicine is not a prerequisite of being listed in the schedule. PHARMAC bases its decisions on the needs of patients in New Zealand and availability of funds, as described earlier (BPAC, 2013). An example of a medicine that was funded when unapproved is benzbromarone for the treatment of gout (BPAC, 2014) or when there are supply issues and another medicine has to be sourced that does not have consent for distribution in New Zealand, for example, in the recent recall of Span K, brand of a slow release potassium chloride tablet (Medsafe, 2016).

12.8 EARLY ACCESS PROGRAMMES

The term Medicine Access Program is used as an umbrella term to describe programmes that are offered by pharmaceutical companies to patients to improve access to specific medications. This improved access may be via deferred cost, cost-free or by subsidised means (Council of Australian Therapeutic Advisory Groups, 2015).

The medicines access programs may include products that are unregistered in the country (Patil, 2016). There may be a paucity of information on the safety, quality and efficacy of the product (Patil, 2016). Establishing quality of a medicine which has shown to be of some benefit is difficult at individual level; without the necessary tools of testing the products and certificates of analysis and without the comfort of the relying on Medsafe to have rigorously reviewed the data to approve registration, clinicians have to make a decision sometimes based on limited information (Patil, 2016).

Many countries have 'early access' schemes; early access programmes, compassionate access or medicines access programmes all that enable patient's early access to medicines that they may ordinarily not be able to afford, that are showing promise in early research (Patil, 2016). PHARMAC states that it "has strong interest in funding promising new medicines with emerging evidence (so-called 'early access'), but the timing and extent of such decisions are always a careful judgement" (Pharmaceutical Management Agency, 2016a, b).

The benefit of access programmes cannot be denied. The specialist is enabled to provide a medicine to a patient who often has exhausted other options and has a direct effect on monitoring progress. Often patients are desperate and it is natural for a doctor to explore every mechanism to enable trial options.

Medicines Access Programs may have both benefits and risks. The patient may benefit from an otherwise inaccessible medicine and the pharmaceutical company may get to promote its medicine, develop a future market share and lobby to obtain a successful listing for funding. However, critics argue that the MAPs are usually not sustainable, create equity issues for those unable to get access to the programme or afford the cost-sharing arrangement and there is the potential for inadequate enrolment of patients (Council of Australian Therapeutic Advisory Groups, 2015). Newer medicines usually do not have a well-established safety profile, have uncertain clinical benefit and carry a risk of toxicity (Lewis et al., 2014a). However, since MAPs in Australia and New Zealand are not required to be formally monitored unlike clinical trials, there may be limited or no systematic recording of health outcomes and adverse drug events.

Once the medicine is approved/registered with the regulatory agency often there is a temptation to review whether it should be state funded and the access programme being withdrawn. The patient is then potentially left with a diagnosis and a medicine that they cannot access due to the high cost (Radio, 2016). In addition, supply issues have also been reported (New Zealand Listener, 2016).

12.9 CLINICAL TRIALS

Another avenue for access to high-cost medicines in New Zealand is via clinical trials. This route may allow patients to access medicines that are in the early stages of development or those that are already developed, but being trialled for new indications. Eligibility criteria and geographical residence is often a limitation to access for certain patients, amongst a myriad of other considerations (Lewis et al., 2014b). Balancing access to appropriate clinical trials and protecting patients from the harms of investigational medicines is not always a seamless process (Darrow et al., 2015).

12.10 RARE CONDITION PILOT

Rare conditions are as by nature rare, and thus it is difficult for PHARMAC to gain sufficient evidence for evaluation (Babar and Francis, 2014). To compound the issue, the unit cost is increased for these low-demand medicines due to the need to satisfy manufacturer ordering and regulatory requirements (Babar and Francis, 2014).

In 2014 PHARMAC requested feedback on medicines for rare disorders (Pharmaceutical Management Agency, 2017a–h). This was the first time that PHARMAC had aimed to improve access to medications for rare disorders in this manner, which was a commercial approach. Feedback was received from suppliers, individuals, prescribers and consumer groups. As of March 2017 there are 10 medicines that are approved for funding via this pilot; evaluation of the pilot will start in 2017 to whether the process should be run again. PHARMAC has reported that it intends to continue to make these medications available to those who are benefitting from these drugs, as measured by clinical benefit (Pharmaceutical Management Agency, 2017a–h).

The medications currently approved via the rare conditions scheme are listed in the table below (Pharmaceutical Management Agency, 2017a–h). Some medicines were noted by PHARMAC as still needing approval by Medsafe (Pharmaceutical Management Agency, 2017a–h).

Medicine approved (brand)	Indication
Betaine (Cystadane)	For patients with homocystinuria who have not achieved an appropriate homocysteine level with vitamin supplementation
Alglucosidase alfa (Myozyme)	For infantile-onset Pompe Disease
Idursulfase (Elaprase)	For Hunter Syndrome (MPS II) to stabilise patients awaiting stem cell transplant
Laronidase (Aldurazyme)	For Hurler Syndrome (MPS 1-H) to stabilise patients awaiting stem cell transplant
Cholic acid (Cholebiol)	For the treatment of rare forms of bile acid synthesis disorders in infants with metabolic liver disease
Sodium phenylbutyrate (Pheburane)	For the metabolic disorders known as urea cycle disorders, which can lead to a fatal build-up of nitrogen and ammonia in the body
Siltuximab (Sylvant)	For a rare form of immune system disorder called HHV-negative idiopathic multicentric Castleman's disease (iMCD)

Medicine approved (brand)	Indication
Bedaquiline (Sirturo)	For a rare extensively multi-drug resistant form of tuberculosis
Galsulfase (Naglazyme)	For people with the rare enzyme deficiency condition Maroteaux–Lamy Syndrome, or mucopolysaccharidosis (MPS) VI
Icatibant (Firazyr)	For hereditary angioedema

12.11 CROWDFUNDING

With long waits to accessing publicly funded medicines, patients are often turning to social media and crowdfunding sites to fund access to healthcare (Snyder et al., 2016). While, this mechanism of raising funds at first glance seems like a great opportunity to access treatment that one may not be able to afford, it is fraught with difficulties and ethical challenges (Young and Scheinberg, 2017). An example of an online crowdfunding website in New Zealand is "Givealittle" from the Spark foundation, established in January 2008. Individuals, charities, schools and businesses can all use the website, and the funding that you market via this site, may include medical-related costs. To date, it reports to have had $69 million of donations over all the projects that have used this site (Spark, n.d.).

12.12 FUTURE OF ACCESS TO HIGH-COST MEDICINES IN NEW ZEALAND

The issue of access to high-cost medicines will be an ongoing challenge worldwide; expensive and specialised medicines for conditions, such as rare disorders, are likely to increase (Pharmaceutical Management Agency, 2014). McCormack et al. (2010) have noted that in the future medicines will be increasingly targeted for fewer patients. Furthermore, the pharmaceutical industry has been suggested to be moving toward "niche-buster" drugs, rather than "blockbuster" ones (Melnikova, 2012). At this stage PHARMAC have indicated that they will be evaluating the rare condition pilot contestable funding in early 2017 before further decisions are made on the commercial processes for medicines for rare conditions (Pharmaceutical Management Agency, 2017a–h).

It has been reported by Babar and Francis (2014) that there are inefficiencies in the processes surrounding the special authority and the NPPA medicines, whereby the authors suggest that PHARMAC may want to consider contracting an evidence-based facilitator to ease the burden for clinicians.

Lastly, McCormack et al. (2010) in their report to the Ministry of Health recommended a number of key points relating to the access of high-cost medicines in New Zealand, including the need to treat high cost, highly specialised medicines the same way as other medicines when it comes to decisions on funding, the need to have greater consistency in decision-making when it comes to funding of medicines and reduced complexity and increased transparency.

12.13 CONCLUSION

Worldwide the population is ageing, which subsequently increases the demand and use of medications. Combined with consumer expectation, both of these aforementioned factors contribute to the challenge of medicine expenditure and the policies that allow access to high-cost medicines. This chapter outlines the avenues to which patients in New Zealand can access high-cost medicines—some of these routes are funded by the government, whilst others are not. In non-funded and in some cases unapproved pharmaceuticals access becomes a limitation to treatment. PHARMAC has recently restructured how factors in which they make decisions on whether to fund a medicine, and in addition have started a pilot scheme for rare disorders. However, as more expensive medicines enter the market the challenge will be to provide equitable access to these high-cost medicines.

REFERENCES

Access to high-cost medicines report received 2010. Available from: http://www.scoop.co.nz/stories/PA1005/S00127.htm.

Babar, Z.U., Francis, S., 2014. Identifying priority medicines policy issues for New Zealand: a general inductive study. BMJ Open 4 (5), e004415.

Babar, Z., Vitry, A., 2014. Differences in Australian and New Zealand medicines funding policies. Australian Prescriber (37), 150–151.

BPAC, N.Z., 2013. Upfront: Unapproved medicines and unapproved uses of medicines: keeping prescribers and patients safe, Available from: http://www.bpac.org.nz/BPJ/2013/March/unapproved-medicines.aspx.

BPAC, N.Z., 2014. Gout update: Febuxostat now subsidised on Special Authority, Available from: http://www.bpac.org.nz/BPJ/2014/July/febuxostat.aspx.

Council of Australian Therapeutic Advisory Groups, 2015. Managing Medicines Access Programs, Guiding principles for the governance of Medicines Access Programs in Australian hospitals 2015 [cited 2016, 7 September]. Available from: http://www.catag.org.au/wp-content/uploads/2012/08/OKA10428-CATAG-Guiding-Principles-for-Australian-Hospitals-FINAL-pdf.pdf.

Cumming, J., Mays, N., Daube, J., 2010. How New Zealand has contained expenditure on drugs. BMJ 340, c2441.

Darrow, J.J., Sarpatwari, A., Avorn, J., Kesselheim, A.S., 2015. Practical, legal, and ethical issues in expanded access to investigational drugs. New England Journal of Medicine 372 (3), 279–286.

Fenton, E., 2010. Making fair funding decisions for high cost cancer care: the case of herceptin in New Zealand. Public Health Ethics 3 (2), 137–146.

Funding of cancer drug 'bad' precedent 2008. Available from: http://www.stuff.co.nz/the-press/756278.

Gillies, J., Brown, J., Byrnes, C., Farrell, A., Graham, D., 2005. PHARMAC and Ventolin in New Zealand. The New Zealand Medical Journal 118 (1220), U1616.

Grainger, R., Harrison, A., 2005. TNF inhibitors for inflammatory arthritis in New Zealand. The New Zealand Medical Journal 118 (1224).

Hynd, A., Roughead, E.E., Preen, D.B., Glover, J., Bulsara, M., Semmens, J., 2008. The impact of co-payment increases on dispensings of government-subsidised medicines in Australia. Pharmacoepidemiology and Drug Safety 17 (11), 1091–1099.

Lewis, J.R.R., Lipworth, W., Kerridge, I., Doran, E., 2014a. Dilemmas in the compassionate supply of investigational cancer drugs. Internal Medicine Journal 44 (9), 841–845.

Lewis, J.R., Lipworth, W., Kerridge, I., Doran, E., 2014b. Dilemmas in the compassionate supply of investigational cancer drugs. Internal Medicine Journal 44 (9), 841–845.

Mayor, S., 2015. WHO includes 16 new cancer drugs on list of essential medicines. Lancet Oncology 16 (7), 757.

McCormack, P., Quigley, J., Hansen, P., 2010. Review of Access to High-Cost, Highly-Specialised Medicines in New Zealand, Available from: http://img.scoop.co.nz/media/pdfs/1005/Review_of_Access_to_High_Cost_Highly_Specialised_Medicines_31_April_2010.pdf.

Medsafe., 2009. Use of Unapproved Medicines in New Zealand, Available from: http://www.medsafe.govt.nz/profs/PUArticles/Use of unapproved medicine in New Zealand Aug 09.htm.

Medsafe. Medsafe's Evaluation and Approval Process, 2013. Available from: http://www.medsafe.govt.nz/Consumers/Safety-of-Medicines/Medsafe-Evaluation-Process.asp.

Medsafe., 2014. Use of Unapproved Medicines and Unapproved Use of Medicines, Available from: http://www.medsafe.govt.nz/profs/RIss/unapp.asp.

Medsafe., 2016. Guidance for Pharmacists Dispensing Prescriptions for Span-K, Available from: http://www.medsafe.govt.nz/hot/RecallActionNoticesNew/20651.asp.

Melnikova, I., 2012. Rare diseases and orphan drugs. Nature Reviews Drug Discovery 11 (4), 267–268.

Ministry of Health. Prescription charges Medications, 2017. Available from: http://www.health.govt.nz/your-health/conditions-and-treatments/treatments-and-surgery/medications/prescription-charges.

New Zealand Government., 2010. Actioning Medicines New Zealand, Available from: http://www.health.govt.nz/system/files/documents/publications/actioning-medsnz-updated-mar2010.pdf.

New Zealand Listener., 2016. Conflicting Agendas, Available from: https://www.pressreader.com/new-zealand/new-zealand-listener/20160902/281809988331577.

Organisation for Economic Co-operation and Development, 2013. Health at a glance, OECD indicators Paris: OECD Publishing; 2013. Available from: http://www.oecd.org/els/health-systems/Health-at-a-Glance.2013.pdf.

Patil, S., 2016. Early access programs: benefits, challenges, and key considerations for successful implementation. Perspectives in Clinical Research 7 (1), 4–8.

Pharmaceutical Management Agency., 2006. How high cost medicine should be funded, Available from: http://www.pharmac.govt.nz/2006/12/15/HCM.pdf.

Pharmaceutical Management Agency., 2013. PHARMAC's decision criteria: summary of submissions. Wellington, Available from: http://www.pharmac.health.nz/assets/decision-criteria-summary-of-submissions-2013-12.pdf.
Pharmaceutical Management Agency., 2014. High Cost Medicines for Rare Disorders, Available from: https://www.pharmac.govt.nz/assets/high-cost-medicines-discussion-document-2014-04.pdf.
Pharmaceutical Management Agency., 2015. Do differences in funding cancer medicines in Australia and New Zealand impact on people's health?, Available from: https://www.pharmac.govt.nz/assets/cancer-comparisons-summary-2015-10-03.pdf.
Pharmaceutical Management Agency. Special Authority Applications. In: New Zealand Pharmaceutical Schedule.2016. 5.
Pharmaceutical Management Agency., 2016b. Early access schemes, Available from: https://www.pharmac.govt.nz/medicines/new-medicines/early-access-schemes/.
Pharmaceutical Management Agency, 2017a. Medicines for rare disorders, Available from: https://www.pharmac.govt.nz/medicines/how-medicines-are-funded/medicines-for-rare-disorders/.
Pharmaceutical Management Agency, 2017b. Supporting Information: Factors for consideration, Available from:https://www.pharmac.govt.nz/medicines/how-medicines-are-funded/factors-for-consideration/supporting-information/#how.
Pharmaceutical Management Agency. PHARMAC Our history. 2017. PHARMAC Our history Available from: https://www.pharmac.govt.nz/about/our-history/.
Pharmaceutical Management Agency. Exceptional Circumstances Framework (including the Named Patient Pharmaceutical Assessment Policy) 2017. Available from: https://www.pharmac.govt.nz/assets/exceptional-circumstances-framework.pdf.
Pharmaceutical Management Agency. Hepatitis C treatments: information about new listings from 1 July 2016 2017. Available from: https://www.pharmac.govt.nz/medicines/my-medicine-has-changed/hepatitis-c-treatments/.
Pharmaceutical Management Agency. How Medicines are Funded: Factors for Consideration Medicines; 2017. Available from: https://www.pharmac.govt.nz/medicines/how-medicines-are-funded/factors-for-consideration/.
Pharmaceutical Management Agency. Inside the Pharmaceutical Schedule, 2017. Available from: https://www.pharmac.govt.nz/about/your-guide-to-pharmac/factsheet-14-pharmaceutical-schedule/.
Pharmaceutical Management Agency. Operating policies and procedures: Special Authorities 2017. Available from: https://www.pharmac.govt.nz/about/operating-policies-and-procedures/.
Radio, N.Z., 2016. Patients left in lurch as Bayer pulls free anti-coagulant, Available from: http://www.radionz.co.nz/news/national/296713/patients-left-in-lurch-as-free-drug-pulled.
Ragupathy, R., Kilpatrick, K., Babar, Z.-U.-D., 2014. Pharmaceutical pricing in NZ. In: Babar, Z-U-D. (Ed.), Pharmaceutical Prices in the 21st Century. ADIS.
Snyder, J., Mathers, A., Crooks, V.A., 2016. Fund my treatment! A call for ethics-focused social science research into the use of crowdfunding for medical care. Social Science Medicine 169, 27–30.
Spark Foundation. About Givealittle. Available from: https://givealittle.co.nz/content/how-givealittleworks/about.
Vogler, S., Vitry, A., Babar, Z.U., 2016. Cancer drugs in 16 European countries, Australia, and New Zealand: a cross-country price comparison study. Lancet Oncology 17 (1), 39–47.
World Health Organisation. Essential medicines and health products. Available from: http://www.who.int/medicines/publications/essentialmedicines/en/.

World Health Organisation., 2015. 19th WHO Model List of Essential Medicines, Available from: http://www.who.int/medicines/publications/essentialmedicines/EML2015_8-May-15.pdf.
Wonder, M., Milne, R., 2011. Access to new medicines in New Zealand compared to Australia. The New Zealand Medical Journal 124 (1346.).
Young, M.J., Scheinberg, E., 2017. The rise of crowdfunding for medical care: promises and perils. JAMA. 317 (16), 1623–1624.

CHAPTER 13

Access to High-Cost Medicines in Wales

Alice Varnava*, Sabrina Rind*, Robert Bracchi*, Karen Samuels*, Philip A. Routledge*, Dyfrig A. Hughes**

*All Wales Therapeutics and Toxicology Centre, Academic Centre, University Hospital Llandough, Wales, United Kingdom

**Centre for Health Economics and Medicines Evaluation, Bangor University, Bangor, Wales, United Kingdom

13.1 INTRODUCTION

Since 1999, the National Health Service (NHS) in Wales has been run by its devolved government which decides on the level of funding, and the structure and governance of how the NHS operates. In 2015–2016, prescribing expenditure in NHS Wales totalled £0.85 billion. This represents 5.7% of total Welsh government expenditure (All Wales Medicines Strategy Group, 2017a). A total of £518 million was spent on prescribed medicines in primary healthcare (Welsh Government, 2017). There were 25.7 prescription items per head per annum dispensed in Wales, which was the highest number of prescription items per head of population among the four devolved countries in the UK (Welsh Government, 2016).

The Welsh Government aims to ensure that patients in Wales have equitable and fast access to new medicines, in an effective, efficient and transparent manner (All Wales Medicines Strategy Group, 2017b, 2014). To facilitate this, Wales established its own health technology assessment (HTA) agency to appraise new medicines for their clinical and cost effectiveness via a transparent and evidence-based process. In 2002, the All Wales Medicines Strategy Group (AWMSG) was established as a statutory committee to provide recommendations on access, management and prescription of medicines to the Welsh Government. The group consists of an expert panel of health professionals, scientists, health economists, industry representatives, patient advocates and lay representatives, who work together to reach a consensus on the use of medicines.

Equitable Access to High-Cost Pharmaceuticals
http://dx.doi.org/10.1016/B978-0-12-811945-7.00013-0

13.1.1 Developments in Wales

The original remit of the AWMSG appraisal process was focused on high-cost medicines, defined as those costing more than £2,000 per patient per year and excluding those on the National Institute for Health and Care Excellence (NICE) work programme (Welsh Medicines Resource Centre, 2010). In 2007, the AWMSG appraisal process was broadened to also include all new cardiovascular and cancer therapies not on the NICE work-programme. In October 2010, the remit was further expanded to include all new licensed medicines. Medicines where NICE intended to publish guidance for the same product and indication(s) within 12 months from the date of marketing authorisation were usually excluded from appraisal (Welsh Medicines Resource Centre, 2010; All Wales Medicines Strategy Group, 2017c). As a result, AWMSG largely considers medicines that are not due to be appraised by NICE [which represented about 60% of new medicines in 2012 (House of Commons Health Select Committee, 2012)] and those for which a final NICE advice is not expected within 12 months of gaining marketing authorisation (All Wales Medicines Strategy Group, 2017c). Should NICE subsequently issue guidance, its final technology appraisal advice supersedes AWMSG recommendations.

The AWMSG has continued to evolve, introducing new policies and developing its processes and criteria in response to the various challenges faced by NHS Wales. One significant change has been the introduction and modification of its policies for appraising medicines for rare diseases (All Wales Medicines Strategy Group, 2015; Welsh Government, 2013) and medicines that may be life-extending for patients with short life expectancy (All Wales Medicines Strategy Group, 2016a). Invariably, these medicines are of high-cost. Based on the assumption of societal preference for treatments being available for affected individuals, AWMSG's policy allows the appraisal committee to take broader considerations into account to facilitate a positive recommendation. Additional criteria are considered, and patients and clinicians are given greater involvement in the appraisal decision-making process. AWMSG recognises that there is more uncertainty with the clinical data and, in acknowledgement of the circumstances, may accept a higher incremental cost-effectiveness ratio (ICER).

The introduction of the Wales Patient Access Scheme (WPAS) in 2012 provides an option for pharmaceutical manufacturers to propose a discount, rebate or other variation from the list price of a medicine that may be linked to the number, type or response of patients, and/or the collection of new evidence. A Patient Access Scheme (PAS), which has been previously approved by the Department of Health in England, will be considered as part of the HTA process in Wales if the medicine is subsequently submitted to AWMSG for appraisal for another indication. This only includes discount schemes where the PAS is already included within a positive NICE Final Appraisal Determination. These schemes allow AWMSG to recommend the use of a medicine within NHS Wales that may not have been considered cost-effective at the list price without such a scheme (All Wales Medicines Strategy Group, 2012).

13.1.2 Recommendations Made By AWMSG

AWMSG has conducted 341 appraisals between 2002 and 2017 (see Table 13.1). Of the 341 appraisals, 287 (84%) were given a positive recommendation for use in NHS Wales and 76 of these had a restricted recommendation for their use. A restricted recommendation (referred to as an optimised recommendation by NICE) is given when the use of the medicine is restricted to a specific sub-population rather than being recommended for the full indication under consideration; the medicine is not recommended outside of the restriction. The number of medicines appraised annually has increased over time, with seven medicines being appraised in 2004 and 43 in 2016.

13.2 THE APPRAISAL PROCESS

The responsibility for engaging with the AWMSG process lies with the manufacturer. The secretariat for AWMSG conducts horizon scanning to identify medicines expected to receive their marketing authorisation (product licence) within 18 months and will alert the manufacturer to the AWMSG appraisal process. Should manufacturers choose not to submit any evidence in support of their medicine, AWMSG will issue a Statement of Advice (SoA) confirming the medicine cannot be endorsed for use within NHS Wales. If there is a service need for advice, AWMSG may appraise the medicine using publicly available information.

AWMSG considers either a full or limited submission from a manufacturer. Limited submissions are considered for a new formulation which has a pro-rata or lower cost per treatment, a minor licence extension of an existing medicine, if the anticipated usage in NHS Wales is considered to be of minimal budgetary impact, and if the estimated difference in cost compared with the appropriate comparator(s) is small.

Table 13.1 AWMSG Recommendations by British National Formulary Chapter and Subsection Between 2002 and 2017

	Number of Appraisals	Recom-mended	Recommended with Restrictions	Not Recommended
All appraisals	*341*	*211*	*76*	*54*
1. Gastro-intestinal system	7	5	1	1
2. Cardiovascular system	27	18	5	4
3. Respiratory system	20	16	1	3
4. Central nervous system	31	18	7	6
5. Infections	70	54	14	2
5.3.1. HIV infection[a]	43	38	4	1
6. Endocrine system	32	18	9	5
6.1.2. Antidiabetic drugs[a]	15	10	4	1
7. Obstetrics, gynaecology, and urinary-tract disorders	8	4	2	2
8. Malignant disease and immuno-suppression	69	32	17	20
8.1.5. Other antineoplastic drugs[a]	36	16	11	9
9. Nutrition and blood	39	20	11	8
10. Musculoskeletal and joint diseases	20	14	5	1
11. Eye	5	4	0	1
12. Ear, nose and oropharynx	0	0	0	0
13. Skin	11	6	4	1
14. Immunological products and vaccines	0	0	0	0
15. Anaesthesia	2	2	0	0

Abbreviations: AWMSG, All Wales Medicines Strategy Group; BNF, British National Formulary; HIV, human immunodeficiency virus.

[a] Only the BNF subsections where most AWMSG appraisals have been undertaken have been included for comparison.

The AWMSG appraisal process is outlined in Fig. 13.1 (All Wales Medicines Strategy Group, 2016b). The secretariat for AWMSG produces a report [the AWMSG Secretariat Assessment Report (ASAR)] which summarises and critiques the evidence submitted by the manufacturer on the clinical effectiveness, comparative safety, cost-effectiveness and estimated budget impact of a new medicine. Evidence from a review of the literature,

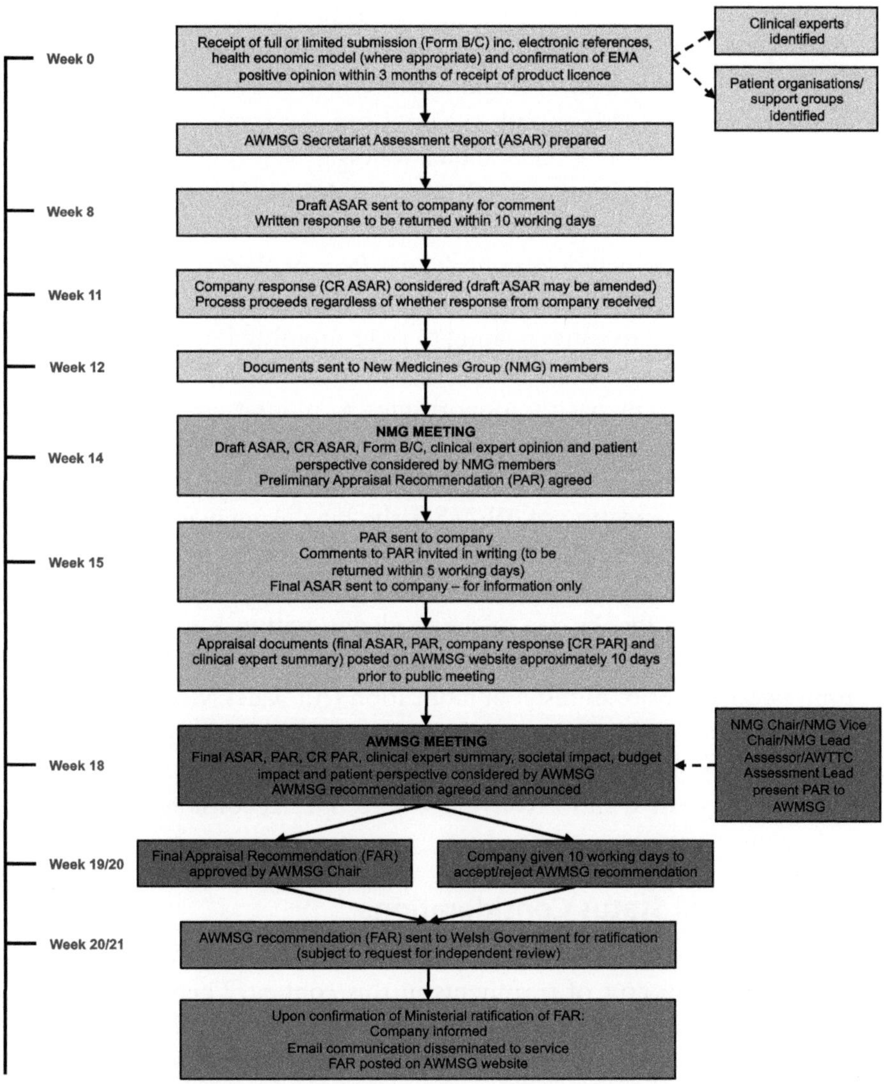

Figure 13.1 ***Summary of medicines appraisal process in Wales by AWMSG (All Wales Medicines Strategy Group, 2017d).***

conducted by the secretariat, is also considered and incorporated into the ASAR if deemed relevant. Views from clinical experts and patient organisations are captured in a questionnaire. A clinical expert is invited to attend the New Medicines Group (NMG) meeting and there is lay representation at NMG and AWMSG meetings.

The evidence is first appraised by NMG, a subgroup of AWMSG which meets in private to consider the clinical and cost-effectiveness of the medicine based on written evidence from the manufacturer, the ASAR, clinical expert opinion, and the views of patients, carers and patient organisations. NMG makes a preliminary recommendation, which is then considered by AWMSG. AWMSG also considers equity, broader societal issues and budgetary impact of the new medicine in Wales, as well as any outstanding issues relating to clinical and cost-effectiveness. AWMSG holds its meeting in public to ensure the transparency of the decision-making process; however, submissions which include a confidential PAS or WPAS are appraised by AWMSG in private. Manufacturers are encouraged to attend the AWMSG meeting to respond to issues relating to their submitted evidence (All Wales Medicines Strategy Group, 2016c).

The manufacturer has the opportunity to request an independent review (IR) to address scientific disputes and/or concerns relating to process; this additional step will extend the appraisal process. If the manufacturer accepts the recommendation of AWMSG, the Final Appraisal Recommendation is submitted to the Welsh Government for ratification. Welsh Government considers the recommendation and decides whether funding should be made available for the use of the medicine within NHS Wales. Health boards in Wales have a legal requirement to implement AWMSG guidance within two months of ministerial ratification (All Wales Medicines Strategy Group, 2017d). AWMSG aims to complete the appraisal process within 6 months; however, there are circumstances when steps are added, which may extend the process, to allow AWMSG to give special considerations to their conclusions.

13.2.1 Special Status Considerations

The AWMSG recognises the clinical needs of patients with rare diseases, and the potential high cost of treatments in this context. Therefore, AWMSG takes into account broader considerations in its deliberations of orphan/ultra-orphan medicines and medicines for a rare disease with an equivalent size population to an orphan/ultra-orphan medicine (see Box 13.1 for definitions). These considerations include, but are not limited to: the degree

BOX 13.1

Definitions of orphan, ultra-orphan and medicines for rare diseases (All Wales Medicines Strategy Group, 2015)

Orphan medicine: *a medicine with a European Medicines Agency (EMA) designated orphan status, which includes conditions affecting not more than 5 in 10,000 persons, which is equivalent to 1,500 patients in Wales where the population is 3 million.*

Ultra-orphan medicine: *a medicine that has been granted EMA designated orphan status and is used to treat a condition with a prevalence of 1 in 50,000 or less in the UK (or 60 patients in Wales).*

Medicines developed specifically to treat rare diseases: *a medicine developed specifically to treat an equivalent size population irrespective of whether it is designated by the EMA as an orphan medicine.*

For orphan, ultra-orphan and medicines developed specifically for rare diseases the definitions apply to the full population of the licensed indication/s.

of severity of the disease, unmet need, whether the medicine can reverse or cure the condition, the ability of the medicine to bridge a gap to future therapy, the innovative nature of the medicine, the added value to the patient that may not be adequately captured in the quality-adjusted life-year (QALY) and the value to the patient's family.

Since 2015, when the policy for appraising medicines for rare diseases was updated, AWMSG has appraised 16 medicines for rare diseases; seven of these medicines were considered as ultra-orphan; five were given a positive recommendation for use in NHS Wales and two were given a non-recommendation. Nine were considered orphan medicines by AWMSG; all were given a positive recommendation and five of these had a restricted recommendation for their use.

When appraising a medicine for orphan, ultra-orphan or rare diseases, if a medicine receives a negative preliminary recommendation from NMG, the manufacturer can request that a meeting of the Clinician and Patient Involvement Group (CAPIG) be convened. The aim of CAPIG is to identify and consider in detail any additional benefits of the medicine from a clinician, societal and patient perspective. Clinicians, patients, the manufacturer and a representative from the public are invited to provide a statement, and to attend and participate in discussions at the CAPIG meeting. A written summary of the meeting is given to AWMSG to consider and a summary of the main issues discussed is presented to AWMSG by the CAPIG Chair.

CAPIG meetings have been convened in six of the 16 appraisals for medicines which treat rare diseases. The meeting gives patients, clinicians and the public, the opportunity to raise in detail the issues that really matter to them. While the HTA process routinely includes input from clinical experts and patient organisations, the CAPIG meeting allows for a fuller discussion of issues that patients and clinicians feel should be taken into account. Discussions at a CAPIG meeting have included clarification of areas of uncertainty regarding clinical effectiveness and the proposed treatment pathway, as well as equity issues if a medicine is available in other devolved countries in the UK. The impact of a medicine's availability on the ability of a patient to return to work and the impact this has on the family and society has been discussed at CAPIG meetings. Clinicians have also provided further information on the likely progression of the patient without the medication and the likely costs involved.

For appraisal of life-extending, end-of-life medicines (see Box 13.2 for definitions) when the most plausible ICER estimate exceeds £30,000 per QALY, NMG and AWMSG consider giving greater weight to the QALYs achieved in the later stages of terminal diseases and the magnitude of additional weight to be assigned in order for the medicine to be cost-effective. A company can request that the appraisal process is suspended so that a panel can be convened to consider whether the conditions for end-of-life have been met. Between 2012 and 2016, six medicines have met the

BOX 13.2

Definition of a life-extending, end-of-life medicine (All Wales Medicines Strategy Group, 2016a)

Medicines qualify for appraisal as life-extending, end-of-life medicines when the most plausible incremental cost-effectiveness ratio (ICER) estimate exceeds £30,000 per quality-adjusted life-year (QALY) gained, and the following conditions are satisfied:

- *the medicine is indicated for patients with a short life expectancy, normally less than 24 months (e.g. estimated from the median survival of patients in the control group of the pivotal study) and;*
- *there is sufficient evidence to indicate that the medicine offers an extension to life, normally of at least an additional three months, compared to current NHS treatment. The estimates of the extension to life should be robust and shown (or reasonably inferred) from either progression free survival or overall survival.*

life-extending, end-of-life criteria and four of these were given a positive recommendation for use in NHS Wales.

13.2.2 Other Routes to Accessing Medicines

If a medicine has not been recommended for routine use in Wales, or cannot be endorsed for use in Wales due to the holder of the marketing authorisation not making a submission, a request for access to the medicine can be made through the Individual Patient Funding Request (IPFR) process. IPFR may be used by clinicians to access a treatment in circumstances when a medicine is not routinely funded on the NHS in Wales (All Wales Therapeutics and Toxicology Centre, 2016). Treatment will only be funded under IPFR if it is expected to provide significant clinical benefit and value for money for individual patients (IPFR, 2017). However, in circumstances where several patients who may benefit from the medicine are identified, a medicine may be accessed through the 'One Wales' commissioning route. One Wales is a process that allows manufacturers who have immature clinical data to collect more robust evidence that will add support to their submission to the HTA process by AWMSG or NICE. Manufacturers can take this route provided they commit to engagement in a future HTA.

13.3 THE APPRAISAL CRITERIA

13.3.1 Clinical Effectiveness

NMG and AWMSG consider a range of evidence to determine clinical effectiveness, from randomised controlled trials to network meta-analyses, observational studies and qualitative evidence related to the experiences of patients, carers and clinical experts who have used the medicine being appraised or are familiar with the relevant condition. The importance given to these various forms of evidence depends on the overall balance of scientific quality and relevance to the decision problem. Where no head-to-head trials against a relevant comparator exist, AWMSG accepts indirect analyses based on rigorous statistical methods to inform decisions on comparative effectiveness. In general, greater importance is given to evidence derived from high-quality studies using methodology designed to minimise bias.

13.3.2 Comparative Safety

Evidence of comparative safety is considered by both NMG and AWMSG. Decisions about a medicine's safety are generally based on the differences in adverse events profiles of the medicine compared to alternative treatments

(All Wales Medicines Strategy Group, 2016d). Evidence from comparative trials is preferred; however, findings from non-comparative studies may be considered relevant. For example, they may demonstrate a relative lack of adverse effects commonly associated with a competitor or the occurrence of adverse effects not significantly associated with other treatments. Additional information available from regulatory summaries on the method of administration, adverse effects, contra-indications, precautions and interactions is reviewed by both committees (All Wales Medicines Strategy Group, 2016d).

13.3.3 Cost-Effectiveness

NMG and AWMSG judgements on the cost-effectiveness of new medicines are made on the basis of the incremental cost per QALY gained (All Wales Medicines Strategy Group, 2016e). Economic evidence is normally derived from a model that combines the available evidence to estimate the expected costs and QALY gains over an appropriate time horizon. A lifetime time horizon is normally used for treatments of chronic diseases or that impact on survival. NMG and AWMSG do not use a fixed ICER threshold above which a medicine would automatically be defined as not cost-effective or below which it would, but rather a threshold range.

Below a most plausible ICER of £20,000 per QALY gained, the decision to recommend the use of a clinically effective medicine is normally based on the cost-effectiveness estimate and the acceptability of a medicine as an effective use of NHS resources (All Wales Medicines Strategy Group, 2016e). However, medicines with presented ICERs less than £20,000 per QALY gained may not be recommended if NMG or AWMSG are not persuaded by the plausibility of the inputs to the economic modelling and/or the certainty around the estimated ICER. This might be affected, for example, by limitations to the generalizability of findings regarding effectiveness. Above a most plausible ICER of £20,000 per QALY gained, judgements about the acceptability of the medicine as an effective use of NHS resources specifically take account of the following factors:

- the nature and quality of the evidence
- uncertainty in the evidence
- the robustness and appropriateness of the statistical analyses
- the possible differential effectiveness or greater risk of adverse events in different subgroups of patients
- the harms and benefits of the medicine from the patient's perspective
- the position of the medicine in the overall pathway (All Wales Medicines Strategy Group, 2016e).

As the ICER of a medicine increases in the £20,000 to £30,000 per QALY range, NMG and AWMSG's judgement about the acceptability of the medicine as an effective use of NHS resources normally make explicit reference to the relevant factors listed above (All Wales Medicines Strategy Group, 2016e). Above an ICER of £30,000 per QALY gained, the case for supporting the medicine based on these factors has to be increasingly strong (All Wales Medicines Strategy Group, 2016e).

Both NMG and AWMSG have a preference for expressing health gains in terms of QALYs (All Wales Medicines Strategy Group, 2016e). Under circumstances where the health gain is expressed in terms of life-years gained, the range of most plausible ICERs that are acceptable will be substantially lower than those described above (All Wales Medicines Strategy Group, 2016e).

13.3.4 Deviation from the Cost-Effectiveness Threshold Range

NMG and AWMSG may consider additional criteria for appraising medicines for rare diseases (see Box 13.1) and medicines which extend the survival of patients with a short life expectancy (see Box 13.2). Where the cost per QALY of an end-of-life medicine is above the threshold range, the committees are able to apply greater moderation in their assessment of its cost-effectiveness (All Wales Medicines Strategy Group, 2016a). They assess the impact of giving greater weight to QALYs achieved in the later stages of terminal diseases, and of the magnitude of the additional weight that would need to be assigned to the QALY benefits in this patient group for the cost-effectiveness of the medicine to fall within the current threshold range. Additional factors taken into account in the appraisal of medicines for rare diseases include the severity of the condition, the availability of alternative treatments and innovative nature of the medicine (see Box 13.3 for criteria).

13.3.5 Budget Impact

An additional remit of AWMSG is to also take into consideration the anticipated budget impact of a medicine (All Wales Medicines Strategy Group, 2016e). When AWMSG considers that a medicine has a large impact on NHS resources within a given disease area, it will want to be increasingly certain of its cost-effectiveness and may require more robust clinical and economic evidence (All Wales Medicines Strategy Group, 2016e).

BOX 13.3

Additional criteria for appraising orphan and ultra-orphan medicines, and medicines developed specifically for rare diseases (All Wales Medicines Strategy Group, 2015)

Where the cost per QALY is above the normal thresholds applied, additional criteria for appraising these medicines are considered. These include:

- *the degree of severity of the disease as presently managed, in terms of survival and quality of life impacts on patients and their carers*
- *whether the medicine addresses an unmet need (e.g. no other licensed medicines)*
- *whether the medicine can reverse or cure, rather than stabilise the condition*
- *whether the medicine may bridge a gap to a "definitive" therapy (e.g. gene therapy) and that this "definitive" therapy is currently in development*
- *the innovative nature of the medicine*
- *added value to the patient which may not adequately be captured in the QALY (e.g. impact on quality of life such as ability to work or continue in education/ function, symptoms such as fatigue, pain, psychological distress, convenience of treatment, ability to maintain independence and dignity)*
- *added value to the patient's family (e.g. impact on a carer or family life).*

13.4 CONSIDERATION OF WIDER SOCIETAL ISSUES

Cost-effectiveness is only part of a wider judgement of the value of a new medicine; societal aspects are also an important component in AWMSG's discussions and deliberations (All Wales Medicines Strategy Group, 2015). Social value judgements are concerned with what is appropriate and acceptable for society in delivering healthcare (Rawlins, 2010). For instance, AWMSG may consider whether the medicine has an impact on non-health benefits that are not captured in the QALY (e.g. impact on families and carers, work and schooling), costs to sectors outside the NHS such as educational services, and productivity losses attributable to changes in health outcomes (All Wales Medicines Strategy Group, 2016e).

AWMSG additionally makes equity considerations regarding whether, by recommending a medicine, inequalities in health will be reduced across Wales (All Wales Medicines Strategy Group, 2016e). It considers, for instance, whether the condition being treated is significantly more prevalent in groups of people who may be socially disadvantaged; for example, members of a disenfranchised racial, ethnic or religious group. AWMSG also takes into account how its judgements have a bearing on distributive justice or legal requirements in relation to human rights, discrimination and equality. Such characteristics include: age; sex/gender or sexual orientation; people's income, social class or position in life; race or ethnicity; disability; and conditions that are or may be, in whole or in part, self-inflicted or are associated with social stigma (All Wales Medicines Strategy Group, 2016e).

These considerations are especially important in the context of high-cost medicines such as those which meet the end-of-life or rare diseases criteria, where health gains in affected patients are valued higher than equivalent gains in other patients. AWMSG recognises that the cost per QALY is only part of a wider judgement of the value of such medicines and wider societal aspects are an important component in AWMSG's discussions (All Wales Medicines Strategy Group, 2015).

13.5 FUTURE CHALLENGES

AWMSG has evolved throughout its existence, demonstrating an ability to respond to the ever-changing challenges faced by healthcare in Wales. The introduction and modification of policies for appraising medicines has enabled AWMSG to recommend the use of medicines which it considers valuable to society but are not cost-effective by conventional cost-effectiveness criteria. One significant challenge has been the growing number of orphan medicines, and AWMSG's new policy for medicines for rare diseases helps to provide access to medicines that are invariably associated with high costs. NICE has also introduced new guidelines for appraising medicines for very rare conditions, which have been adopted by AWMSG.

Given the financial pressures faced by the NHS, more attention than ever needs to be given to the opportunity cost associated with the introduction of new technologies with increasing costs. The facilitated access of high-cost medicines may result in the reduction, dilution, and closure or withdrawal of other services, and identifying what is foregone as a consequence of AWMSG decisions is important for understanding the effects of HTA decisions on the health care system.

The budget impact estimates are important to the seven health boards (and one Health Trust) in Wales in planning their resources and allocating budgets. However, there is a general tendency for manufacturers to overestimate expected costs in their submissions to AWMSG, possibly reflecting their overestimation of future market share. Improving forecasting of the costs associated with a new medicine is just one of the important steps required to further inform decisions regarding access to new medicines for patients in Wales.

REFERENCES

All Wales Medicines Strategy Group, 2012. Wales Patient Access Scheme: process guidance. Available from: http://www.awmsg.org/docs/awmsg/appraisaldocs/inforandforms/Wales%20Patient%20Access%20Scheme%20process%20guidance.pdf.

All Wales Medicines Strategy Group, 2014. AWMSG five-year strategy 2013–2018. Improving the patient's experience of medicines in Wales. Available from: http://www.awmsg.org/docs/awmsg/awmsgdocs/AWMSG_Five-year_Strategy_2013-2018.pdf.

All Wales Medicines Strategy Group, 2015. Process for appraising orphan and ultra-orphan medicines and medicines developed specifically for rare diseases. Available from: http://www.awmsg.org/awmsgonline/docs/awmsg/appraisaldocs/inforandforms/AWMSG Orphan and Ultra Orphan process.pdf.

All Wales Medicines Strategy Group, 2016a. AWMSG policy on appraising life-extending, end-of-life medicines. Available from: http://www.awmsg.org/docs/awmsg/appraisaldocs/inforandforms/AWMSG%20policy%20on%20appraising%20life-extending,%20end%20of%20life%20medicines.pdf.

All Wales Medicines Strategy Group, 2016b. Appraisal process and timeline—full and limited submissions. Available from: http://www.awmsg.org/docs/awmsg/appraisaldocs/inforandforms/AWMSG%20appraisal%20process%20flow%20diagram%20&%20timeline.pdf.

All Wales Medicines Strategy Group, 2016c. AWMSG appraisal process. Frequently asked questions. Available from: http://www.awmsg.org/docs/awmsg/appraisaldocs/inforandforms/AWMSG%20appraisal%20FAQs.pdf.

All Wales Medicines Strategy Group, 2016d. Form B guidance notes. Available from: http://www.awmsg.org/docs/awmsg/appraisaldocs/inforandforms/Form%20B%20guidance%20notes.pdf.

All Wales Medicines Strategy Group, 2016e. Guidance on appraisal structure and evidence considered. Available from: http://www.awmsg.org/awmsgonline/docs/awmsg/appraisaldocs/inforandforms/AWMSG summary guidelines for appraising medicines.pdf.

All Wales Medicines Strategy Group, 2017a. Medicines identified as low priority for funding in NHS Wales. Available from: http://www.awmsg.org/docs/awmsg/medman/Medicines%20Identified%20as%20Low%20Priority%20for%20Funding%20in%20NHS%20Wales.pdf.

All Wales Medicines Strategy Group, 2017b. About AWMSG appraisal process. Available from: http://www.awmsg.org/industry_about.html?jqprselect=button1.

All Wales Medicines Strategy Group, 2017c. Medicines outside of the AWMSG remit. Available from: http://www.awmsg.org/docs/awmsg/appraisaldocs/inforandforms/AWMSG%20exclusion%20criteria.pdf.

All Wales Medicines Strategy Group, 2017d. Welsh Health Circular. The New Treatment Fund—access to medicines recommended by the National Institute for Health and Care Excellence (NICE) and the All Wales Medicines Strategy Group (AWMSG). Available from: http://www.awmsg.org/docs/awmsg/appraisaldocs/inforandforms/Welsh%20Health%20Circular%20(2017)%20001%20The%20new%20treatment%20fund%20Access%20to%20medicines%20recommended%20by%20NICE%20and%20AWMSG.pdf.

All Wales Therapeutics and Toxicology Centre, 2016. Improving access to medicines for patient cohorts. One Wales interim commissioning process. Available from: https://openrepository.awttc.org/app/serve/resource/dvua4779.

House of Commons Health Select Committee, 2012. Written evidence from the Ethical Medicines Industry Group (NICE 23). Available from: https://www.publications.parliament.uk/pa/cm201213/cmselect/cmhealth/782/782vw21.htm.

The Independent Patient Funding Request (IPFR) Review Group, 2017. Independent review of the individual patient funding request process in Wales. Available from: http://gov.wales/docs/dhss/publications/170117ipfrreporten.pdf.

Rawlins, M., 2010. Pharmacoeconomics: NICE's approach to decision-making. Br. J. Clin. Pharmacol. 70 (3), 346–349. doi: 10.1111/j.1365-2125.2009.03589.x.
Welsh Government, 2013. Written statement—access to new medicines: availability of ivacaftor (Kalydeco) within NHS Wales for the treatment of cystic fibrosis. Available from: http://gov.wales/about/cabinet/cabinetstatements/previous-administration/2013/kalydeco/?lang=en.
Welsh Government, 2016. Prescriptions dispensed in the community, 2015. Available from: http://gov.wales/docs/statistics/2016/160518-prescriptions-dispensed-community-2015-en.pdf.
Welsh Government, 2017. Health statistics Wales, 2016. Available from: http://gov.wales/docs/statistics/2017/170131-health-statistics-wales-2016-summary-en.pdf.
Welsh Medicines Resource Centre, 2010. The medicines appraisal process in Wales. Available from: https://www.wemerec.org/Documents/Bulletins/DrugAppraisal2010Online.pdf.

INDEX

N

O

P

Q

R

CPI Antony Rowe
Chippenham, UK
2018-10-11 20:12